Barrington Stoke would like to thank all its readers for commenting on the manuscript before publication and in particular:

Michael A.
Emma Andres
Ross Atkin
Janine Bennetts
Emma Bennetts
Ben Bradshaw
Claire Brash
Cameron Burgess
Paul Clark
Daniel Dean
Jennifer DeBues
David Dinwoodie
Jools Eastwood
Sue Hall
Lysette Harman
Marion Hellewell
Jack Johnstone
Russell Jones
Keren Jones
Yvonne Keeping
Jack Lister
Mrs Martin
Joseph Martin
Chloe Mason
Steven Mclean
Brogan McPherson
Ben Oliver

Steven Ormiston
Francesca Page
Shane Read
Kieran Read
Shauri Reed
Shaun Richards
David Riley
Lee Roberts
Ashley Sand
Sarah Sewell
Nichola Shannahan
Sean Sherlock
Daniel Siall
Matthew Smith
Aroon Sothikvmar
Sam Spray
Daniel Stace
Kathlee Sweeney
Gina Taylor
Luke Thomas
Dean Vagg
Mrs Waters
Craig Watson
Mesbach Williams
Benjamin Woollacott
Martin Wren
Henry Wright

Become a Consultant!

Would you like to give us feedback on our titles before they are published? Contact us at the email address below – we'd love to hear from you!

Email: info@barringtonstoke.co.uk

... sell more!"

—Hermann W. Braun, Director of Category Management and
Shopper Marketing, Ferrero Germany

"This is a unique book that examines and explains the need for the measurement of actual shopper behavior in retail environments. Based on real shopper studies, this takes analysis beyond POS data. Herb Sorensen pays particular attention to precise measurement of nonintuitive aspects of shopper interaction with the shelf."

—Franz A. Dill, Former Manager and Founder of
Procter & Gamble's Retail Innovation Center

"Herb Sorensen's ideas and observations about in-store shopper behavior have been instrumental in shaping my recent research. He has an uncanny ability to see beyond surface details and detect meaningful patterns of genuine interest to front-line managers and senior executives. It's great that so much of his wisdom—and that of other researchers he has influenced—is collected together here."

—Peter Fader, Professor of Marketing, The Wharton School
of the University of Pennsylvania

"Every year retailers disrupt their customers by spending time, money, and resources remodeling stores. Before remodeling one more store, read what Herb Sorensen has learned about how customers shop and how you can use it to improve your customer's shopping performance and your earnings.

One hundred years ago retailers ran their stores by watching their customers closely. Somewhere during the last hundred years, spread sheets, slotting allowances, and quarterly performance replaced the basic principles of the business. Sorensen's book puts you back on the floor of the store and allows you to see how the customer sees your store. What Sorensen shows you will make your stores better and more efficient for the customer and will maximize the money you are investing in design and remodels."

—No
Sa

Windsor and Maidenhead

9580000046512

"This book is priceless for anyone in retailing. It is based on 40 years of retail experience, and Herb Sorensen opens the doors to a new world. He serves us with masses of empirical data and examples, but also with new metrics and a new theory of shopper behavior. I am certain that he will challenge most retailers as well as researchers and force them to check if what he states can really be so. He challenged me, I had to check, and he was right!"

—Jens Nordfaült, Assistant Professor, Stockholm School of
    Economics; Dean, Nordic School of Retail Management; CEO,
    Hakon Swenson Research Foundation

"*Inside the Mind of the Shopper* is the preeminent handbook for any marketer or retailer seeking to understand why people do what they do when they shop. Armed with the knowledge in this book, marketers and retailers can work together to predict how shoppers will respond (or not!) to package and label design, selling messages, shelf plans, and the entire retail space."

—Matt Ohligschlager, Senior Manager, Consumer and Market
    Knowledge, Procter & Gamble

"A must-read for anyone who is passionate about understanding shopping."

—Joe Radabaugh, Director, Shopper Marketing, Nestlé USA

"From his 40 years of observing shoppers, Herb Sorensen has given us the gift of understanding shoppers. Now, we clearly see that the store layouts merchants want are not what shoppers want. On the ground, managers THINK they know their shoppers, but anyone who follows Herb's handbook on shopper insights will know them a lot better."

—Joel Rubinson, Chief Research Officer,
    The Advertising Research Foundation

"Herb Sorensen is the dean of behaviorally responsive shopper marketing. Crammed with stats and crisp insights, his book guides retail professionals through the maze of motivations that lead shoppers to locate, stop, and buy."

—James Tenser, Principal, VSN Strategies

Praise for the Second Edition of
Inside the Mind of the Shopper

"The Second Edition of *Inside the Mind of the Shopper* is a goldmine for anyone trying to wrap their heads around the disruptions reshaping retail in the 21st Century. It provides much-needed clarity to a variety of hotly contested issues, from a pragmatic approach to 'moments of truth' to a dispassionate assessment of how physical and digital retailing can co-exist, compete, and (most importantly) be managed. But, for me at least, while there is much new ground broken here, none is more fertile than Sorensen's notions of shopping as a 'directional search' and the idea of the retail area as the interface of products' and shoppers' competition for space. The author has given us many things to learn and even more to think about."

—Ryan Mathews, CEO, Black Monk Consulting; author of *The Myth of Excellence; The Deviant's Advantage; and What's Your Story?*

"The author's new chapters really contribute to making his ideas about active retailing even clearer, and making the book more up to date with the comparisons between online and offline. The book is so refreshing due to the author's unique perspective and approach to retailing. I am used to both the practitioner's ways of reasoning as well as academic literature on retailing, but the author's perspective is distinct. He seems to have the mind of both an engineer as well as that of a retailer."

—Jens Nordfält, Head of Research, Hakon Swenson Research Foundation; Assistant Professor, Stockholm School of Economics

"The Second Edition of *Inside the Mind of the Shopper* is version 2.0, not 1.1. Rarely does an update pave so much new ground that it could be considered an entirely new book. In the first edition, the author summarized the wisdom he developed from watching shoppers across close to a million shopping trips. In the second edition, the author examines today's most pressing questions for retailers—how to rapidly evolve into a hybrid world of bricks, clicks, digital, social, and mobile. The second edition is an essential read whether or not you've read the first edition. Most of the information is new and virtually all of it is essential."

—Neale Martin, CEO, Sublime Marketing; Professor of Innovation, Coles College of Management, Kennesaw State University; author of *Habit: The 95% of Behavior Marketers Ignore*

"Herb Sorensen's seminal first edition of *Inside the Mind of the Shopper* has not only become prescribed reading for our consultants, but it has also become the go-to read for many of our clients. This is not a cover-to-cover read but rather a constant companion for any retail or shopper marketing practitioner, as it is packed with valuable insights drawn from over 40 years of shopper understanding. The updated second edition takes into account the dramatic changes technology has brought about since the launch of the first edition seven years ago. Technology has not only changed shopper behavior, but it has also played a significant role in how retailers and marketers engage the shopper. The author's recommendations for how bricks and mortar retail should venture forth in this digital age are both reassuring and energizing. One thing that hasn't changed over the two editions is the message that the shopper should be at the heart of everything we do as retailers and brand owners."

—Peter Wilson, Director, koji

"I found this book to be a very important part of the industry. I also think it is a must-read for every merchandiser and category manager and would be the right text book for any retail merchandizing course for retail management programs, and even for management trainee programs. I spent time at Grand Union stores years ago in each of their four phase training programs, and this book would have helped me understand a lot more of how shoppers control the store."

—Frank Riso, formerly with MSI/Symbol Technologies

"This fresh update to Herb Sorensen's seminal book *Inside the Mind of the Shopper* is especially timely as retailing in the digital age begins to mature. While the second edition (rightly) still puts emphasis on the shoppers' time and on 'Big Head' categories, there is a new, deep analysis of both digital and bricks-and-mortar retailing. This book is a must-read for every student of shopping, from aspiring marketers and merchants to seasoned veterans."

—Liz Crawford, SVP Insights MATCH; author of
The Shopper Economy

"*Inside the Mind of the Shopper* gathers the insights of decades of research into shopper behavior by one of the world's leading retail experts. It pulls off the difficult trick of blending science with immediately accessible descriptions of exactly what is happening when shoppers interact with goods in a retail environment. As you read, you experience a succession of 'Aha! So that is what is happening!' moments as realization dawns that your personal experience has a scientific underpinning. This is a must-read for any researcher in the field, and for any store owner or manager."

—**Professor Alan Penn, Dean The Bartlett Faculty of the Built Environment, University College London**

"Anyone interested in retail marketing, shopper behaviour, or evidence-based marketing MUST read this book. Here is the evidence you've been looking for, and more."

—**Professor Byron Sharp, Director of the Ehrenberg-Bass Institute, and author of** *How Brands Grow*

INSIDE THE MIND OF THE SHOPPER

Second Edition

INSIDE THE MIND OF THE SHOPPER

Second Edition

The Science of Retailing

Herb Sorensen

With Mark Heckman, Accelerated Merchandising,
and James Sorensen, Kantar Retail

Study questions by Svetlana Bogomolova,
Ehrenberg-Bass Institute of Univ. So. Australia

Associate Editor: Kim Boedigheimer
Senior Marketing Manager: Stephane Nakib
Cover Designer: Chuti Prasertsith
Managing Editor: Sandra Schroder
Senior Project Editor: Lori Lyons
Project Manager: Dhayanidhi
Copy Editor: Christopher Morris
Proofreader: Srimathy Rajmohan
Indexer: Erika Millen
Compositor: codeMantra

For information about buying this title in bulk quantities, or for special sales opportunities (which may include electronic versions; custom cover designs; and content particular to your business, training goals, marketing focus, or branding interests), please contact our corporate sales department at corpsales@pearsoned.com or (800) 382-3419.

For government sales inquiries, please contact governmentsales@pearsoned.com.

For questions about sales outside the U.S., please contact intlcs@pearson.com.

Company and product names mentioned herein are the trademarks or registered trademarks of their respective owners.

Some of the data reported in this book has been produced by methods that may be covered by one or more of the following U.S.patents: 7,006,982; 7,606,728; 7,652,687; 7,933,797; 7,944,358; 8,041,590; 8,140,378; 8,666,790; 8,873,794; 9,076,149; and others pending.

1 16

ISBN-10: 0-13-430892-1
ISBN-13: 978-0-13-430892-0

Pearson Education LTD.
Pearson Education Australia PTY, Limited
Pearson Education Singapore, Pte. Ltd.
Pearson Education Asia, Ltd.
Pearson Education Canada, Ltd.
Pearson Educación de Mexico, S.A. de C.V.
Pearson Education—Japan
Pearson Education Malaysia, Pte. Ltd.

Library of Congress Control Number: 2016945007

Dedication

This book is dedicated to Bob Stevens of Procter & Gamble (P&G), the man who set me on the path of "active retailing" and who is also widely viewed as a pioneer in the field of shopper research.

He was a man of many talents: A consummate researcher, he was also an avid sports fan. Indeed, at 15, he began a short career as a professional wrestler, assuming the name "Rocky Stevens." Later in life, his love of basketball took him to Israel, Italy, and Alaska to cheer on his teams.

Bob was a devout Christian, a loving husband, father, and grandfather, and a philanthropist, too. He raised money for education and, post-retirement, taught and lectured often on market research and management, donating his honoraria to charity. For a time, he served on the board of Hope Cottage, a temporary shelter for abused, abandoned, or neglected children.

The greatest portion of his life, however, was spent at P&G where, beginning in 1951, he spent nearly 40 years as a consumer research manager. Bob was known as an inveterate people-watcher, fascinated by consumers' behavior both in-store and out, and especially their interaction with products.

His retirement did not put a stop to his professional involvement. He continued to write about marketing and research in a periodic newsletter called "Views from the Hills of Kentucky," which he emailed or faxed *gratis* to subscribers.

So, what made this man special? He was an advocate for the shopper, for understanding their needs and for doing the right thing as a researcher, often acting as a role model for his peers. He was always curious about what people *did* as opposed to what they *said*. And in many ways, his work has stood the test of time, as brands began to focus more on ethnography.

Bob would always dig a little deeper when it came to research. Bob Goodpaster, who was Vice President of Global Insights for The Hershey Company, recalls that when he worked with him at P&G, Bob would focus on research at one or two stores, giving people coupons to go in and buy products, while collecting their names and phone numbers for follow-up research.

What he was trying to do was to predict potential repeat purchasing, but working it out over a weekend, without having to wait months and months to read the normal statistical print-outs. He was way ahead of his time.

It couldn't have been easy because, as with any pioneer, there were those who were enthusiastic about change and those who were afraid of it. But Bob persevered, and rarely turned down the chance to innovate. For P&G, this resulted in insights that the company might never have achieved otherwise. Indeed, P&G is one of the most innovative research organizations around today, and Bob played a part in laying the foundations of that continuing innovation.

Bob's philosophy lies at the heart of this book, too. His enthusiasm for researching shoppers, for knowing what goes on when they enter a store, is translated in these pages into a modus operandi for retailers (and brand owners) who want to make the most of their businesses.

Earlier, I mentioned his newsletters, which inspired new ways of thinking and working. Two of his favorite topics were, distinguishing between "testers" and "users" and the need for "assessment in context." Bob's views on these issues matched my own major concerns as a scientist transplanted to market research. We believe that customers should be studied in their native environment: This means researching supermarket shoppers in supermarkets; food service patrons in restaurants, schools, and other commercial and non-commercial locations; food service operators in their kitchens; schoolchildren in their schools; and so on. Also, we prefer direct observation of "users," and asking questions, converting them into "testers" as follow-ups, rather than as the foundation of the research.

Our learnings about the messy process of testing in context were inspired by Bob, and became integral to my business following discussions with him. It was Bob who turned my narrow focus from the shoppers and the products, to also include the stores, their natural habitat. I hope that, from whatever lofty peak he's now operating, he feels that I'm still taking his work forward in the ongoing search for truth about shoppers.

Contents at a Glance

Contents

Chapter 2   **Transitioning Retailers from Passive
to Active Mode 49**

Acknowledgments

I was born at an early age....

What might have been seen as precocity in the first half of my life has evolved into a certain independence in this half. Here I want to give tribute to some of the key players in bringing this book to fruition.

From my mother, I inherited a drive for improvement, and from my father, hard work as the proper and justifying role of man. I met my wife when I was fourteen, and was blown away by her wise and serious essay on the stages of life, read by her to our English III class in high school. Now past our fifty-fifth wedding anniversary, she has been the tether that keeps me connected to those most important things in life. Five years after our first meeting, we had our first daughter Kris, while I was finishing my senior year in college.

All of my five children grew up inside the business that evolved to deliver this book. Kris managed the operations side of the business during some of the most explosive growth we ever experienced. Beth, even as a pre-teen, was helping with keeping those rows and columns straight, in the days when we did manual tabulation of survey data. Later, she and I set a personal record of 130 respondents recruited and interviewed in one hectic day in Santa Monica.

Jon is the philosopher-musician-writer who helped me begin contributing reports and articles to the marketing research press. This work laid the foundations of this book, helping me to think through some of the issues covered here. James is the right hand that built Sorensen Associates, "The in-store research company®," which the world has come to know. He is the one who transmuted my scientific curiosity into something of practical value for our clientele, which has swelled under his ministrations.

Paul is an award-winning nuclear physicist who wrote the software for our TURF analysis (Total Unduplicated Reach and Frequency). We continue to use the procedures he developed for shopper flow analysis in our PathTracker® Tool Suite.

Beyond the core of my family, the towering influence from my early professional years was Lloyd Ingraham, my major professor at the University of California at Davis. His was an open and searching mind that encouraged the same for me. What an incredible experience, to be given free range and funding to follow my nose into nuclear quadrupole resonance, chick embryo metabolism, the quantum chemistry of small ring heterocycles, the role of thiamine in muscular dystrophy, and radio-carbon and dendrochronology, all resulting in peer-reviewed scientific papers in one three-year period.

Leaping forward nearly 30 years found me with an eclectic history encompassing university faculty positions, board-certified clinical chemistry, which evolved through a food laboratory and sensory science to market research. The logical connection through all this is curiosity.

In 2000, three things converged: my long-standing curiosity about the overall movement of shoppers through stores, my acquaintance with Peter Fader at Wharton, and client support by Sandy Swan at Dr. Pepper/7UP for an initiative to conduct the study. Although a few others followed, it was Sandy's immediate financial encouragement that launched PathTracker®, the most extensive study of shopper paths (and much more) ever conducted. Sandy was with me on the early work when the insights were accumulating, but the knowledge of how to use the insights profitably was slow to coalesce.

And then, Peter Fader's immediate and enthusiastic support for the project rendered the objective, academic *imprimatur* that I valued more than the money. His practical views on the relation of online and offline retailing are covered in our interview in Chapter 4, "Integrating Online and Offline Retailing: An Interview with Professors Peter Fader (The Wharton School) and Wendy Moe (University of Maryland)."

Mike Twitty of Unilever was another major influence. Mike and I both participated in the first IIR Shopper Insights Conference (2001), and I recognized early on that Mike was a *serious* student of the shopper. Mike Twitty has had the "quick trip" as a focus for several years, and my own overwhelming data forced me to recognize the unclaimed potential in this area. Mike is making a tremendous contribution to the entire industry through the insights he shares from this work in Chapter 7, "The Quick-Trip Paradox: An Interview with Unilever's Mike Twitty."

I've mentioned the role of curiosity in my career and this book. Science is, of course, another prominent motif. But *independence* is perhaps as important. Not caring what anyone else thinks is a strength and flaw encouraged by a decade or more of living, like Thoreau, in my own mountain-forest semi-isolation. My independence, however, is tempered by a healthy dose of personal insecurity, which always secretly seeks confirmation and approval. But I am very picky about whose approval and confirmation I care about.

This is the significance of Fader, Twitty; and later of Bill Bean, then at Pepsi; then Mark Heckman, who preceded my shopper tracking work at Marsh—the "Marsh Super Study" in the early '90s and now a partner with me in Accelerated Merchandising LLC; and even later of Cliff McGregor of Nestlé; and, finally, Siemon Scammell-Katz of ID Magasin, then at TNS/Kantar. In any budding and exciting field like "shopper," there are always plenty of thin poseurs. But these folks are genuine gold, having their own independent and advanced expertise in the shopper that I know and care about.

Bill Bean, while at Pepsi, sponsored a study of four supermarkets using the RFID tracking technology, while it was still cutting/bleeding edge. Bill took the raw data from those four stores and did his own independent study, using intelligent agent modeling with Icosystem, which confirmed and went beyond many of the things I was learning myself. (The Wharton group under Fader has also operated independently, following its own curiosity and analytical strengths.)

My professional collaboration with Mark Heckman over the past decade, has deepened considerably. His real-world retailer perspective included years actually incorporating our joint insights into profitable retail practice at Marsh and other retailers. This gave us tools for looking, not only from the outside in on the business, but from the inside looking out. Mark has collaborated extensively on this second edition, including focus on the "*The Five Vital Tenets of Active Retailing*," a blueprint for his second chapter in this edition, ***Transitioning Retailers from Passive to Active Mode***.

Siemon Scammell-Katz is the first person I ever met who knew many of the principles and truths that were emerging from PathTracker® but had no prior exposure to the intricacies of our work. His knowledge was a result of having spent more than a decade studying shoppers' behavior on a tenth of a second by tenth of a second basis (fixation by fixation) from point-of-focus eye tracking studies, primarily in Europe. Siemon's independent work not only served as confirmation, but also stimulated me to a renewed interest in eye tracking, particularly linking the foot-path to the eye path.

Finally, Cliff McGregor at Nestlé and I have had many illuminating (to me) discussions. These interested me greatly, initially, because of Cliff's former participation in the Envirosell organization in Australia before he joined Nestlé. I've mentioned in the book my great respect for Paco Underhill's work, although we have never been connected professionally, other than my reading his books and sitting in his audiences.

Cliff did me the kindness of reading the entire first draft of the first edition and commenting, to my profit, on various features. I spent a very pleasant day in 2007 chatting with Cliff about our mutual views on shoppers. This was very helpful because of my own newness to the global scene and his wide experience of global retailing, as well as a more detailed view into the cultural anthropological approach to studying shoppers. In this sense, Siemon and Cliff, both enhanced my own study and focus by broadening my scope to a bigger, global picture, as well as a more detailed focus on the individual shopper.

In my mind, I have something of an artificial boundary between myself and "my" company, which in reality has been run for quite a few years by my son, James. But at the same time, there is an obvious connection, beyond family. Frankly, I could never have learned what I have about shoppers if I had stayed tethered to our clients' questions and interests. On the other hand, had the company not focused on those, we wouldn't exist. It is James and his staff that have mediated the learnings from PathTracker® to the world of our clients. But James has been the stern "client" that always disciplines me with, "So what?" And it has not been an indifferent "So what." This is why Chapter 10, "Brands, Retailers, and Shoppers: Why the Long Tail Is Wagging the Dog," is in reality a collaboration between myself, James, Siemon, and Ginger Sack, our senior researcher on the client side.

There was a significant lapse in our focus in the first edition: and that was the lack of attention to the substantial amount of retail focusing on major, and typically, infrequent purchases. James Sorensen, now Executive Vice President, Shopper Insights, at Kantar Retail, has remedied this with his chapter 6, "Long Cycle Purchasing."

Of course, many at TNS Sorensen played crucial roles in supporting my studies, and I thank them all, but three have been the heavy-lifters in research and development. Dave Albers is the concept and numbers genius that always improved every idea I brought him, Jamin Roth is my database right hand, and Marcus Geroux is the creative talent who does the same with devices, electronics, and anything requiring "making." I told Marcus once that he must have apprenticed with James Bond's "Q." All three have played key roles in one or more of the suite of patents underlying the PathTracker® Tool Suite.

I must mention also my increasing involvement with Byron Sharp, director of the Ehrenberg-Bass Institute at the University of South Australia, and many of his staff, but particularly with Svetlana Bogomolova, who joined this second edition team as we were doing the final editing. But in addition to helpful reviewing of the work, added two sidebars in chapter 2, and stimulated very wide thoughts, leading to an Afterward, which is in reality a survey of the research needed going forward. Svetlana, Mark Heckman and I have collaborated in that final work of this second edition.

My sincere thanks to the giants mentioned here, upon whose shoulders I have stood.

I am yet grateful to Laura Mazur and Louella Miles, who spent the better part of a year coaxing and encouraging me in the writing of the first edition, drafting content from my interviews, rewriting and stitching together a vast quilt from the multifarious pieces I had assembled willy-nilly over the years. It was then that Robert Gunther added his creative polish to the first edition. My nephew, Ray Sorensen, a very fine writer in his own right, recently undertook the formidable task of integrating my new work, and that of Mark Heckman and James Sorensen, in moving the content from that appropriate to 2008, to the real world of global retail of 2016, that is, now *Convergent* Online, *Mobile* and *Bricks* (COMB) retail. Of course, I retain all responsibility for the content of the final document, so send any brickbats my way. Kudos to the rest!

About the Author

Herb Sorensen is a preeminent authority on observing and measuring shopping behavior and attitudes within the four walls of the store. He has worked with Fortune 100 retailers and consumer packaged-goods manufacturers for more than 40 years, studying shopper behavior, motivations, and perceptions at the point of purchase. Sorensen's methods are helping to revolutionize retail-marketing strategies from a traditional "product-centric" perspective to a new "shopper-centric" focus. As *Baseline* magazine commented, "Herb Sorensen and Paco Underhill are the yin and yang of observational research."

Herb has conducted studies in North America, Europe, Asia, Australia, and South America. His research has been published in AMA's *Marketing Research, The Journal of Advertising Research, FMI Advantage Magazine, Progressive Grocer,* and *Chain Drug Review.* He has also been utilized as an expert source for *The Wall Street Journal, Supermarket News,* and *BusinessWeek.* Herb appeared on the television show Dr. Oz as an expert on the movement of the eyes as part of the shopping process. Additionally, he is currently a panelist of Retail Wire's "Brain Trust" and blogs at www.shopperscientist.com.

Herb's career intertwines the world of science with the world of business. His Ph.D. in biochemistry from the University of California at Davis, 1970, resulted in publications ranging from metabolism, to chemical and electron structures. He is also a Diplomate of the American Board of Clinical Chemistry. In 1972 he launched a food laboratory, specializing in nutrition, safety, and HACCP quality programs.

His second company, Sorensen Associates, "The In-store Research Company™," grew at an annualized rate of nearly 30% from 1979–2009. In the 90s a mentor, Bob Stevens of P&G, encouraged a sharper focus on "assessment in context." This led to the invention and patenting of PathTracker®, a second-by-second method of electronically studying shopper behavior in stores. Early on, PathTracker® enjoyed mentoring and advice from Peter Fader, and Herb shared in the honor of the AMA's EXPLOR award in 2007, with Fader and his group at the Wharton School of Business of the University of Pennsylvania.

In 2004 *Fast Company Magazine* named Herb one of its top 50 innovators. In 2013, he received the Charles Coolidge Parlin Marketing Research Award, "honoring distinguished academics and practitioners who have demonstrated outstanding leadership and sustained impact on the evolving profession of marketing research over an extended period." In receiving this prestigious award, Sorensen joined other marketing research legends such as Robert Wood Johnson, Peter Drucker, Arthur C. Nielsen, George Gallup, August A. Busch III, Paul E. Green, John A. Howard, Philip Kotler, Robert J. Lavidge, and Jagdish Sheth.

Globalization of Herb's work expanded when he sold his company to TNS/Kantar and published the first edition of *Inside the Mind of the Shopper* and through affiliation with the Ehrenberg-Bass Institute at the University of South Australia as an Adjunct Senior Research Fellow. Herb is collaborating with Mark Heckman on Accelerated Merchandising™, increasing sales and profits through shopper efficiency.

Preface

Who Is #1?

As you read the second edition of *Inside the Mind of the Shopper*, consider the various players at retail: shoppers, retailers, brand suppliers, and other supporting businesses. Ask yourself, out of these players, who is the top dog? Who is the most important? *Who is #1?* The answer(s) to that question will provide insight necessary for understanding many of the concepts we discuss in *Inside the Mind of the Shopper*.

First of all, #1 is a coveted position in most human endeavors. Clearly, in the world of retail, Walmart is #1, approaching a half trillion in annual sales. Costco is #2, with about a quarter of the sales volume of Walmart. You might consider Amazon a distant competitor, but their outsized annual growth makes clear that it is only a matter of time before they reach #3, globally. You could study just these three global retailers and learn a large share of what you need to know. If we want to add a fourth, it should be Kroger, because of their steady quarter after quarter growth in the United States alone.

Caution should weigh heavily on anyone who considers this through a historical perspective. As British Prime Minister Benjamin Disraeli remarked on ascending to the office: "'At last I have reached the top of the greasy pole." One hundred years ago, a new retailer, The Great A&P, with a new business model, quickly became the first retailer in the world to reach a billion dollars of sales. And just recently they filed their final liquidation bankruptcy, after decades of descent, with fruitless reorganization. The caution is that retailing is *still* a greasy pole.

It is my intention with this book to provide a very new perspective on who is #1. I'm quite confident that the shopper is #1, and I'm not saying that as some kind of feel-good PR fluff. Each of the four retailers first mentioned here, and many others, have all risen to their stature through making *some* aspect of the shopper #1, at some point in time. Walmart efficiently leveraged price, groceries, and a large selection to achieve their dominance. Costco *efficiently* leveraged price, groceries, and a limited selection, much of it non-grocery, to drive their growth. Amazon has *efficiently* leveraged novel technology for all three basic components of retail sales: a meeting of the minds of buyer and seller; close the sale with payment; delivery of the goods to the customer. And as the "Everything Store," Amazon effectively has an infinite Long Tail. Kroger is in the chase because they have focused on the efficiency of the shopper, without neglecting their own efficiency.

You will see in Mark Heckman's chapter on the *Five Tenets*, exactly what we mean about building your own sales through the efficiency of your shoppers. But here I want to put a spotlight on the reality of everyday retail, on what happens behind the screen, unseen by the shoppers. Indeed, many managers within the industry probably haven't given adequate consideration to these facts.

These three graphs (Figure P.1) show some solid illustrative data on who is #1. From these, it is important to see how the views of shoppers are related to, but radically different than, those of the typical

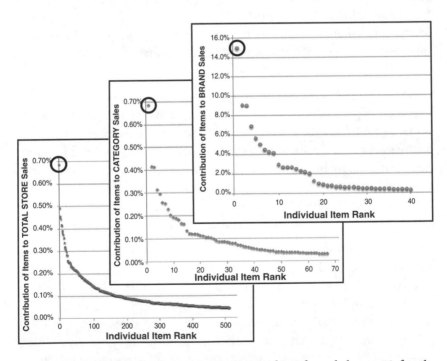

Figure P.1 Whether total store, category, or brand, each has a #1 for the shopper

bricks-and-mortar retailer. In the first graph on the left, the share of the store's sales contributed by single items is displayed. The circled high point is in fact the #1 selling product in that store. In the second, middle graph, we see only the contribution of items in a *single category* to sales of that particular category. And the circled high point is the #1 selling item in that category. The third graph, in the upper-right, is the same type of graph, but in this case it includes data for only a single *brand* in the category. As with the other graphs, the circled high point is the #1 selling item *for that brand manufacturer.*

Each one of these #1s has a special significance for one of the three major manager categories at retailers around the world. The first major manager type is management representing the retail store itself. The stark fact is that many of these managers may not know just what that #1 selling item is. The reason is simple: That item is probably one of anywhere from a few thousand to hundreds of thousands of items in one of possibly hundreds or thousands of stores under their purview. Management is focused on a *massive* undertaking that scarcely makes allowance for focus on any one item.

The second type of manager we want to notice is the one associated with the manufacturers brand, the *brand manager*, whose product suite is illustrated in the upper-right graph. Brand managers have a greater opportunity for focus, with possibly anywhere from dozens to hundreds of items managed across a wide variety of retailers. The relatively tiny brand catalog—tiny in comparison to the retailer catalog—means that no retailer can be expected to have the knowledge of individual brand items that the brand manager does.

Now comes a major complicating factor. No one can reasonably manage 50,000 items. This can be thought of in terms of management span-of-control theory. Basically, supervisors work most effectively with 3–10 employees. As the number of employees increases, span-of-control increases—supervision becomes more problematic. Products are not people, but the general principle applies there also. In the interests of managing 40,000 different items in a store, retailers have been grouping them together into a couple hundred different categories. This reduces the problem from one of a totally unmanageable 40,000 items to one of maybe 200 categories with more like 500 to a few thousand items. For the past 30 years, the *science* of category management has come a long way.

NEW IN THE 2ND EDITION

In this edition of *Inside the Mind of the Shopper* we still explore the insights gained through the scientific study of shoppers and the shopping process and we discuss how retailers can apply these insights to increase sales in their stores. But, now, we inspect these insights through the prism of the evolution currently taking place within retail. Dramatic changes in technology and society are quickly propelling this evolution. These changes recall the seismic societal and technological shifts that transformed the industry a century ago in the wake of the Industrial Revolution. That transformation saw the demise of thousands of small retailers and the emergence of a few industry giants. By understanding how history shaped the current state of retail and how modern developments such as online retail and its convergence with bricks and mortar retail continue to mold the industry, retailers can better position themselves to exploit this evolution and thrive in the 21st century.

However, there are still embedded serious conflicts that keep anyone from focusing on the shoppers. Please recognize that if you were buried under 40,000 items, or even a couple thousand items in a category, as a category manager, you would be overwhelmed from a span-of-control point of view. And this is exacerbated by the fact that all those different brands in the category are *competitors*. Competitors are not your friends, even if you are all polite. I don't want to overemphasize the angst, but I have actually seen a grown man cry in a store because of what he believed his competitor was doing to him—through his "little children," the brand products he was responsible for managing, on behalf of his manufacturer employer.

This is to give meaning to my statement that what is going on in the aisles of the stores is brand-on-brand mayhem, a gladiatorial contest with civilizing rules. Now, the interesting thing is that the retailer has someone assigned to each category, who ultimately has responsibility for what happens in that category. But every brand knows that only a certain amount of shelf space is allotted to the category, and to put it simply, every slot Brand A doesn't fill, Brand X, Y, or Z will.

Note too that federal law forbids, under the threat of severe punishment, any collusion among the brands that *might* be disadvantageous to the shoppers. Another possibly shocking fact: Retailers do not want any one supplier to be too successful in selling their products to the shoppers. The reason for this is obvious when you realize that most of the retailer's profits come from what are basically advertising fees paid by the brands supplying products to the retailer. These fees are totally legitimate, but they have to be negotiated independently with each supplier. This leads to the retailer essentially managing a serial blind auction in which each supplier comes in and makes a deal for his products with the retailer armed with no knowledge of the deals the retailer is making with others (as specified by law).

The result is that each supplier is essentially a "customer" for the retailer's services: store, shelves, shoppers, and displays. And the retailer does best with a good number of healthy suppliers, with no one being dominant.

Now, obviously, this is not as neat as I have outlined here, but it reasonably accurately explains why *no one is paying much attention to the shopper*, other than being polite and pleasant and operating a store that is reasonably convenient to the shopper. After all, the retailer is essentially a merchant warehouseman who makes his money on that basis. And for self-service retailers, the shopper is an unpaid stock-picker who picks the products she wants and takes them to the exit to make payment. (All this means that the retailer mantra of 100 years ago, "Pile it high, and let it fly!" is still deeply embedded yet today in an industry that's poorly understood, even by the global hordes employed in the industry.)

With all this in mind, you should see that any item that is #1 (or #2, #3, #4, and so on) actually got that way because the shopper, the true #1, gave that product the sales and rank it has. The shopper is always the real #1, and it is their innermost feelings and desires that are manifested in the total sales occurring in the store.

As you read this second edition of *Inside the Mind of the Shopper* and consider the concepts and ideas, the history and trajectory of global retail that we explore, remember: With all the power, money, and products at retail, *it is the shopper that is #1!*

—**Herb Sorensen, Ph.D.**
  Shopper Scientist

Introduction

From time to time a researcher has the opportunity to see their earlier ideas combine in a way that brings the current subject of study into sharper focus. This was the case as I sat down to write an issue of my occasional online publication, *Views on the World of Shoppers, Retailers, and Brands*. As I thought about my endeavors to look at shopping from a strictly scientific point of view—but, at the same time, with tremendous commercial significance—three earlier ideas came together and brought into focus the issue of *navigability* through stores.

Before exploring each of these ideas, let's set the scene with a single shopper purchasing a single item (see Figure I.1). All of retail, whether bricks or clicks, builds on this as the basic unit of sales:

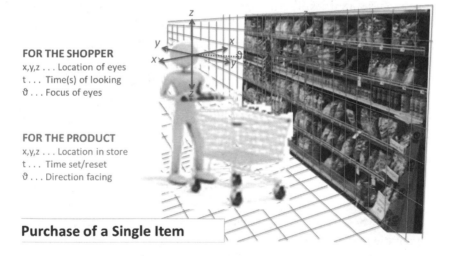

FOR THE SHOPPER
x,y,z . . . Location of eyes
t . . . Time(s) of looking
ϑ . . . Focus of eyes

FOR THE PRODUCT
x,y,z . . . Location in store
t . . . Time set/reset
ϑ . . . Direction facing

Purchase of a Single Item

Figure I.1 The three-dimensional shopper interacts with the three-dimensional shelf.

The illustration above shows the two parties to the purchase, the shopper and the product. Note the complementarity between the two. In other words, if you take either one of them out of the picture, the purchase will not happen. Here we balance the interests of the two. By diagraming this complementarity dimensionally, we capture both parties to the purchase in a common metric system, rather than in a separate one for each. This will be very significant going forward in understanding the *process* by which purchases occur. Purchases are not simply events to be tabulated. They are examples of a process to be understood.

Bidirectional Search

The first idea that demonstrates how navigability drives shopping is what I call *bidirectional search*. This idea is important because it is the fundamental process of shopping, whether online or in bricks-and-mortar stores. In bidirectional search, as the illustration above shows, retailers and suppliers are searching for shoppers, while at the same time shoppers are searching for products. Much of the time the industry does not properly recognize the first part of this bidirectional search, primarily because of the relatively passive role retailers and suppliers play at the final point of purchase.

I've written about this passivity in my post, *"Googling" the Store*,[1] in the aforementioned *Views* (in this edition of this book, I frequently reference material that I and others have previously published. We provide notes and links to all of these sources). Passivity, in turn, leads merchant warehouse retailers, whose neighborhood warehouses merely store merchandise until a shopper puts it in her basket, to fail in reaching their full potential in sales. This stark description is my attempt to break through the mechanical way we tend to look at retailing, particularly the accounting, or more accurately the *counting* of events, that has become deeply embedded in the industry's thinking and retail metrics.

Retailers and suppliers are of course not physically present to search for shoppers. Instead, they rely on their surrogates, the displays and products, to do the searching for them. For the retailer, a display is a display, whereas for the supplier it is more about products. That is, the suppliers are sending in their brands and individual products to represent them, whereas the retailers take a more aggregate approach, with entire displays, aisles, and departments representing them.

So all the displays and products in the store do their best to shout at shoppers as they pass by: "Buy me! Buy me!" "No, no, no, *buy me!*" It's no wonder shoppers typically shop the store so superficially. They have to in order to retain their sanity. The shopper's *clutter filter* maintains a state of obliviousness by screening from consideration everything except the little bit of information that makes it through the cacophonous roar that retailers and suppliers orchestrate in their search for shoppers to buy their products.

Never forget this bidirectional perspective: shoppers looking for products; products looking for shoppers. It should drive store design and operations. Mr. Retailer, Ms. Brand Supplier, you can be far more effective on your side of the search by working *with* the shopper, rather than by indiscriminately shotgunning from your side of the aisle and display interface.

Products/Shoppers Competition

The second idea that brings navigability into focus here is that there is an actual competition occurring in the store between the products and the shoppers. This competition gets very personal, particularly in the selection process when it is *this* shelf or product display talking to *this* specific shopper or passerby (see illustration above.) I won't discuss this in detail here because that personal communication between products and shoppers has more to do with package and planogram design than store design, which is what we focus on here. I will, however, mention one at-the-shelf principle: *Shoppers do not like to be talked down to!*

This is why top shelves are typically very poor places to sell anything. Shoppers do not want their products staring at them from eye level. Rather, the products should be humble supplicants looking up to the shopper from 30 to 60 inches above the floor. That is where most purchasing occurs. Those products have the decency to respectfully look up to their masters, the shoppers. One way to achieve this proper product humility is to place the bottom shelf protruding into the aisle a few inches, with a slight tip upward. This is an excellent way to give that bottom shelf a bit more prominence. The products are well displayed, humble supplicants to the shopper at the cost of only a few inches of crowding of the shopper's feet, something they really don't mind at all.

A little intrusion into the aisle down there is no serious offense: The feet scarcely notice!

Other than right at the shelf, the competition between products and shoppers is almost totally under the control of the store designer. The store designer manages this competition through how much space the designer allocates to displays and products versus how much space he allocates to the shoppers. Here we are talking about the total area of the store, and its division into shelves, displays, and other *product* areas versus the actual square footage in which the *shoppers* can walk, navigate, and shop. We call this measure *product/shopper allocation.*[2] The more products and displays you jam into the store, the less space for shoppers.

This ratio, product-space to shopper-space, is a major controller of the efficiency of the store. (See Figure I.2, below.)

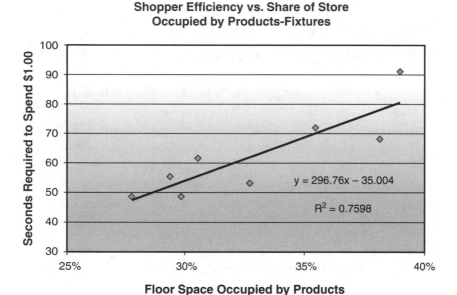

Figure I.2 The mathematical effect of the competition between products and shoppers.

All stores must have space for both shoppers and products. But this chart shows that at a certain point the amount of space allocated to products can actually suppress sales rather than increase them. This is not a simple relationship, but it further demonstrates how open space attracts shoppers and generates sales.

Although retailers may be unaware of it, they have learned to provide lots of open space on the perimeter, in produce, and other areas of their stores where the vast majority of sales occur. Increased sales in these areas are not due to the specific merchandise offered there, only, but rather, also, to the attractive way retailers display the products in these locations.

Open Space Actually Attracts Shoppers—Think Navigation!

The third idea that supports navigability of the store is that shoppers are subconsciously drawn to open space. This happens because shoppers shop through their eyes. They do not look for products through careful, rational thinking, but by habit and instinct. This is why I often urge, "If the shopper does not see it, it's effectively not in the store." The shopper sees only a small fraction of the store up close and personal. If you are going to manage the sales process, you better know what that small fraction is.

Everything about store design is about seeing. An ideal store design includes a wide, open track that circumnavigates the store. Low displays on at least one side of that track allow a wide vista so that shoppers see to the furthest areas of the store. It's okay for shoppers to see lots of merchandise at a distance. Let the shopper go that distance if that merchandise resonates with them. Don't jam it all into their faces, limiting their ability to see more of the store and more available products. See Chapter 3 of this book.

Professor Allen Penn of the University College of London showed exactly how open space moves shoppers around the store.[3] Professor Penn and one of his students ingeniously illustrated how shoppers respond to the space in an IKEA floor plan by creating a model store that consisted of only floor space and blank blocks representing the displays and fixtures. (Upper left of Figure I.3) They then sent bots programed to seek out open spaces through the floor plan. Here you can see how their open-space sensitive bots created the exact same paths that real shoppers walked in the real, fully stocked store:

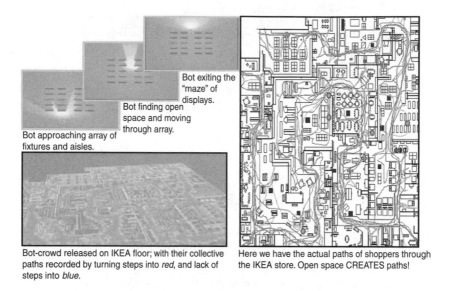

Bot exiting the "maze" of displays.

Bot finding open space and moving through array.

Bot approaching array of fixtures and aisles.

Bot-crowd released on IKEA floor; with their collective paths recorded by turning steps into *red*, and lack of steps into *blue*.

Here we have the actual paths of shoppers through the IKEA store. Open space CREATES paths!

Figure I.3 Open space driving the shoppers' navigation. (Images provided by Professor Alan Penn, UCL.)

In the upper-left of Figure I.3, you see three successive scenes of a bot approaching an array of shelf displays that block vision, with seeable open spaces indicated by the lights penetrating the array. The bot moves in the direction of the most light and seeable space and makes its way to the widest aisle, and down that to the exit of the array of displays.

On the lower-left you see this principle applied with a crowd of these bots making their way through an IKEA store model with fixtures matching a real store. The steps of the bots on the floor turns the floor redder, and areas where they don't step, over time, turn bluer. On the right, the white lines on the same floor plan is the recorded paths of actual shoppers in the real IKEA store. Open space *drives* the paths of the shoppers. There may be multiple major paths, but all of them will have the characteristic of wide visual accessibility.

We have discussed three ideas that should drive store design and impact selection at the shelf:

- **Bidirectional search**—Products search for shoppers; shoppers search for products.

- **Products/shoppers compete for space**—They occupy interfacing spaces.

- **Open space actually attracts shoppers**—Think navigation!

We have recognized and appreciated these principles before, but we have not recognized them as part of the mosaic of shopping, and particularly navigation, in the store. This reminds me of something J. R. R. Tolkien observed about a beautiful painting that you might buy and hang in a prominent place for your regular enjoyment. As time goes by, and you see it again and again, the painting gradually fades from your consciousness, until, possibly, a guest seeing it for the first time exclaims, "What a beautiful painting!" And then you look at it anew and say, "Yes, it is quite lovely!"

This principle applies to the wonder and joy of this incredible thing we have, self-service retailing, which came into being only about 100 years ago. It had a massive and positive global impact for consumers, retailers, and their suppliers. In fact, a century ago, some people understood the glories of self-service retail going on around them, and didn't just see it as "pile it high, and let it fly!" In 1916, an American visionary filed a patent for a self-serving store.[4] You can still find that spirit of innovation and efficiency today.[5] (See also: The "Path-to-Purchase" is Often a U-Turn[6].)

For retailers, the reduction or elimination of their sales team/staff, meant that their focus moved to logistics, supplier management/negotiations, and matching merchandise selection with their shoppers. No real selling was needed. Again, self-service means, "shopper, sell yourself." But the death of retailer *selling* (as contrasted with merchandising) was resisted by a few retailers. One in particular, Clarence Saunders, continually pressed for more efficiency in selling, and patented the store design represented here:

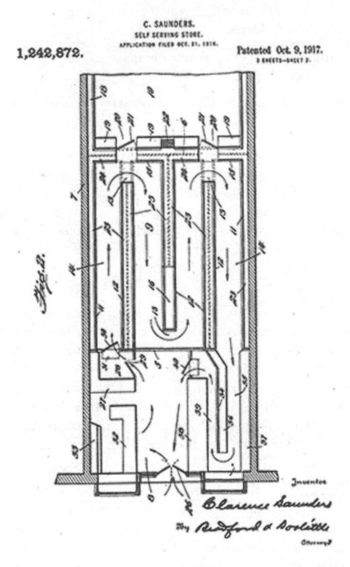

Notice the vestibule area at the front of the store, where shoppers can enter the display area, on the left, and pass in a serpentine path up and down a series of aisles. The purpose of this serpentine path was to allow the merchant to introduce the shopper to an "appropriate" offering of merchandise in a systematic way. In this way, Clarence Saunders retained control of the selling process, and was able to assist the shopper with their purchases. In effect, in these serpentine stores, the retailer assumed responsibility for selling, to an extent, instead of passively abdicating this responsibility for the sale to the shopper.

Obviously, instead of following this lead, retailers the world over abandoned Saunders' serpentine path, multiplied aisles, for which manufacturers generously rewarded them, and turned shoppers loose, to their own devices, in mini-warehouses. Retailers became passive in the process of shoppers making purchase decisions, essentially allowing selling skills to atrophy.

It is no wonder shoppers waste 80% of their time in the store, wandering about seeking something to buy - not to mention vast options when they finally arrive in an area where a purchase will actually occur. But there are modern incarnations of the serpentine store. Ikea is probably the best known global example. But for the CPG/FMCG market the pre-eminent example is Stew Leonards, where they achieve something like $100 million in sales with the serpentine path.[5]

By studying that history, and by measuring everything going on in the store, I like to think we have scraped the dull overfamiliarity off of this marvelous painting, to once again stand in awe at the view. It might seem odd that it would take a scientist, mindful of Lord Kelvin's dictum, "If you cannot express your knowledge in numbers, it is of a meager and unsatisfactory sort!" to understand the *art* of modern self-service retailing. But I am hoping an increasing number of fellow viewers will delight in the perspective—to see the obvious, again, possibly for the very first time.

My colleague, Mark Heckman, and I are getting closer to rolling out a comprehensive retail management system we call *Accelerated Merchandising*. Thinking things through from scratch again—in particular, putting the science of retailing into an historical perspective— has been a privilege. Every principle discovered can be validated by the successes and failures of the past 100 years, and accounts for the rise and fall of the retail giants in our own time. We believe it shows the way from where we are today to increased performance for all self-service retailers, both bricks and online, going forward. Here we want to share a significantly different view of the self-service sales process going on in stores around the world. I hope you find this useful to your own thinking!

Review Questions

1. Discuss what the term *bidirectional search* means. What are the two components of bidirectional search?

2. How does bidirectional search look in a passive store?

3. What does the author mean by a shopper's *clutter filter*? Why is this coping mechanism necessary in a contemporary store?

4. Is eye-level the best place on a shelf? What areas of a shelf are potentially more appealing from the shopper perspective?

5. What is meant by *product/shopper allocation*? Why does a store designer need to consider space for shoppers, not just a space for store fixtures and products?

6. What is the role of open space in in-store navigation and product visibility?

Endnotes

1. Sorensen, H. (2012, June 11). *"Googling" the Store.* Retrieved from http://www.shopperscientist.com/2012-06-11.html

2. Sorensen, H. (2008, August 16). *The Aisleness of Stores.* Retrieved from http://www.shopperscientist.com/2008-08-16.html (We now refer to "aisleness" as "product/shopper allocation.)

3. Penn, A. (2011, January 18). Who enjoys shopping in IKEA? *UCL Lunch Hour Lectures.* Retrieved from https://www.youtube.com/watch?v=NkePRXxH9D4

4. Saunders, C. (1916, October 21). U.S. patent application for the self-serving store. Retrieved from http://pdfpiw.uspto.gov/.piw?Docid=01242872&homeurl=http%3A%2F%2Fpatft.uspto.gov%2Fnetacgi%2Fnph-Parser%3FSect1%3DPTO1%26Sect2%3DHITOFF%26d%3DPALL%26p%3D1%26u%3D%2Fnetahtml%2FPTO%2Fsrchnum.htm%26r%3D1%26f%3DG%26l%3D50%26s1%3D1242872.PN.%26OS%3DPN%2F1242872%26RS%3DPN%2F1242872&PageNum=&Rtype=&SectionNum=&idkey=NONE&Input=View+first+page

5. Leonard, S. (2009). *Stew Leonard: My Story.* Colle & Co., Publishers.

6. Sorensen, H. (2010, March 27). The "Path-to-Purchase" is Often a U-Turn. Retrieved from http://www.shopperscientist .com/2010-03-27.html

PART I

Toward Total Convergence of Bricks-and-Mortar and Online Retailing

1

How We Got Here
and Where We Are Going

I n the seven years since we published the first edition of this book, society has evolved significantly. Some of that evolution is a consequence of the continual integration of technology into our lives, and some a consequence of major geopolitical events. The two are intertwined. Although this book is not about societal evolution, we do intently explore one of the greatest forces at work for the advancement of free societies. We refer to this force as *Retailing: The Trojan Horse of Global Freedom and Prosperity*.[1]

In this chapter, we look at how retailing changed in the last century to accommodate and facilitate the growing prosperity and freedom of Western societies. We focus on how retailing, and retailers, must continue to evolve to meet the demands of newly prosperous societies around the globe as they apply new technologies that change how they shop for and acquire an ever-growing list of available products. We do not spend a lot of time prognosticating on the future. As Niels Bohr noted, "Prediction is very difficult, especially about the future." This should not deter us, however, from noting obvious trajectories and preparing ourselves for the inevitable zigs and zags as society and retailing continue their *pas de deux* into an exciting and promising future.

A RECIPE FOR GROWTH

I built my more than 40-year career on three foundational stones:

- Science
- Selling
- Growth

The first two stones support the third. The more than 25% annual growth of our company, Sorensen Associates, for the 20 years from 1989 to 2009 when we sold to TNS (now Kantar Retail), adequately speaks to the effectiveness of this approach. And my science has been widely applauded and endorsed.

We begin by defining *selling* in microdetail. I assume if you are reading this book that you are prepared for a series of deep discussions on various topics concerning the present state of retailing. The meaning of *selling* is perhaps the single most important of these topics. In this chapter, I offer my own paradigm for thinking about selling.

We examine how and why the self-service retail business, magnificent engine that it is, got to its current state. The foundations of modern self-service retail were laid 100 years ago. Without knowing something of the history, it is impossible to understand why things work the way they do today.

And finally, we look at how the science of selling, and basic economics, define the way online and offline retail, clicks and bricks, must converge into a single, even more efficient retail engine than either one alone could possibly achieve.

What Is Selling?

Think about the 360-degree view in the aisle of any self-service store in the world, as seen in Figure 1.1:

Now, ask yourself what the retailer wants to *sell* the shopper in that aisle? Think about it and you will realize the absurdity of the question. The retailer is not selling the shopper anything! The retailer cares very little about what the shopper buys. His function is not to sell any one thing; rather he is here to provide a wide range of products from which the shopper may select. The shoppers sell to themselves. This is how self-service retail evolved and nothing in its history would have caused the retailer to think about the actual sales process, with few exceptions.

Figure 1.1 One shopper, thousands of items, yields only one, or a few, purchases. (Image by fStop Images—Patrick Strattner).

Selling Requires a Salesperson, Not a Retailer

The selling that we refer to here is what automobile, life insurance, and real estate salespeople do. In these industries, professionals assist their clients in identifying and selecting the products that best meet their desires and needs while simultaneously working to move product and generate profit. This is true selling. Those in the business of selling study and celebrate their craft as an art and science. The general public has a poor understanding of the fine intricacies of this type of selling. Most retailers fall into this category as well. I am fortunate in having been indoctrinated very early in life in the principle that nothing happens until somebody sells something! You can learn more about personal selling from Joe Girard, who holds the Guinness World Record as the World's Greatest Salesman, averaging more than two automobile sales per day over a 15-year period.[2]

Let's return now to our shopper standing alone in an aisle surrounded by hundreds, possibly thousands, of products and trying to decide what she wants to buy. Bear in mind that if she buys anything in this aisle at all it will most likely be just *one* item. At most, she will purchase two or three items in this aisle. Half of the shoppers that walk down this aisle on any given day will buy five or fewer items from the entire store.

This is a hard fact that, fortunately for you, most of your competition absolutely refuses to believe. One retailer told me, "Our target demographic is the stock-up shopper." In other words, he ignores *half or more* of his shoppers as non-target. The flaw in this common thinking is that a large number of those one-, two-, or three-item purchasers are stock-up shoppers. They simply are not on a stock-up trip on this occasion. Focusing on the efficiency of those small baskets is the key to substantial increases in the large baskets, too. (See Mike Twitty's "The Quick Trip Paradox," Chapter 7 of this book.)

The good news is that when you think about the challenge for the shopper and how you, as a good salesman and a *ghost in the aisle*,[3] can assist her in deciding on what to purchase, it is not difficult to increase those small baskets. Do away with the fiction that what the retailer wants bears anything but a remote relation to what the shopper wants. The reason Joe Girard sold two automobiles a day, day after day, is that he obsessively focused on what the shopper wanted, not on what Joe himself might have wanted.

SELLING: Focus on the Big Head of What the Shopper Wants to Buy

We can begin to think this way in a self-service environment by thinking about the total shopping crowd. What does the *crowd* want? We can simply answer that—for the crowd—based on what they have already been buying. In relating to the individual shopper before us, we can use the crowd's desires as a guide to satisfying the most individuals. Whatever the crowd wants in the greatest quantity means they have an *itch* for those products, which we will help them scratch. So our *selling* is first motivated by focusing only on items that are already appealing to lots of shoppers, generating lots of sales. This is the *crowd* component of our selling to shoppers. Leveraging the crowd component is illustrated in Figure 1.2a, where "Top" Seller refers to what "the crowd" has selected, not us.

Figure 1.2a The "whispering" silent Top Seller salesman—the "ghost in the aisle."

The second component is to recognize that people mostly do not have the time or interest to do deep thinking about what they buy. Any little clue that will help them to quickly make a selection is genuinely useful to the shopper. Letting them know that *this* specific item is the one most people buy here is hugely helpful. *Aha! So* most *people buy this,* or *"Choosy moms" buy this,* or *Connoisseurs prefer this one;* these are powerful triggers. This then is the *social* component of our selling—creating an association with others the shopper is likely to respect or want to emulate. Hence, we refer to this as *crowd-social* marketing.

Figure 1.2a illustrates the way our crowd-social marketing, TopSeller technique, works in a store. In this case for Juanita's Triangle Chips, the lift was actually 25% (see Figure 1.2b)!

UPC	Description	Lift $$$*
20168300000	'BEEF PATTIES 16% FAT'	390%
30400773778	'ANGEL SOFT 12 DBL ROLL'	179%
30955062044	'ROMERO'S CHUNKY SALSA'	129%
4124400006	'MARTNLI SPRKLNG CIDER NON'	109%
89293100014	'A to Z Pinot Gris'	83%
87356510124	'CLOS DU BOIS CHARDONNAY'	82%
52603054256	'PACIFIC RTS CH BR 32 OZ'	41%
71279301006	'CAESAR SALAD'	37%
71990320003	'COORS LIGHT 6 PK 16 OZ CANS'	33%
72830002011	'TILLAMOOK CHEESE CHEDDAR LOAF MED'	33%
71514150349	'EGGLANDS BEST LG EGGS'	32%
20662500000	'BREAKFAST SANDWICH'	31%
76187091506	'WEF BRN EGGS AA LRG 12 CT'	25%
48867312249	'Juanita's Triangle chips'	25%
73130028558	'OROWEAT OAT NUT BREAD'	22%
72830070218	TILL Van Bean IceCream	17%
72830011044	'TILL SHRD. SHARP'	16%
20167100000	'LEANEST GROUND BEEF 7% FAT'	16%
28080900000	'OREGON FRYER THIGHS'	14%
80660956152	'CORONA 12 PK'	14%
72830008013	'TILL. SLICED MED. CHDR.'	12%
24105590051	'GNP JUST-BR BNL/SKL BRST'	11%
Average across all 83 items		**41%**

Figure 1.2b The 83 items tagged Top Seller averaged 41% lift, year over year. This does not include the halo effect, due to more efficiency wherever the tag is used.

The full deployment of TopSeller tags in this store involved more than 80 carefully selected products, from those *most* purchased by shoppers, and resulted in an average sales increase of 41% across the featured items.

Note that we don't expect for the shopper to necessarily notice this tag on the shelf on first sight. In fact, we don't care if no one notices it. But the *subconscious mind of shoppers who already are buying this product will note the tag and add it to their repertoire of subconscious triggers* associated with that product. If they need some conscious help with this process, the text, "This item picked by our customers as one of Lamb's bestselling products," defers to "our customers," who alone have made this a bestseller. This is what we refer to as "crowd-social" marketing with the shopper, although with a bit different context than is usual for these terms. In this case, we are leveraging the fact that most shoppers really do not have the time or interest to conduct a serious, rational evaluation of the products they buy. Stores provide all kinds of highly suspect cues, but the shopper is instinctively attracted to "The Wisdom of Crowds,"[4] (See James Surowiecki.) So we are providing a gentle nudge to encourage the shopper to quickly drop in their basket something there is already a good probability that they were going to do.

This brings us to the almost certain mechanism behind the increasing sales, even if our speculation about the subconscious is not totally correct. This is the relation between the speed of making the purchase, and the quantity of purchases made. From many careful measurements, we know that shoppers have some kind of internal clock, that must have a subconscious allocation of time for tasks in the store. So, for example, if we sell more quickly in a department, the shoppers do *not* leave until their "budgeted" time is up. Typically this leads to buying more of what they were buying, or of nearby products—increasing surrounding sales. This halo effect is of tremendous importance.

> The general rule is that shoppers' time is not elastic, but their money is. If you save them time, they will spend more money. If you impede their purchasing, they will do less of it.

An important thing to note is that the TopSeller program does not involve "paying the customer to buy," also known as *promotional pricing*. We discuss this issue further in the navigational section of Chapter 2, (Tenet 3 describes the use of TopSeller to help move shoppers along the dominant path), but there is a wholesale, unwarranted expectation among retailers that splashing big signs proclaiming "price reductions" is the best way to "promote" anything. This is done while ignoring large amounts of data showing that it is not the price that drove increased sales, but the calling of attention to the product, often in a variety of ways. Promotion should never mean price alone, and in the majority of cases, price adds little to the value of the promotion.

Stop Shouting at Your Shoppers

The most powerful selling does not involve obnoxious, abrasive shouting at the customer. Far too many voices shout at shoppers in an effort to get their attention. This shouting is so pervasive in self-service stores that shoppers have developed what we call a *clutter filter* that operates at the subconscious level and discards the noise, leaving it unheard by the shopper. We encourage retailers to employ a more effective style of marketing that *whispers* to the shopper.[5] This type of selling operates at the subconscious level, relying on the shopper's instinctive responses. Most importantly, it does not try to get the shopper to buy anything they have no natural inclination to buy. It works with the shopper to help them do what their habits and instincts reveal *they want to do*. But there is also a stark difference in the time it takes to impact sales. This is a sure method whose impact builds over weeks and months. It is *not* a costly flash-in-the-pan, but a true *nudge* method whose effects compound over time.

The example of whispering shown below represents the tip of the iceberg of the potential increase in sales and profits that more efficient self-service retail can achieve through leveraging the shopper's subconscious instincts. Figure 1.3 shows a photo of the shelf where our Top Seller tag whispered to shoppers on behalf of the "salesperson" and shows the impact of our technique:

Figure 1.3 Out-of-stock (OOS) means the shopper needs more facings/ inventory!!!

The promoted item is nearly out-of-stock, or OOS, which is the best proof of extraordinary sales. We regularly see OOS with this nonfinancial promotion. What's the solution to this problem that costs retailers 4 to 8% of sales across the board, other than more diligent stocking? You can double the display size for products that consistently go OOS. Never mind your deals with suppliers. This product has earned the love of the shoppers. The bricks store is a warehouse and allocation of storage, represented as shelf space, that should follow the needs of the shoppers as shown in the sales of merchandise.

From Opportunity to Final Purchase

This study tracks the behavior of the shopper's eye as it moves from point-to-point in the final few seconds before their purchase goes into the basket. See figure 1.4. Notice that, as this process begins, the initial fixations are 0.3 to 0.4 seconds in duration, increasing to about 0.7 seconds as the product goes into the basket. Fast eye movement at the start, and much slower in the end.

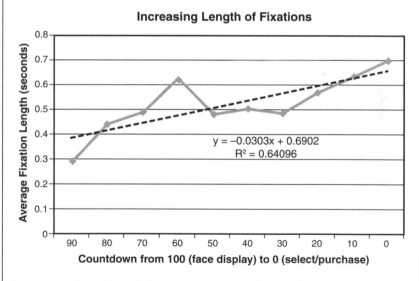

Figure 1.4 From first sighting (point of focus) to final focus-purchase, the length of fixations tend to increase.

Turning our attention now to what the shopper focuses on, Figure 1.5, sorted into six broad categories: brand name or symbol, picture or graphic design element, verbal description of the product, price, variety or flavor, or other package element.

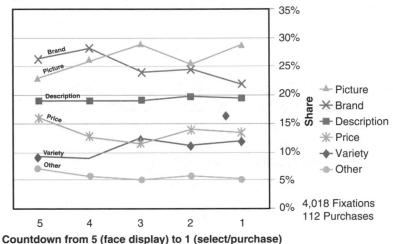

Figure 1.5 From first sighting to final focus-purchase, brand and graphic/photo dominate shopper consideration.

The entire process is dominated by either the brand (including the logo) or a picture. Initially, the brand name or logo dominates, and then the photo identification of the product dominates later in the process.

The actual amount of time it takes broadly varies from as few as five seconds to the quite-long 60 seconds. Dividing these into three categories—short, medium, and long time—Figure 1.6, notice that the shortest purchases focus heavily on the picture and textual description. This suggests that the picture element is the quickest way to communicate to a shopper, and a brief description, along with the brand, is enough to close the deal quickly. The more time the sale takes, the greater the role the brand will play.

Notice that in every case, the price is at best the fourth influencer (as evidenced by the shopper's attention.) So when retailers want to sell something to shoppers, what is their first idea? *Price.* Hmmm!

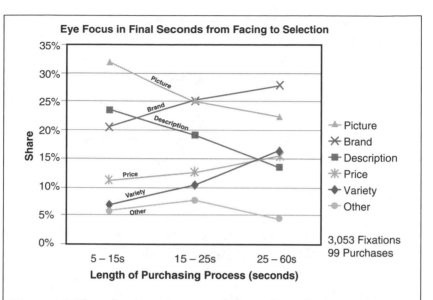

Figure 1.6 The more time taken to make a purchase, the more attention is given to the variety and brand. Perhaps multiple options for a brand (varieties) slow the decision process, with continuing reference to the brand itself, to assure that the shopper is still considering within their brand of choice.

Also, note that the longer the purchase takes, in total seconds, the more attention is invested in brand, variety, and price. This may suggest that the more variety (brands, prices, and flavors) the longer it takes the shoppers to make up their minds—almost certainly suppressing sales. (Refer to Figure 2.2 in Chapter 2.)

The complete study can be seen online at: "From Opportunity to Final Purchase" at www.shopperscientist.com/2014-03-24.html.

How We Got This Way

No matter its incarnation, from the rickety, fetid, fish merchant's stall in a dusty, cacophonous, medieval open-air market, to the sleek, computerized, Amazon drone that delivers a cellophane-encased DVD to your front door, retailing has always been about getting a product some people have produced into the hands of other people who want the product and are willing to pay for it. By studying how society has managed this process in the past, and how we developed the current system of self-service retail, we can better understand the evolution taking place now that's driven by online retail and other advances in technology. The better we are able to see this bigger picture, the better we can position ourselves to thrive in the new retail landscape.

Here I look at the final mile of this process through a scientific lens and focus on the *meeting of the minds* of the retailer and shopper, the most critical function in retail, where the shopper agrees to purchase a specific product and the retailer agrees to provide the product for a specific price. From there, I work backwards through the mental process of the shopper to the origin of that need or desire. I also look at the process preceding the shopper's trip to the store by which the retailers and suppliers play their part in making the products available, eventually leading us to the *inside of the store* and to that final transaction.

Early Shopping in America

One hundred years ago there were a half million small stores in America whose proprietors and clerks personally assisted each shopper in selecting the products they wished to purchase. Clerks often developed personal relationships with their customers and knew their preferences and dislikes. Clerks also had to have extensive knowledge of the products they made available in their shops. They knew which products they were most likely to sell to which shoppers. Products were usually displayed on shelves behind the counter and out of reach of the shoppers who relied on the clerks to guide them in their purchasing decisions by narrowing the selection and dismissing any products that would not meet their needs or desires. The clerk eventually passed selected products across the counter to the shopper for closer inspection or for purchase. In this way, clerks sold products to shoppers.

The Birth of Self-Service Retail

In the early twentieth century, increased production, efficient supply and distribution chains, and lower prices for most products expanded the store shelves tremendously. To accommodate this massive increase in available products, the clerk was replaced by the merchant warehouseman who arranged products on shelves accessible to the shoppers. This model continues today, as shoppers navigate aisles filled with unprecedented amounts of inventory, ever-increasing variety at ever-decreasing prices. Instead of helpful clerks providing individualized assistance, a cacophony of voices in the forms of labeling, advertising, and promotions assault shoppers from all sides. Shoppers must rely on the products themselves for assistance in determining which best meet their needs or desires. Their interactions with the merchant are reduced to a brief transaction at the check-out stand.

The massive increase in productivity brought about by the Industrial Revolution and the subsequent transformation of society drove the transition from service retail to self-service retail. Several important players had a hand this process, but one dominated the field of retail in the early twentieth century. The impact on retail of The Great Atlantic & Pacific Tea Company, better known as A&P, was outsized, and A&P ultimately became the first billion-dollar retailer in the world.[6]

A&P began as a tea merchant in the nineteenth century. In 1870, many years before the self-service retail revolution, the company introduced the first consumer packaged good, although at the time they only sold it to the wholesale trade (Figure 1.7).

Figure 1.7 Thea Nectar, packaged tea introduced in 1870 by the Great A&P. Advertisement © Great Atlantic & Pacific.

Think of that package of tea as the harbinger of the explosive growth of branded, packaged goods 50 years later. Branding and prepackaging products was a prerequisite for the efficient distribution and selling of products by self-service retail. The efficiency of mass production and mass packaging demanded efficiency in distribution and retailing, both of which were seriously fragmented and inefficient in the early years of the twentieth century.

At this point, the two Hartford brothers, John and George, heirs to the A&P tea business, began what would eventually become the world's first billion-dollar retail business. John was the marketing genius who could presage the movement of society and read the evolving market like a book. George was a number cruncher, running a data-driven business with paper, pencil, and mimeograph long before electronic calculators or computers.

Together, the Hartford brothers built a business model that would influence self-service retail for the next 100 years. Their revolutionary strategy did not rely on return on margins, the basic foundation of most businesses. Instead, they built on return on capital. This was a huge issue, the misunderstanding of which leads to a lot of misunderstanding of retailing today, even by many within the industry. As Marc Levinson explains:

> The preference for volume over margin was a matter on which the Hartford brothers [initially] did not see eye to eye. George hewed to a traditional understanding of retail profitability, preferring to maintain a generous markup on each item sold. Profits averaged an impressive 3% of sales from 1921 to 1925, appearing to show the success of the high-markup strategy. John, though, downplayed return on sales as a measure of profitability. He preferred to watch the company's return on investment. Historically, A&P's pretax return on investment had exceeded 25% in most years, and John set that as the norm. The way to boost return on investment, he thought, was to make better use of capital by pushing more merchandise through A&P's stores and warehouses.
>
> Rather than trying to increase profits per dollar of sales—the conventional strategy of the day—A&P was deliberately seeking to reduce profits per dollar sold in hopes of creating more sales.
>
> The two brothers' strengths were in unique alignment. John Hartford's high-volume, low-price strategy, executed with George Hartford scrutinizing every financial detail, represented a radically new model for retailers.

This business of measuring profitability based on revenue per capital deployed rather than revenue per margins (on dollar sales) is at the heart of driving prices down, down, down while driving volume up, up, up.

Think about this in relation to Amazon nearly a century later. Capital efficiency is driving the next wave of retailing—not the mode of selling or delivery.

This business model was made to order for a self-service retailer, who stocked the warehouse (store) and used unpaid stock-pickers (shoppers) to sell themselves the merchandise they wanted with the retailer collecting payment at the exit. The retailer turned merchant warehouseman. This was *efficiency*!

A&P drove that efficiency as their volume increased across large numbers of stores. They expected their suppliers to be more efficient, too. Where they could not find suitably efficient suppliers, A&P built their own plants and manufactured their own products. Kroger was another retailer active in manufacturing. The same principle applied to the distribution and warehousing aspects of the business. No one who continued to do retailing according to nineteenth-century paradigms was spared under the new, more efficient system introduced by chains like A&P. The slaughter was complete from the mom and pop stores, up the chain through the distributors, wholesalers, and to the manufacturers themselves. Joseph Schumpeter described the process as *creative destruction*. We are experiencing another wave of creative destruction today.

Today, we take for granted many of the features created as a part of the self-service retail evolution. We fail to recognize how and why they came into being, and possibly more importantly, how they interrelate. Really low prices came from not trying to make profits based on margin sales, but instead on super-efficiency of the capital investment. This meant that the return on capital was high with prices being low, driving traffic of both shoppers and products through the stores.

We All Need to Eat!

Today advertising remains the number-one source of profits for self-service retailers. Though Walmart continued A&P's philosophical legacy of focusing on operating efficiency, they mostly took their profits in the traditional mark-up way. But rather than marking prices up for their shoppers, they convinced suppliers to share *their* healthy margins through lower wholesale prices, to create more Walmart profits.

Walmart could never have achieved its astounding ascendancy at retail, eventually pushing nearly half a trillion dollars, if it had continued to rely on store efficiency and low prices to drive sales. The reality, which we discuss in a later chapter, is that prices are an ambivalent and costly tool in driving store traffic and thence sales. Walmart did not go to the head of the pack based on a pricing strategy alone. Rather, Walmart built its empire on a *grocery strategy!*

It's a scientific fact that humans have certain biological and hierarchical needs. Air is at the top of the needs pyramid. Without it, human survival is limited to a few minutes. Water is nearly as critical a need, with humans requiring it on a daily basis. Next on the hierarchy is food, which humans can go without for, at most, a couple of weeks. We are used to satisfying our need or desire for food and water every few hours. It is no wonder that the average American family visits a supermarket twice or more a week.

Walmart could not drive the traffic needed to reach the pinnacle of retailing without selling food. Although it is valuable to have the meme *"Always low prices, Always,"* associated with a store, shoppers will not go to that store if it does not have what the shoppers need. And all shoppers, no matter where they live or how much money they have, will always need food.

But there is another source of income for a retailer like A&P. The company advertised and promoted the merchandise in their stores in weekly circulars and newspapers. Brand suppliers realized the tremendous benefit in getting their own products featured in A&P's print advertising. And A&P expected their brand suppliers to help pay for that advertising. But think about this: If the brands were paying to promote their own products through A&P advertising, why shouldn't A&P also charge the brand for various other promotional services inside the store?

Remember, A&P was aiming for as close to zero mark-up on products as they possibly could, to keep prices low and drive traffic through the stores. At the same time, the brands were aiming for—and achieving—relatively high margins. So why shouldn't the retailer who was stocking and delivering those products to the customer share in some of that brand margin as a reasonable share of advertising money?

As well as becoming merchant warehousemen 100 years ago, in the same process, retailers also became major *media* companies. Stores offered a way for a brand manufacturer to reach his audience. Stores could sell the access to their shoppers in the same way that a newspaper sold advertising on the basis of their circulation.

The evolution of self-service retailers into media companies selling access to an audience was a direct consequence of merchant warehousemen choosing not to make the majority of their profits by marking up the prices of the products, but rather by getting as close as they could to giving away products in order to generate massive traffic. To John Hartford, this amounted to 2.5% net profit from selling products to shoppers, an absurdly low level if this was their only revenue. But this was a media company now.

This arrangement—merchant warehousemen providing brand suppliers with access to large numbers of shoppers in exchange for financial consideration from those suppliers, while offering products at low prices to the shoppers—has not changed in the past 100 years. Not really, of course. But self-service retailers still operate in the paradigm that A&P created. A decade after the Hartford brothers died, a new player, adopting a modified form of the Hartford plan, broke on the scene—Sam Walton.

Although Walton pursued the same ferocious low price strategy that the Hartford brothers had, he did not follow their model of selling his suppliers access to his shoppers. He expected suppliers to give him all that media money in the form of lower wholesale prices. He would promote Walmart stores and the products he sold without direct supplier participation. Suppliers could only buy favor with Walmart by cutting their own prices.

Although we cannot fully understand self-service retail without understanding the advertising component of the business, we must also consider that for the brand suppliers, retailer advertising was only one component of the reach business. The need of suppliers to reach the self-service retail shoppers had a significant impact on the development of radio and television. Major brand sponsorship of programming such as soap operas, sporting events, and news funded the rapid growth of those media. Figure 1.8 illustrates the classic Tide advertisement.

Figure 1.8 Classic Tide advertisement.

The *selling* by major brands through mass media represented an efficient means of communicating with their customers. But through the programing it made possible, and even through the commercials themselves, it also helped knit disparate regions of the country into a unified whole and created a new national consciousness. Retailing may have been an unwitting and unintentional force behind this transformation, but that does not alter the fact that retailing has been at the cutting edge of social evolution for the past century. In a sense, efficiency and convenience are the glue that binds the United States together. And, the glue of commerce will work its will on the global population regardless of political forces to the contrary.

Can Selling Make a Comeback in the Twenty-first Century?

By the second half of the twentieth century, the selling that was once practiced in small retail stores across the country was now ensconced in the national media and driven by the troika: brand manufacturers, advertising agencies, and major broadcast networks. But any professional salesman lives for the final moment of the sale, in the close, when the sale is consummated! Hence the mantra, "close early and close often." Unfortunately, it is not possible for even the most super-selling mass media to actually close the sale for the self-service retail shopper, because they cannot be in the aisle where the sale is ultimately consummated.

We began our discussion of the consummation of the sale by explaining why no one is actually selling to shoppers in self-service stores and how shoppers must actually sell to themselves with little assistance from retailers or suppliers. We demonstrated one remedy for this situation with the example of using Top Seller tags allowing the retailer to be a *ghost in the aisle* and actually sell a product by tapping the habits of current buyers. We now look at the next evolution self-service retailing must make in order to remain the effective force for global freedom and prosperity it has been for the past century.

First, let's begin with the reasonable assumption that we are going exactly where we are already heading. For this purpose, we will divide all the purchases made by all the shoppers in all the stores in the world, regardless of product category or class of trade, into four general categories. This is necessary because most of my facts and figures and my science of retail is driven by the study of high-volume self-service retail. However, the *principles* can be applied broadly. But they are easier to apply if we recognize the classes of purchases made in any store. These principles can guide your thinking in any store in the world. (See Chapter 6, "Long Cycle Purchasing.")

The Four Dimensions of Purchasing

Before we examine how to sell in a self-service store, we need to better understand the shoppers and how the absence of selling manifests to them. We also need to understand the shopper's online selling experiences and how those experiences translate to the bricks world. We can think of the shopper's experience, both online and bricks, in terms of a *hedonic-time dimension*. A hedonic dimension, one driven by elements such as enjoyment, convenience, and pleasure, alone is inadequate for our purpose because time is often the most important element to the shopper.

NOW!!!

Surprise
Delight

Routine
Autopilot

Frustration
Angst

Figure 1.9 The four purchase states: 1-Immediacy (Now!); 2-Pleasure (Surprise/Delight); 3-Routine (Autopilot); 4-Frustration (Angst). (In order from left to right: © bokasana / Fotolia, © puhhha / Fotolia, © Kirsty Pargeter / Fotolia, © Dieter Hawlan / Fotolia).

We can express the Hedonic-Time Dimension in four purchase states: Now!, Surprise/Delight, Routine/Autopilot, and Frustration/Angst (Figure 1.9). These four states have parallels in the personal sales world. Think of self-service as unmediated selling, and personal sales as mediated selling. If you have a personal sales store, you simply have that personal layer over the underlying self-service structure I am describing.

Because the four purchase states describe the psychic state of the shopper and say nothing about the class of merchandise they are shopping for and purchasing, this paradigm works for retailing "shoes or ships or sealing wax" as Lewis Carroll might have described it. It transcends all self-service retail, whether supermarkets, electronic stores, clothing, auto parts or any other class of trade.

Click-and-Collect

Although bricks retailers currently enjoy the advantage over online when it comes to Now! purchases, online retailers are making continuous improvements upon their one inherent weakness in this key purchase state: *delivery of the item*.

As we discuss in later chapters, online retailers such as Amazon are building their success on a foundation of helping their shoppers select specific, individual items from their inventory of hundreds of thousands of items, quickly and efficiently. A shopper no longer has to be her own stock-picker, wandering through aisles of thousands of warehoused items and picking the few she wants from the shelves. She now only has to click her mouse and wait for Amazon to deliver her selection to her via UPS, FedEx, or even by automated flying drone.

The bricks retailer's answer to the online stock-picking service is *click-and-collect*. Under this system, shoppers who do not wish to wait for delivery can select their items online and then collect them, at the store, on their own schedule.

Many bricks retailer's experiments with click-and-collect have proven less than stellar. This is because bricks retailers still operate in a merchant warehouseman culture where their function is simply to stock pallets of products from which shoppers pick items for themselves, whereas online success is driven by a culture of bringing individual shoppers together with individual items.

Throughout this book, we explore ways in which bricks retail culture can change through innovation and understanding the mind of the shopper. To quote Pope Francis, "Things will not return to how they were before." The culture of retail is changing before our eyes. Bricks retailers must change with it.

These four purchase states are a key to understanding how bricks retailing is currently intersecting with online retailing. As we define these states and map out an ideal path for bricks retailers and online retailers, a paradigm emerges in which the two converge rather than merely intersect.

Now! Purchases (Advantage—Bricks Retail)

From the traditional trade in early development markets to the most advanced markets in the world, stores have always functioned as communal pantries, a place where everyone in the community can go to get things that they do not presently have in stock in their own homes or workplaces. There is a stage in our evolution from the minimalist living of primitives when growing wealth allows the population to begin storing excess provisions of all types in their own homes. This storing of excess, for later use, is done in the *pantry*. Later, when abundance becomes more common, and stores more ubiquitous, it makes a lot less sense to store things in either home or office, and then society moves back in the direction of the communal pantry in which the store *stores* everything you need, and you simply come and get it.

We do not readily recognize that we live in such a system, because when we ask shoppers how many items they purchased at the store on their most recent trip, no one says "one" and most say "five" or even more. But as we will see, studies show that the most common number of items purchased from any store in the world is *one*. We won't provide a full psychological explanation for this fact, but usually shoppers do not buy a single item in a store for use the next day, week, or month. Single items are purchased to fill an immediate need. Immediacy drives the single-item purchase, which is inextricably then linked to Now!

The Now! factor heavily favors bricks retailing. Hence, the large focus of online retailing on same-day or next-day delivery. But, for genuine immediacy, other than electronic delivery of music, books, and the like, it is hard to see how bricks retailing can totally lose their immediacy advantage.

Surprise/Delight Purchases (Advantage—Bricks Retail)

You might think of Surprise/Delight as the domain of clothing, electronics, sports gear, or other non-grocery type merchandise. But we can reasonably apply the classification to a large range of merchandise. Often, retailers single-mindedly focus on price for this function. That can obviously be costly. Other experiential factors, however, can play a role here. For example, something as simple as quality customer service might be a Surprise/Delight.

There is a 360-degree experience attendant on bricks shopping that strongly supports Surprise/Delight. But the most common bricks retailer experience, in which shoppers navigate through rows and aisles filled with tens of thousands of items, is not impenetrable to online. This means that even though bricks has some inherent advantages for this purchase state, the typical bricks store is highly vulnerable to online Surprise/Delight challenges.

Routine/Autopilot Purchases (Advantage—Online Retail)

This state refers to what Neale Martin[7] describes as anything the shopper habitually buys, whether by frequency or by a consistent pattern of behavior. Anything purchased routinely can be automated or semi-automated, at tremendous relief to the shopper, making all such purchases the natural bailiwick of the online retailer.

This category of merchandising is heavily weighted toward groceries. Remember, groceries drove Walmart to nearly half a trillion dollars in sales. People did not spend all that money on groceries, but the frequency of their trips to buy groceries drove a lot of other purchases. The efficiency with which online retailers can tap into the Routine/Autopilot purchase represents the bricks retailer's greatest vulnerability.

Frustration/Angst Purchases (Advantage—Online Retail)

The frustration and angst purchases are often phantom purchases, meaning that they don't happen, even though the shopper *wants* them to happen. Have you been to a store recently and left without something you really wanted or needed but couldn't find? Maybe you couldn't find the right color, flavor, or size. Maybe the store didn't have anything close to what you wanted. Or possibly it was a price issue. That's a phantom purchase, a purchase that never happened!

These purchases will never go away. But Amazon, with its Everything Store strategy, backed up by a host of other online merchants a Google search away, means online will own the Frustration/Angst purchase. This doesn't mean that bricks will not continue to play a part. Remember, immediate need favors the bricks retailer in nearly all cases.

Where Is Selling Going?

So with these purchase psychology principles in mind, let's get into the pivotal facts that are driving retail where many do not want to go. There are three basic sets of data that tell the tale, Figure 1.10:

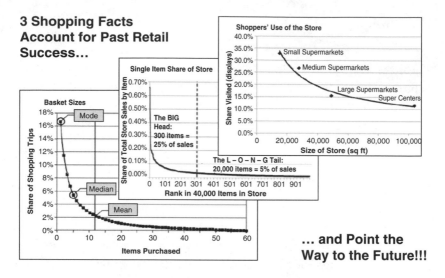

Figure 1.10 Look to the past to understand the future!

The first chart (at the lower left) shows just how many items shoppers buy in the store. This curve looks the same for any store in the world, except that the scale on the bottom varies depending on the type of store. The one here shows a supermarket, but a drug store or a supercenter would have the same curve shape. Just the median moves, with smaller medians for smaller stores and larger medians for larger stores. This chart tells us a lot about current retail and where it is going. The rule here is that the largest number of trips buys very little. This is definitely driven by the Now! type purchase.

The second chart (in the middle) describes the *Big Head*. This represents what is bought in large quantity. Shoppers across the spectrum share a lot of characteristics: Most everyone buys milk, eggs, butter, bread, and so on. This leads the crowd of shoppers to buy certain products in large quantity; hence, Big Head. On the other hand, everyone is unique in some ways and they buy distinctive items for themselves. Some of us like macadamia nuts and others prefer cashews. Or very few shoppers buy many items rarely and others not at all. This creates the *Long Tail*. Nearly all bricks retailers do a poor job of distinctly managing these two entities. This spells large opportunity for those who choose to do it right. Hint: Some of the most successful stores in the world have just lopped off the Long Tail. Costco, the second largest retailer globally, has only

4,000 items in the store. However, I have long believed that any Big Head plus Long Tail store could outperform a Big Head only store. Amazon is certainly proving this online.

The third chart (at the upper-right) reflects the retailers' poor management of the Big Head and the Long Tail by showing the larger the store, the less of it is visited by shoppers. Although shoppers do tend to buy more items per trip in larger stores, the overall efficiency of the store plummets. Nearly all bricks stores are squandering two types of capital: real estate, such as buildings and fixtures, and static inventory. The larger the store, the more capital it squanders. I refer to this capital as *parked*, because it is very inefficient in delivering sales.

Online retailing addresses the parked capital problem. Amazon does not have unpaid stock-pickers wasting warehouse space along with unmoving inventory. Notice they *do* pay their stock-pickers, which is an online disadvantage to bricks, where they are unpaid.

Given the natural advantages of bricks retailers for one share of purchase states and a natural advantage of online for a different share of purchase states, any serious retailer must manage both modes under their banner. The problem is that skilled retailers like Amazon are essentially mediating sales to shoppers automatically but in a personal sales mode. Their selling strategies tap into the intuitive, instinctive, and habitual tendencies of shoppers and rival the mediated personal sales occurring in the service-type bricks store. The challenge lying ahead is to figure out how bricks retailing can be more efficient and at the same time supercharge that efficiency by a blended online presence within the bricks store. We take a closer look at how retail is struggling with this challenge in our chapter on Amazon's bricks store in Seattle.

While bricks retailers are struggling, often in ineffective ways, to bring online to their bricks stores through *click and collect*, where shoppers order products online then pick-up their orders at the store, Amazon is moving to become an overt bricks retailer.[8] Any bricks retailers looking to thrive through the next evolution in self-service retail will adopt an approach complementary to the one in those Amazon stores. That is, bricks retailers must be looking to encroach on Amazon's business, from within their bricks stores!

We will now consider in some detail a phased plan for converting a bricks store into a store that retains its brand but with the retail potential of the pending Amazon bricks stores.

Like the early twentieth-century mom and pop store that fell to the relentless efficiency of retailers like A&P, unless today's bricks store learns to un-park its capital and improves shopper efficiency it is a sitting duck for the predatory intentions of Amazon. Successful online retailers such as Amazon will learn the basics of Big Head bricks retailing much easier than successful bricks retailers can learn to meet the *minds* of their shoppers, because of their long-learned merchant warehousemen ways. By applying its automated personal selling process, without the wasteful capital, Amazon could become the world's largest retailer in just a few years.

The Selling Prescription

As successful as online retailing has been to this point, online is not going to swallow up the entire world of retail. I like to say that as long as people live in bricks houses, they will be shopping in bricks stores. Eventually, however, online and bricks must converge in an ideal store that leverages the strengths of both modes and taps into all four purchasing states. Anyone who can successfully manage that evolution will own retail in the twenty-first century.

I have great confidence that someone will actually build and operate many thousands of these ideal stores. But they will not be cookie-cutter stores. Populations and markets have great similarities which we want to leverage. But they also have differences, which is what drives the Long Tail. So our prescription will have some rigid and invariant principles, but also lots of flexibility, both in final execution and in getting from where each store is to the varied form of *ideal* that will be its evolving future.

If we could even semi-automate half of the routine/autopilot grocery purchases made in stores, we could drastically reduce the square footage of selling space needed while massively increasing shopper efficiency. At the same time, we could turn our attention to the Surprise/Delight function. For starters, let's just focus on the shopper's efficiency.

The Shopper's Ideal Self-Service Retail Experience

A convergence between bricks and online might work like this: At the beginning of each week, the retailer sends every shopper enrolled in the program a list of items they most likely need to buy this week based on their prior purchases and the seasonal calendar. Think of this list as their "stock-picking" list. The shopper can strike off what items they do not want and add anything they do want that is not already on the list. The majority of any soft upselling should be done in the retailer's creation of the list itself. Then the shopper return-emails the list to the store. The bricks retailer confirms the order in the same way Amazon does, including the time for pick-up.

Quite a number of bricks retailers are already facilitating shoppers ordering from the store using the Internet. The shopper simply comes to the store to pick up their order. There should be no special attempt to get them to order everything, especially fresh produce and other products that are an important component of Surprise/Delight.

If you intend to continue to be a bricks retailer, you should not encourage shipping. The reason for this will become clear in the following process. The orders themselves are stock-picked by low-wage employees during slow times in the store, prepackaged in clear plastic bags so the shopper can see what they are getting, charged to the shopper, placed in a shopping cart with the shopper's name and list prominently affixed, and held in a secure area near the entry of the store but well within the shopping area. We will call this pick-up area the *convergence depot*. This crucial step is potentially as important as Amazon's one-click ordering. The goal is to encourage the shopper to put additional items in the basket and add them to the checkout total when they come to the store for pick-up. If curbside delivery is offered, the delivery staff should always offer appropriate add-on items. Remember: never stop selling, Ms. Active Retailer!

We do not want to hurry the shopper away from the store. Rather, we are accelerating the Routine/Autopilot purchases through the online mode. At the same time, we do not want to obstruct shoppers from leaving immediately, recognizing the time factor of the hedonic-time dimension in which the four purchasing states exist. This is the essential element of the convergence of online and bricks retailing. Bricks retailers must not think of themselves as running bricks stores with the alternative of shopping at their online store. It must be one smoothly integrated operation, and the simple process described here will facilitate the convergence by taking the drudgery of routine purchasing off the table, allowing what time is devoted to bricks shopping to be diverted to Surprise/Delight and Now! shopping.

What Does the Ideal Self-Service Retail Store of the Future Look Like?

To show how our ideal store is divided into two separate functions, consider this diagram, Figure 1.11:

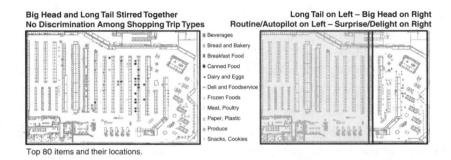

Figure 1.11 Conceptual migration from current store to a new, smaller, more efficient store.

The store on the left is an actual supermarket, and the dots show the locations of 80 of the top 500 sellers, to illustrate dispersion across the store. Those dots represent the named categories, starting with the number-one seller (bananas). The top 500 altogether represent about one third of total store sales. The store on the left has dispersed the items that are most important to the shoppers across the entire store. The store on the right concentrates those items in a smaller area about one-third the size, which is devoted to efficiently serving the shopping crowd. This store is targeting the Surprise/Delight/Now! shopper.

What we are doing here is moving every one of those individual items into the one-third of the store nearest the entrance and leaving the Long Tail in a new "warehouse" area. This doesn't mean there is a hard and fast rule that no Big Head items can be in the Long Tail area, or that no

Long Tail items can occur in the Big Head area. Secondary placements will make sense on a very selective basis. But let me point out that one of the major reasons produce outsells every other category in the store is simply because the total number of items on display in this relatively large area is miniscule compared to what is typical of center-of-store aisles. I'm not detracting from the value of fresh fruit and vegetables but simply pointing out that the way they are merchandised has a lot to do with their very large sales. And this is why Big Head stores around the world vastly outperform the typical Long Tail store—95% of the stores in the world.

What we have done here is create a means for distinct management of the Routine/Autopilot sale, those sales that need to move to online ordering and ultimately to automated, or even robotic, stock-picking. This is the path to radically downsizing the parked capital in store area and inventory. Do not hesitate in testing the waters by restructuring your merchandise to align with this plan. Remember, though, this is an evolutionary process in which the shopper must take the lead by ordering their Routine/Autopilot purchases online. They are going to do it with Amazon, or someone else, if not with you.

The Dark Store

Bear in mind that retailers in the United Kingdom and France have already significantly leveraged the *dark store* concept, in which the store shelves are not open to the public but rather house goods to fulfill online orders. In Europe, the dark store primarily facilitates click and collect.[9] These examples bear little relation to the *convergence of online, mobile, and bricks-and-mortar (COMB)* retail that we examine here. In the U.S., the Toys-R-Us dark store effort uses existing stores as warehouses, struggling blindly to make some use of their parked inventory in an online mode.[10] *Retailers need to realize that a large portion of their store is already dark in the sense that shoppers make very little use of it.*

What we prescribe here is the gradual evolution to a store that does not need such a large dark store component, but allows that function to be shared across large numbers of their former Big Head and Long Tail stores (refer to the left illustration in Figure 1.11). We want to build a very large volume of online sales by nudging shoppers to replace the shopping they normally do in in the dark portions of the supermarkets they already frequent with online shopping. Don't shove them out of your dark store. Just make it more convenient for them to buy the dark store products from you online while they continue to buy Surprise/Delight/Now! purchases in your smaller, more efficient, higher velocity, store. And, they often begin those purchases when they pick up their shopping carts prefilled with their online orders, with *their* name on it, in your convergence depot!

Step-by-Step

Next we outline the probable phases in moving from current self-service retail store to a store that leverages the Surprise/Delight/Now! purchase states while reducing the parked capital of the dark and Long Tail store (refer to the right and left side of Figure 1.11).

- **Phase I—Existing store with significant online fulfillment:** Quite a few stores—particularly in the UK, but around the globe, already have the option to order online and pick-up at the store, or click and collect. As a retailer managing your store's evolution into a fully converged online and bricks store, your first step is to begin the process by adding the convergence depot near the front of the store but within the current first shopping area, that is, wherever most shoppers now actually begin selecting items for purchase, often the produce area. The convergence depot should be attractive and highly visible so that all shoppers in the store can see how online shoppers benefit from preordering their purchases by having the orders ready for them when they arrive at the store. But also so they can watch these shoppers possibly picking up a few more items to add to those carts with an express checkout just for the preorder customers. Keep in mind that payment systems will continue integrating near field communication and other technologies that will eventually eliminate check-out as we know it. Retailers will need to keep up with these developments while at the same time implementing the necessary changes to leverage them.

- **Phase II—Bidirectional migration of Big Head and Long Tail merchandise:** Notice that there is no need to shuffle merchandise while you are building your online base of shoppers, who are also smoothly transitioning from online to bricks when they pick up at the store. As this process builds, closely monitor what additional items shoppers are buying in the store along with their online orders as a guide to decide what products would be best moved from the dark, Long Tail store to your budding Surprise/ Delight/Now! store. At the same time, anything crowding the Surprise/Delight/Now! store but moving slowly is parked merchandise and should be targeted for migrating to the dark, Long Tail section of your store. These movements can begin early and should be driven by close monitoring of the transaction logs.

- **Phase III—Making the Surprise/Delight/Now!–Dark/Long Tail distinction explicit to the shoppers:** At some point, you will have enough volume from online sales coming out of the store that you will be able to pool online orders from multiple stores. For example, the shoppers picking up their online ordered merchandise from your convergence depot really don't care where that merchandise came from. You may use the dark, Long Tail section of a single store to service a group of maybe 10 or more stores. Phase III tees up the ball for that move by perhaps distinctly partitioning all dark, Long Tail sections in the individual stores and eventually selecting one of the stores to be the dark, Long Tail mothership for all the others. This is also the phase in which to semifinalize just what the composition of the Surprise/Delight/ Now! is going to be, probably no more than a few thousand SKUs.

- **Phase IV—Nearly all stores are only Surprise/Delight/Now! with dark stores abandoned or repurposed:** The final, ideal neighborhood store will be around 10,000 square feet with a heavy focus on fresh deli, bakery, produce, and high volume purchases. Shoppers select most of their purchases before leaving their home, nudged by whispers from the *ghost in the cloud*, the twenty-first century version of the helpful clerk reminding them what products they might need and which products they might desire. They arrive at the store to find their shopping cart waiting for them in the welcoming convergence depot already stocked with all their Routine/Autopilot purchases. Rather than tediously meandering up and down aisles of shelves stocked with thousands of products, immediately upon entering the store shoppers encounter a plethora of Surprise/Delight purchasing

---

opportunities. They browse through pleasantly arranged selections of high-volume, low-priced products that make them want to buy for the joy of it! Perhaps they decide to indulge in a treat tonight and wander through the bakery or look in the ice cream display to satisfy that Now! impulse. After adding several products to their cart, they head to the express checkout.

It is possible that many of these new communal pantries will be built by new players in the self-service retail game, perhaps Amazon, Google, or other aggressive global players that successfully mastered the convergence of online and bricks retail.

Something like this four-phase process must almost certainly happen, given global retail trends today. A huge driving force will be the shoppers who will *love* the convenience—and probably savings. For the retailer reducing the untenable amount of capital currently parked in inefficient space and inventory, this will level the playing field against pure online retailers as well as the traditional bricks competition.

The Ever-Changing Retail Landscape Favors an Evolving Retailer Species

We have examined how at the beginning of the last century retail changed from a personal sales model to a merchant warehouse model to accommodate and facilitate the growing prosperity of Western societies. That revolution saw the slaughter of small, inefficient stores unable to compete with advances in supply chain management, large merchant warehouse stores, and resulting lower prices. We have also shown that at the beginning of the twenty-first century we are experiencing yet another retail revolution as shoppers adopt new technologies that offer even more efficient ways to shop for and acquire the products they need and desire. And we have mapped out a possible strategy for retailers willing and ready to join the revolution and fully exploit the potential of a new *selling* paradigm that leverages the convergence of online, mobile, and bricks retailing (COMB).

Change is never easy. Many retailers have not yet gone beyond the tentative first phases of adopting a new model for selling. Others are struggling for survival, blaming a global economy for decimating their businesses while failing to recognize a fundamental shift in the very functions of buying and selling. But this revolution is just getting underway. In the years to come, it will drive us to new heights of efficiency beyond anything Joseph Schumpeter could have imagined when he described the last century's revolution as creative destruction.

Our next chapter provides a set of five vital tenets as a suite of metrics that will define those retailers surviving, and even thriving, in the twenty-first century retail landscape.

Review Questions

1. What does the author mean by a self-service retailer? How does this view differ from our traditional expectations of retailing and selling? What are the implications for shopper's satisfaction with customer service or shopper's ability to complete a shopping task efficiently?

2. Reflect on the preference for sales volume and shopper traffic over high margins on every product as business performance indicators. How did the Hartford brothers' business model for A&P influence the development of self-service retail in the early twentieth century?

3. Why does the author consider retailers to be the biggest media companies? Explain how and why retailers are able to charge brand manufacturers for in-store promotions and catalogue advertisements.

4. Think of the examples the author uses of whispering (instead of shouting) at shoppers in a self-service grocery store. Can you think of other techniques to achieve the same result?

5. Describe the four purchase states. How can retailers use the understanding of these states to sell to shoppers more efficiently? What are the advantages and disadvantages of online and brick retail for each of the four purchase states?

6. Ponder on the convergence of online and bricks retailing. How can the efficiency of online shopping for Routine/Autopilot trips be combined with the immediacy (Now! and Surprise/Delight) of brick stores?

Endnotes

1. Sorensen, H. (2013, April 5). *Retailing: The Trojan horse of global freedom and prosperity.* Retrieved from http://www.shopperscientist.com/2013-04-05.html

2. Girard, J. (1989). *How to Close Every Sale.* New York, NY: Warner Books, Inc.

3. Sorensen, H. (2009, July 31). *The Amazonian Ghost.* Retrieved from http://www.shopperscientist.com/2009-07-31.html

4. Surowiecki, J. (2005). *The Wisdom of Crowds.* New York, NY: Anchor Books.

5. Sorensen, H. (2013, January 4). *Whisper, don't shout (or mumble!).* Retrieved from http://www.shopperscientist.com/2013-01-04.html

6. Levinson, M. (2011) *The great A&P and the struggle for small business in America.* New York, NY: Hill and Wang.

7. Martin, N. (2008). *Habit: The 95% of Behavior Marketers Ignore.* Upper Saddle River, NJ: Pearson Education, Inc.

8. (2015, November 2) *Introducing Amazon books at University Village.* Retrieved from http://www.amazon.com/gp/browse.html?ref_=pe_2270130_154133930_pe_button&redirect=true&node=13270229011&pldnSite=1

9. Benedictus, L. (2014, January 7). "Inside the supermarkets' dark stores." *The Guardian.* Retrieved From http://www.theguardian.com/business/shortcuts/2014/jan/07/inside-supermarkets-dark-stores-online-shopping

10. Dorf, D. (2014, May 13). "Dark Stores." *Oracle: Commerce Anywhere Blog.* Retrieved from https://blogs.oracle.com/retail/entry/dark_stores

2

Transitioning Retailers from Passive to Active Mode

By Mark Heckman

Over the span of more than 30 years in the food retailing business, I have come to grips with the concept that good merchandising will likely remain a mix of art and science. More than 30 years ago, as an eager but inexperienced assistant supermarket manager, I took great pride in planning and building impactful displays throughout the store. After completion, I would step back and admire my work. I took care to ensure the display was *shoppable*, meaning that the customer could easily access the items. The display had to be *impactful*, meaning it had to have a subjectively noticeable presence. And it had to be clearly priced. If my work met those basic thresholds, it was deemed a success (see Figure 2.1).

Fast forward 30 years. Those basic thresholds still rule the day in retailing. Retailers place products on the shelf or on special display with little or no regard to those products' ultimate performance. Of course, retailers look at aggregate metrics such as item and unit sales, but for the most part, the process of retail merchandising remains much more of an *art* than a *science*. If a display looks good and it's shoppable, the retailer has fulfilled their end of the retailer-shopper relationship.

Do these long-standing practices adequately serve retailers and their brand partners? Can retailers afford to rely on these practices alone, given the rapid rise of the data-rich, shopper-assisted, shopping environment presented by e-commerce competitors?

Figure 2.1 The shoppable display.

Passive Merchandising No Longer Suffices in a Shopper-Driven World

In Chapter Four of the first edition of *Inside the Mind of the Shopper*, Dr. Sorensen introduced the contrast between active and passive retailing. *Passive retailing,* in which retailers place products in stores for shoppers to find without knowledge of where the shopper would like to encounter those products, has been the norm for more than a century.

Contrast that with *active retailing,* in which the retailer understands who the shopper is and what the shopper is looking for when they take their predictable path through the store. By measuring the shopper's in-store behavior, we generate the data the retailer needs to drive active retailing, guiding where to best locate displays, product placements, and cross merchandising efforts. As an example of active retailing, consider the top e-commerce sites that use past shopper behavioral data to place the right categories, products, services, and even advertisements in front of the shoppers.

As shoppers become more accustomed to online shopping and its shopper-driven environment, their online experiences affect their expectations when shopping at bricks and mortar stores accordingly. They increasingly expect their in-store experience to mirror their online engagement. Bricks and mortar retailers that make the transition to active retailing and, correspondingly, to active merchandising will grow market share and be in a position to meet the demands of today's dynamic shopper. The most compelling reason for active retailing is purely selfish: Active retailers sell more. The more efficient the retailer (shopper seconds per dollar), the higher the total store sales (see Figure 2.2).

> Efficiency breeds sales, and in turn, higher sales drive further efficiencies.

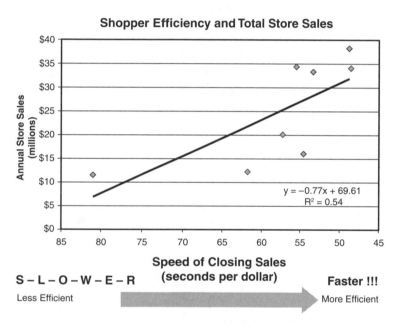

Figure 2.2 The faster you sell, the more you will sell.

The Journey to Active Retailing and the Five Vital Tenets of Active Retailing

Retailers seeking to become successful active retailers have decades of compiled shopper data and new technologies to enable them in their journey. Among the most critical metrics are those that involve shopper time management. In passive retailing, the retailer implicitly believes that the shopper has an unlimited amount of time to shop, read hundreds of signs, wander up and down aisles looking for products, and explore new departments. Based upon this false assumption, retailers bombard the shopper with new products, aisles, programs, signs, and now shopping apps, believing the longer they can keep the shopper engaged and in their stores, the more they will spend.

In active retailing, the retailer acknowledges that the vast majority of shopping trips are fill-in trips, in which shoppers buy fewer than five items. Even on longer, planned trips, the shopper's internal clock ultimately determines when the shopper stops shopping and moves toward the checkout.

> In passive retailing, the retailer is oblivious to the amount of time shoppers spend in their stores. In active retailing, they are obsessed with it.

Any retailer seeking to successfully engage the new in-store shopper should adhere to the Five Vital Tenets of Active Retailing. I offer these tenets not from the perspective of a scientist but rather as a retailer who has experienced over the years what the application of good science can do for the art of merchandising.

The Five Vital Tenets of Active Retailing

Each of these tenets (Figure 2.3) is independently important, but also inextricably linked to the others. Together, they form a road map for the retailer to follow on the journey to active retailing.

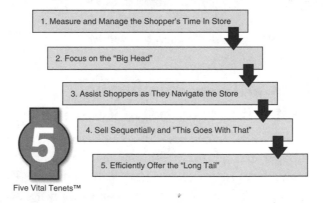

Figure 2.3 The Five Vital Tenets of Active Retailing are the yardstick for measuring the retailer-to-shopper relation.

The link that binds these tenets at the core of active retailing is grounded in three dimensions:

- **Store geography:** Physical attributes of the store such as left, right, center, front, and back.

- **Shopper behavior:** Where they go, what they buy, how long and how fast they shop.

- **Product performance:** What products are purchased and how those products perform across the store.

I am convinced that the Five Vital Tenets of Active Retailing, as we explain them in this chapter, will transform the retail industry and propel the retailer into a new relationship with the shopper. The Five Vital Tenets are:

- Measure and manage the shopper's time in store.

- Focus on selling more of what we already sell the most.

- Assist shoppers as they navigate the store.

- Offer selling events in a sequential manner.

- More efficiently manage those items that sell the least, but occupy the majority of space and inventory costs.

As we examine each of the Five Vital Tenets of Active Retailing, the dimensions of store, shopper, and product will synergistically produce new success metrics, a new merchandising approach, and new ideas to drive sales and shopper satisfaction.

Tenet 1: Measure and Manage the Shopper's Time in the Store

Retailers of all stripes will likely agree that what you cannot measure, you cannot manage. So is the case with managing the shopper's time in the store.

As a retailer, I do not recall ever talking about shopper trip length or why it might have a role in successful merchandising. Retailers assumed the longer the trip the better because the shopper had more time to spend more money.

In actuality, most high-volume retailers are surprised to learn how few items shoppers purchase on any particular trip. Figure 2.4 shows that the median number of items shoppers purchase in a supermarket is just five items. But more importantly, the trend line is moving dramatically in the direction of smaller, more frequent trips to most retailers. This is especially true for supermarkets. Smaller transaction sizes mean a shorter amount of time spent on each trip.

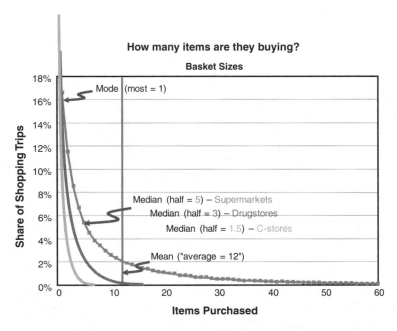

Figure 2.4 The median trips (half larger baskets, half smaller) are a good index across individual retailers and classes of retail including across countries.

Time In-Store: Bluetooth Is a Valid and Convenient Measure

The ability to track shoppers as they move through retail environments using signals emitted by their communication devices (such as mobile phones) can be useful to shopper researchers. This method is inexpensive and has the ability to supply big data for shopper insights. However, this non-probabilistic sampling method could possibly under- or overrepresent certain groups of the shopper population.

A new study[1] assesses the validity of the data describing the length of shopping trips and representativeness of the sample of shoppers carrying Bluetooth-enabled devices. The authors track unique Bluetooth logs in-store and compare to simultaneously collected data from a manual, systematic sample of 324 shoppers observed and interviewed in the same supermarket.

A comparison of the results obtained from the two samples (auto-logging and manual systematic) drawn from the same population indicates automated Bluetooth tracking produces very similar ($r = .92$, $p < .001$) trip lengths to those observed manually. Basket size, dollar spend, and occupation of Bluetooth trackable shoppers are similar to those with no Bluetooth-enabled devices. These findings present compelling evidence that the Bluetooth auto-logging method holds great potential for retail practice and research. An expected underrepresentation of the oldest demographic (66 years old and older) in the Bluetooth discoverable sample calls for complementary methods of data collection to minimize representation bias in real-time tracking technologies for shopper research.

A Shopper's Time Should Be as Important to the Retailer as It Is to the Shopper!

Retailers are sharing their shopper's time with other retailers, both online and in-store, as well as with many other non-shopping demands for the shopper's time. As just one example of the scant amount of time supermarket retailers have to reach their shoppers, Figure 2.5 indicates the average trip length in this particular store is just a tick over 16 minutes per trip, with the specific store involved in this measurement being approximately 50,000 square feet. Some quick math reveals that spending that little amount of time in a store that large does not provide the shopper adequate time for a casual stroll, let alone for a thorough exploration of all the merchandise the retailer placed out for the shopper to buy.

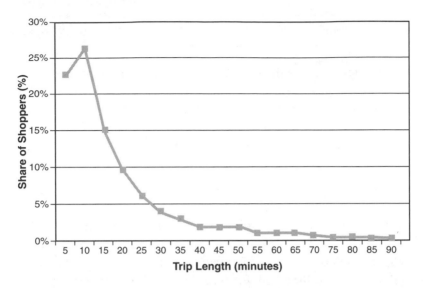

Figure 2.5 Tenet 1 requires that you manage the time (efficiency) of shoppers in your store.

Measuring and Learning from Shopper Efficiency

Time is one of the resources shoppers bring to a store (along with money). Enabling shoppers to complete their grocery shopping more efficiently, spending less time to buy the desired number of items, could result in higher shopper satisfaction and continued patronage.

A recent study[2] developed a novel approach to measuring shopper efficiency. The shopper's time in store was split into "fixed" and "per-item" times, associated with different shopper tasks. *Fixed time* refers to time spent navigating and checking out; whereas *per-item time* is the time spent in choosing and buying. This split allows for a deeper understanding of where and how retailers can make shopping more efficient for their consumers, thus improving the overall in-store experience and outcomes.

A systematic sampling of 1,176 shoppers across three Australian supermarkets provided entry/exit interviews. The shoppers' total time was objectively recorded from their checkout receipts and entry time stamps. Receipts also provided data on items purchased. Researchers used linear regression to model the fixed and per-item times, while ANCOVA analysis provided statistical confirmation of observed differences across the subgroups.

The results revealed females were more efficient than males on a "per item" basis, while males had shorter fixed times associated with entry, navigation, and checking out. Older shoppers were less efficient than younger shoppers. Unemployed respondents tended to spend more time in-store and were less efficient than employed shoppers. There was also a difference between part- and full-time employees. Shopping efficiency in and out of peak periods was not significantly different. Contrary to the assumption in popular media that weekend shopping is more time consuming and hence inefficient, researchers found that weekend shopping was no less efficient than weekday trips.

The identified differences in efficiencies across subgroups have important implications for benchmarking and comparing the performance of different stores, because these will be influenced not only by the time of day and the days of the week, but also by differences in the demographics of the customer base.

Wasted Days and Wasted Nights

Country-western singer Freddie Fender must have just finished shopping for groceries when he recorded his most famous song, "Wasted Days and Wasted Nights." Crudely (but aptly) put, shopping in bricks and mortar stores is a big waste of time. Studies reveal that depending upon the size and layout of the physical store, as much as 85% of the time shoppers spend in a store is spent searching, not buying. This is a problem for retailers for two reasons:

- Shoppers have only so much time to spend shopping. If they are spending only 15% of that time actually *buying*, and the rest of their time is wasted searching, then retailers are suppressing their own sales.

- In the past, when every store was equally inefficient, there was no significant risk of losing shoppers due to their frustration of not finding what they are looking for more quickly. These days, however, Amazon, other online retailers, and smaller bricks-and-mortar formats now offer more efficient alternatives.

After they're confronted with the trip length and the basket size item count, the intuitive reaction from most retailers would be to take steps to slow the shopper down and to use promotions to lure shoppers down aisles typically not traveled. Both practices represent the old thinking of passive retailing.

Active retailing dictates that retailers do the hard work of making it easier for the shopper to buy more in the same or less amount of time they usually spend in the store. Why does this work? The simple answer is: *because that's what the shopper wants*. The deeper answer, however, taps into the shopper's habits. To effectively bring the product to the shopper, the retailer must reach the consumer within their habitual behavior. Anytime a retailer can sell to the shopper as a matter of habit, good numbers follow. I will discuss understanding the shopper's habits as we explore the other tenets of active retailing.

Implications for Active Retailing

Being an advocate for the shopper and their time is the essence of active retailing. After you have measured shoppers' time and their spending efficiency (dollars per second, or its inverse, seconds per dollar), the next steps involve using the other four tenets of active retailing to sell more to shoppers without extending their time in store. Just as important, it is in neither the retailer's nor the shopper's best interest to try to manipulate shoppers into areas of the store where they have no interest in going on that particular trip.

We derive shopper time management metrics from shopper behavioral data that is now available due to improvements in both technology and process. As with any new metric, its importance is commensurate to its link to existing key performance indicators, including sales, margin, transaction size, item counts, and even dollars per space.

Steps for Managing Shoppers' Time in Store

There is an old saying, that what you do not measure, you cannot manage. So here is a brief outline of how to use the *measurement* of time, incorporated in your retail metrics, to gradually and surely increase the efficiency of the shopping process—and thereby the amount of sales produced.

1. Measure trip length in a representative sampling of each store format or layout design.

2. Through shopper tracking (through human observation or through technology), establish where shoppers are predominantly shopping, navigating, and spending time in the store. This will determine the Dominant Path.

3. Create benchmarks of performance, particularly dollars/minute, from the list of metrics provided; and merchandise with a focus on improving the speed in which shoppers are buying.

4. Develop an understanding of new time-related metrics and their links to traditional metrics such as sales, customer count, and basket size.

Tenet 2: Focus on the Big Head

When I think of supermarket merchandising, I think of the amazing amount of products that retailers manage to place in their stores, with the knowledge that each of those products carries an expense or holding cost. Despite the heavy cost of inventory, some of the very best retailers have expanded both the size of their stores and the inventory that populates the many aisles and departments.

The big-store strategy is founded on the belief that bigger is better and variety attracts shoppers. But with e-commerce competing with bricks-and-mortar stores in an already overstored marketplace, their unspoken strategy must be that their size and might will also eliminate the vast majority of their bricks-and-mortar store competition.

The big-store strategy carries with it significant risk. A demonstrated unwillingness to spend precious time navigating large stores reveals a shopper that is screaming at retailers to bring them what they want to buy without making them wade through miles of aisles. The numbers do not lie. Fewer than three hundred items comprise the list of frequently purchased items in the supermarket (see Figure 2.6).

Club stores like Sam's, Costco, and B.J.'s directly addressed this issue by selectively carrying only bestselling items. Rather than having dozens of brands in a category, they pick the top-selling one, two, or three items

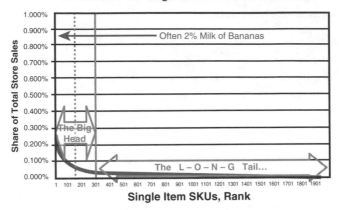

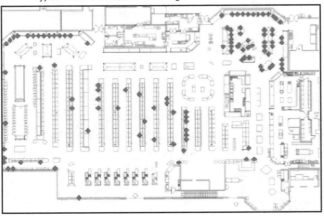

Figure 2.6 Tenet 2 is about managing the Big Head, what shoppers are most interested in, those few items that generate an outsize share of total store sales.

to offer to shoppers. These Big Head stores predictably produce very efficient shopping trips in large part because they don't handle the thousands of items that produce a scant few of actual sales.

We appropriately call these slow-selling items the Long Tail, and we specifically address a strategy for active retailers to address the Long Tail later in this chapter. Think of the Long Tail as the thousands of items that populate the shelves of the supermarket only to be purchased by a scant few shoppers on a scant few shopping trips, as opposed to the few items that make up the Big Head, which most shoppers purchase on most shopping trips. Passive retailers deem Long Tail items necessary to establish an image of significant variety and to provide the shopper with confidence that even infrequently purchased items are available as needed.

In active retailing, the Long Tail becomes an opportunity for the retailer to conveniently make many items available on demand and yet not stored in the physical store, or on the customers' immediate path. We discuss managing the Long Tail later in this chapter.

Implications for Active Retailing

Retailers do not do themselves any favors by burying the Big Head among the Long Tail. But that's exactly what most retailers do as they stubbornly rationalize that shoppers will do the hard work of finding what they need among the clutter. They tell themselves that although shoppers must wander through miles of aisles, they may pick up a few Long Tail items not on their list for this particular trip.

Active retailers take the opposite approach. They understand, as most marketers have learned over the years, that it is much more productive and sales advantageous to enable shoppers to buy more of what they are already buying than to burden them with a time-consuming fishing trip, trying feverishly to lure the shopper into buying items not on their list. That is not to say that smart cross-merchandising is a bad idea. In fact, later in this chapter we discuss how product adjacencies and category affinities are essential to executing smart cross-merchandising.

The quintessential active retailer, Amazon, and other online retailers have opened a new world to shoppers who are quickly becoming accustomed to having their favorite items presented to them based upon past shopping trips. Bricks-and-mortar stores must respond in kind. Like it or not, Amazon is changing the shopper's expectations.

Many retailers have recognized that sales in their big stores have either peaked or the rate of growth has slowed. In response, retailers such as Walmart, Raley's, Whole Foods, and Ahold/Delhaize are experimenting with smaller store formats in hopes that these stores reinvigorate the sales productivity necessary for growth and long-term profitability.

Shopper behavioral research, coupled with an understanding of the ways shoppers' activities in the stores are linked to actual sales at the checkout produces a wealth of information—not just about the shopper, but also about the product category and the in-store real estate in which that product resides. As a retailer, I was an unwitting advocate of many category management segmentation practices, the most common of which involved determining whether a category was a *destination category,* meaning whether shoppers would seek out this category no matter where in the store it was positioned, or an *impulse category,* meaning that the category was more discretionary. As the name implies, shoppers usually do not plan to purchase items from the impulse category. Rather, they purchase those items because they are enamored with the merchandising or product as they pass by.

As a passive retailer, I was a firm believer that this rather intuitive perspective on categories was not only accurate but was a core rationale for placing Big Head items throughout the store, thus manipulating the shopper to these areas and thus increasing the exposure of these often higher-margined, impulse items.

Retailers Attempting to Manipulate or Extend a Shopper's Trip Are on a Fool's Errand

I have no doubt, even today, that some key departments and categories remain destinations for shoppers and that collateral impulse sales can be created by forcing shoppers to make long treks back to the dairy for milk or the produce department for bananas and lettuce. Shoppers, however, are becoming increasingly less malleable when it comes to their convenience. With this more disciplined shopper, retailers who sprinkle Big Head items throughout large store footprints run much greater risk of losing the sale of the Big Head item altogether, not to mention losing any residual impulse sales along the way.

I also believe retailers lose sight of the fact that shoppers don't buy "categories"; they buy specific items. With the advent and maturation of category-management practices, retailers have been able to deal with merchandising and handling 75,000–100,000 items per store by grouping and managing them categorically. The shopper does not have that luxury. Active retailing does indeed recognize the critical importance of managing the store by departments and categories, but it also encourages retailers also to understand the importance of identifying the top selling *items* across categories, because it is the item that the shopper will buy . . . not the category.

Smaller store footprints logically create an inherently more efficient shopping environment, because there is less in-store real estate to navigate. However, simply creating a smaller version of a store designed for passive retailing is not the comprehensive solution active retailers must attain. The mandate for both large and smaller physical store footprints is to become more shopper-centric as they merchandise and plan their stores.

Steps in Managing the Big Head

Managing of the Big Head *alone* is the reason Big Head only stores like Costco are super-successful. Managing the Big Head in the presence of the long tail, but not "hidden" in it, is the key to superior performance Big-Head-*plus*-Long-Tail stores.

1. Identify those items that drive the majority of sales and frequently find their way into your shopper's baskets.

2. Insure many of those items are within convenient access, and readily, distinctly seen on the established Dominant Path of shoppers.

3. Do not position these items as magnets to manipulate shoppers into specific, less trafficked areas of the store, but rather merchandise these items where the shoppers currently go in the store.

4. Understand which Long Tail items have strong affinities with specific Big Head items and create smart cross merchandising opportunities to exploit those affinities.

Tenet 3: Assist Shoppers as They Navigate the Store

When the active retailer is in position to measure and manage the shopper's time in-store and is armed with the knowledge of which Big Head items drive the majority of sales, he is poised to take the next logical step by creating a *shopper-assisted environment*, much like the online environment with which shoppers are becoming enamored.

In a sea of thousands of items and messages, shoppers are often challenged to find what they are looking for in the small amount of time they have in the store. In fact, most shopping studies reveal that up to

85% of the shopper's time in store is spent moving and searching, not buying. Because the average supermarket trip is just a tick more than 16 minutes, this leaves the actual buying time in the average trip at about two and a half minutes.

Tenet 3 is all about helping the shopper find what they are looking for. In doing so, we do not address or advocate the use of digital signage, shopping apps, and other technologies designed to communicate to the shopper along their in-store trip. Rather, we acknowledge that those shopper aids have value only if they save the shopper time and effort instead of adding additional steps in their shopping process. Most importantly, these technologies are only successful if the store layout and the merchandising are positioned to make the shopper's trip more efficient.

When enhancing shopper navigation, the best place to start is with some startling facts. Consider these results from a recent shopper behavioral study from Forrester;[3] many of the findings were sourced from Dr. Sorensen's work.[4]

- The typical shopping visit lasts only 13 minutes.
- 80% of a shopper's visit is spent looking for items in a store.
- There is a direct correlation between the speed at which people shop and total basket size. Short trip shoppers spend faster and tend to buy more (higher per unit of time).
- Only 25%: the amount of store typically walked per visit.
- Average number of SKUs purchased monthly per household is only 150 (total); 83 (in grocery).
- As many as 50% of all grocery trips result in five or fewer items purchased.
- In grocery, as much as 30% of sales come from endcap displays.
- As few as 80 items can constitute 20% of a large grocery's sales.
- Open space and wide aisles and checkouts attract more attention from shoppers.
- Shoppers read very little while shopping, responding more to colors, shapes, and images.
- Three to five seconds: How quickly humans process a scene.

Volumes could be written about the impact of any one of these observations. In my practice as a retailer, I can best relate to the observation of how we tend to merchandise and sign a store as if the shoppers have all day to spend with us while having no clue as to the short amount of time each shopper actually spends in the store, and how much we retailers provide for them to process in just a few minutes out of their day, that they will spend with us.

I assumed that shoppers were being efficient as they shopped my store, because people tended to be efficient with their lists and coupons in hand and because we were not getting complaints from shoppers about the store being poorly designed. Perhaps if I had known then that as much as 60% to 80% of a shopper's thirteen-minute trip is wasted looking for products instead of buying, I might have been compelled to do something to improve shopper efficiency, although I would have had no idea where to begin. As a retailer, being continually exposed to towering runs of merchandise (Figure 2.7) in my own and competitors' stores, didn't encourage me to recognize how they were impeding access to those few high volume items the shoppers wanted to buy.

Figure 2.7 Tenet 3: Towering long runs of product hinder exposure and access (navigation) to other areas of the store.

Some years later, armed with some basic precepts from Dr. Sorensen's past work, I had an opportunity to put some of what I had learned into action. As the marketing vice president at Marsh Supermarkets in

Indianapolis, I was called to a fixture plan meeting with the center store merchandising director and his space management team.

Knowing that I had worked with Dr. Sorensen on past projects, they were looking for ideas to improve the merchandising and price image of an older store that was finally getting a much-needed remodel.

Figure 2.8 Tenet 3: Replacing a wall of values with drop pallets opens sight lines to the center-store aisles.

Taking a quick glance at the fixture plan, and having spent some time in the store in question, I was immediately drawn to the very front of the store. As shoppers entered the store they were forced to take a hard left to move through a passage that had a wall-of-values promotional area called *Stock Ups* on one side and a long run of backlit shelving that housed breads and buns on the other. After shoppers had traversed at least sixty feet of this tunnel-like area of the store, they passed into a small floral department and then took a hard right through the produce department towards the back of the store.

Mr. Retailer, Tear Down This Wall!

This type of promotional presentation is not that unusual and arguably serves the purpose of presenting a strong visual price image to the shopper as they enter the store.

Conversely, past work done by Dr. Sorensen established that long, enclosed aisles naturally repel shoppers. I borrowed a famous challenge from President Reagan and encouraged my colleagues to "tear down that wall" of values and replace it with an open approach that enabled shoppers to have access to the promotional deals, but also to see what's ahead of them in their shopping journey. Thankfully, that's just what we did (Figure 2.8).

The new configuration accomplished several positive results. More shoppers were drawn to the promotional area and more importantly, with the wall of values gone, the shopper had open sightlines to many of the critical center-store aisles and categories that were previously low traffic areas. Sales went up, more importantly; shoppers began accessing some of the key center-store aisles that were previously blocked from their initial view. Assisting shoppers as they navigate the store always pays benefits back to the retailer. Unlike this example, which involved removing aisles and fixtures, most navigational assistance can be done more easily and in a less costly manner.

Implications for Active Retailing

We have shown that creating open spaces and sightlines for the shopper is an area of opportunity by which many retailers can improve shopper navigation. It is also an important early step in becoming an active retailer because this move brings the product more aggressively to the shopper and enables the shopper to buy faster.

A second essential element of accomplishing accelerated buying is to identify something that every store has: a *dominant shopping path*.

Shopper tracking reveals both the direction and the intensity of shoppers as they navigate the store. Ideally the *Dominant Path* is established by measuring the direction of the shopper, the speed of their movement, the number of shoppers in a given area, and the time they spend in a given area. As Figure 2.9 indicates, the path typically forms a U-shaped pattern representing a dominant flow of shoppers from the front of the store to the back, along the back of the store some distance until a wide, inviting aisle is encountered, taking the shopper to the checkouts.

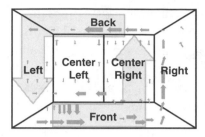

Figure 2.9 Tenet 3: A single Dominant Path is the virtual definition of efficient, convenient navigation.

When the Dominant Path is in place, the active retailer has a powerful tool to leverage. The path, exploited wisely, serves as a launch pad to build basket size, shopper count, and, consequently, sales, without keeping the shopper a second longer in the store than is helpful and comfortable *to them*.

> The Dominant Path also serves as a bridge to the shopper's habitual buying practices, where buying happens faster and more efficiently.

Activating the Dominant Path

The Big Head plays a vital role in activating the path where the majority of shoppers navigate and dwell. As an initial practice, most retailers have the means of identifying those categories with substantial Big Head presence, the categories that drive a disproportionate amount of item and dollar sales. These are the categories that should predominate the Dominant Path because these categories will increase the buying efficiency as measured by dollars or items purchased per minute spent in the store, and correspondingly they will increase the retailer's sales and transaction size.

Obtaining a list of top-selling categories and items allows the retailer to consciously merchandise these items to the Dominant Path and to other high traffic areas in the store. We also know that the earlier in the shopper's trip progression you can present these items, the higher the likelihood for sales conversion.

Although it is understandably impractical to position every Big Head, high volume category in the store along the Dominant Path, it *is* possible to consciously position top selling *items* along the way as secondary displays, cut ins, and in-aisle bump outs, thus avoiding, at least initially, upheaving entire departments and categories in the process of activating the path.

The Dominant Path provides the retailer with an enormous venue to build incremental sales by bringing product actively to shoppers. But the remainder of the store has plenty of potential to do the same.

Figure 2.10 is a snippet from a category report that illustrates how to select items—in this case, salty snacks—to potentially be featured on the Dominant Path. The last three columns here tell the story for the category; these top 11 (of 88) items contribute one-third of the category sales. Simply stated, if we can increase the sales of this small group of items by 10%—a modest goal for *focused* TopSeller promotion—we will get a 3% lift for the full category. In achieving that 10% lift for these *few* items, it is better to focus on maybe only three of them, because getting outsize increases of 20+ percent for that small selection will lift this group by 10%. This is the way we focus on the few to lift the whole show, with modest increases in efficiency. The key to efficiency is focus, focus, focus!

| UPC | Item Description | Total $$$ | Total Store | | | Category | | |
			Share	Cum	Share	Cum	Share	Cum
	Total Store Sales >>>	$30,282,665						
	Total Category Sales>>>	$210,233						
	Total Category Sales>>>	$210,233	0.694%					
4886731216	JUANITAS TORTILLA CHIPS	$17,343	0.057%	16.6%	137	8.2%	8.2%	1
4886731224	JUANITAS FIESTA BAG TORT	$15,129	0.050%	18.3%	161	7.2%	15.4%	2
0686300000	CRISPITOS	$6,139	0.020%	35.2%	599	2.9%	18.4%	3
1410008547	PF GFISH CHS CSD ZTF 6.6 OZ	$4,611	0.015%	41.6%	852	2.2%	20.6%	4
8411400998	KETTLE CHIPS LIGHT SALT	$4,404	0.015%	42.7%	914	2.1%	22.7%	5
2840007122	NO DESCRIPTION AVAILABLE	$4,141	0.014%	43.9%	979	2.0%	24.6%	6
2410044068	SS CHZ IT 13.70 UN	$4,062	0.013%	44.5%	999	1.9%	26.6%	7
2840004768	ROLD GOLD CLASSIC TINY TWISTS	$3,971	0.013%	45.1%	1033	1.9%	28.4%	8
2840004770	ROLD GOLD CLASSIC STICKS	$3,935	0.013%	45.4%	1046	1.9%	30.3%	9
2840006404	NO DESCRIPTION AVAILABLE	$3,743	0.012%	46.4%	1106	1.8%	32.1%	10
2840006399	Tostitos	$3,645	0.012%	47.2%	1141	1.7%	33.8%	11

Figure 2.10 Tenet 3: Top-selling categories and items provide a "seed list" for retailers to plant on the Dominant Path.

As a retailer, I found it difficult to accept the scientific fact that the location of an item within the context of other items in the physical retail store had as much to do with the category's performance as the price of the product or even the product itself. In my discussions with brands and retailers, this provable premise rocked their world. We have all been indoctrinated into believing the 4 P's of marketing: Product, Price, Place, and Promotion. Place was the least significant factor, not the most.

Working with Dr. Sorensen's Vital Quadrant, which segmented categories according to their ability to convert passersby to shoppers and then shoppers to buyers, changed my view of drivers of category performance.

For the first time in my career, I could manage a category's performance by the element of its position in the store. This is very important information for an active retailer.

As Figure 2.11 indicates, categories in specific locations fall into one of four buckets. We should note that the majority of categories are considered average performers and are excluded because there is much more potential available with the outlier categories.

Niche Few stop o shop, but those who do…buy	Leaders Shoppers who pass here stop and shop *and* buy
Underdeveloped Few stop to shop, few who stop…buy	**High Interest** Shoppers stop to shop, but *do not* buy

Figure 2.11 Vital Quadrant analysis based on the Atlas[5] modeling of category performance is a powerful tool in determining which products should be on the Dominant Path.

The result of this new category-segmentation system enables merchandisers to better understand the value of the real estate within their stores and to identify and leverage this information as a tool for cross merchandising, store layout, and category placements.

For example, if a retailer observes that the juice category is classified as a Leader category in one store but falls into the Niche bucket in another, a location change in the second store is worth pursuing because the category earned a Leader classification in the other store.

As the Vital Quadrant relates to the Dominant Path, the items and categories that earn leader or Niche classification in that store would be great candidates for placement or cross-merchandising along the Dominant Path. These categories tend to convert shoppers to buyers, and we know there are shoppers aplenty on the Dominant Path.

Steps in Assisting Shoppers as They Navigate the Store

Following is a good checklist of just what to do to work with shoppers' intuitive, instinctive, distinctive shopping path. It is "the road *most* taken!"

1. Avoid displays and fixtures that hinder the shopper's ability to see "what's next."

2. Provide the shopper options to navigate with wider, short aisle runs, if possible.

3. Identify the store's Dominant Path in which the retailer can reach shoppers in the midst of their habitual shopping behavior.

4. Position and merchandise a strong mix of Big Head categories *and items* along the Dominant Path.

5. Cross-merchandise Long Tail items with strong affinities to the Big Head items that populate the Dominant Path.

6. After a category's performance is identified in the Vital Quadrant analysis, merchandise Niche and Leader categories along the Dominant Path.

7. Do not spend great energy and effort attempting to lure shoppers to areas they do not heavily traffic. The investment of time and promotion will not produce positive results.

Tenet 4: Sell Sequentially

It is obvious that items are purchased one after the other. But it is also clear that items have affinities or attractions among themselves, so that purchase of some items may prompt the purchase of an affinitive item. Active selling means leveraging these relations, by proximities, but also serial order of presentation to the shopper.

What Comes First, The Chicken or the Egg?

In my 30+ years in retail, I have never understood the rationale (assuming there is one) that determines where retailers put things in the store. Not since 1915, when the Alpha Beta grocery chain introduced products stocked in alphabetical order, has there been any real attempt at clarity as to what should come first, the chicken or the egg? (Figure 2.12)

Figure 2.12 Tenet 4: Which comes first? The order in which offers are made to shoppers seriously affects sales. (Image © S-F)

Does the Order of Things Matter?

Having visited stores all over the world, I have seen seemingly as many different views and practices on product location as there are stores. The science of Sequential Selling states that the order and cadence in which shoppers encounter categories and items along their journey can either hasten or hinder their purchase efficiency.

Vital Tenet 4, Sell Sequentially, recognizes that overall department and product placement may be determined in part by the marketing objectives of that store or banner (that is, price, fresh, club). By understanding shopper behavioral science and category performance, however, we can present categories and items in an order that leverages the shopper's habitual practices.

Sequential Selling is simply the practice of using shopper behavioral science to know how to place items in a store according to how the shopper habitually buys. Every shopper's trip through the store has a cadence, whether it is just for a few items or for a stock-up journey.

To better understand Sequential Selling, imagine the store layout with the classic Dominant Path U-turn. First and foremost, a Sequential Sales plan is based upon the shopper's journey. In our example store, the trip begins in a counter-clockwise fashion.

We describe the trip progression in four stages: Early, Mid, Late Mid, and Late (see Figure 2.13).

To effectively build a Sequential Sales plan around the Dominant Path, several shopper behavioral precepts serve as an effective context:

- The Dominant Path provides the medium through which to merchandise during the shopper's trip progression.

- Understanding trip progression is critical. Shoppers spend faster earlier in the trip progression and, conversely, move faster and purchase less frequently towards the end of the trip.

- Shoppers spend only a few seconds focusing on each sale event. Concise, well-placed signage and fixtures designed to communicate to the shopper's subconscious, will most effectively engage the shopper and foster purchases.

- Sequential Sales events should be adequately spaced apart to allow the shopper time to focus on their planned needs and should be limited in number in order to create a presence and an aura of importance.

- Big Head items and Leader and Niche categories serve as the best candidates for Sequential Sales events because they have a strong track record of converting shoppers to buyers.

Implications for Active Retailing

Sequential Selling serves as a natural extension of active retailing because it serves to bring Big Head and other categories with high conversion rates to shoppers as they traverse the store. Key to the success of a

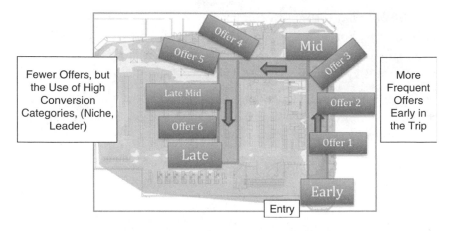

Figure 2.13 Illustration of a Sequential Sales plan built around the store's Dominant Path.

Sequential Sales plan is the creation of a visual image that is recognizable and memorable to the shopper, one that even reaches shoppers on a subconscious level where 95% of shopper decisions are actually made.[6] Creating progressive sales events requires a level of discipline to avoid the temptation to over-merchandise and over-sign the store.

Many successful retailers traditionally flood their shelves with messaging to support new price programs, continuities,[7] and the like. Although the overall impact of this approach presents an exposure for their programs, it does little to register in the shopper's subconscious or to make a lasting impression about any one product in which they may be interested.

Finally, a silent, clean shelf look (Figure 2.14) creates the platform for effective communications when it is important to do so.

Starting from the position of a clean shelf, a simple but effective sign such as *Top Seller* (Figure 2.15) alerts the time-crunched shopper that other shoppers have made the choice to buy this product, thus giving the shopper confidence to do so as well.

A simple approach geared to send a subtle but effective message to the consumer helps the shopper wade through the thousands of choices presented to them and can be an integral part of a Sequential Selling plan.

Programs like *Top Seller* work due to their message design and the strategic and limited placement of signs. Too much of a good thing can certainly diminish the intended impact of the program.

Silent, Clean Aisle

Shouting Display

Figure 2.14 A silent, clean aisle (on the top) vs. a shouting aisle (on the bottom).

Figure 2.15 The active retailer understands and connects with the shopper at a subconscious, habitual level. A few low-impact tags, well selected and placed, can drive a lot of out-of-stocks! (And that's a good thing!)

In his book, *Habit: The 95% of Behavior Marketers Ignore*, Dr. Neale Martin writes that marketers are bombarding the consciousness of the shopper with signs, specials, displays, flashing lights, and great deals, even though it is the subconscious or habitual shopper that makes the majority of the decisions.

Although the passive retailer markets to the conscious shopper with thousands of signs and color-coded programs, the active retailer understands and connects with the shopper at a subconscious, habitual level in each phase of the shopper's trip.

Steps for Sequential Selling

Summarizing a plan for sequential selling:

1. Begin with understanding the dynamics of shopper flow through the store and identify the Dominant Path of the shoppers in the store (Vital Tenet 3).

2. Use the same shopper observational research that provided the shopper traffic flow to assess where purchase conversion rates are strongest (Vital Tenet 3).

3. From there, tap the Big Head to identify a collection of categories and items that have high consumer interest and those that have a strong history of conversion (turning a shopper into a buyer).

4. Before making more cost-intensive decisions about moving entire categories in new, more shopper-centric locations, begin first with experimentation through placement of high conversion, Big Head items/categories in secondary displays, in-line cut-outs and endcaps.

5. Lastly, create a concise and disciplined communication plan to effectively reach the shopper during their trip progression, a plan that eliminates excess clutter and noise and focuses on messaging that helps the shopper make quicker purchase decisions.

Tenet 5: Managing the Long Tail

In our exploration of the first four tenets, we focused on efficiently bringing to the shopper the products that they buy on a regular basis. This strategy entails offering more of what the shopper is already buying instead of coaxing and prodding the shopper to try something new.

So Where Does This Leave the Tens of Thousands of Other Items That Populate the Shelves of the Store?

As a recovering passive retailer, I am not ready to advocate giving up on the Long Tail. Many of those items create the much-needed aura of variety that shoppers value and upon which some retailers build their reputations. There is cachet in having everything under the sun, but there is also danger.

I could fill the next few pages with charts and graphs that speak to the negative impact fostered by huge amounts of inventory on labor, holding costs, and cash flow. Those of us with retail experience well understand that. We do not need to turn this discussion into an economics lesson. We must recognize, however, that forces are at play in the marketplace that put bricks-and-mortar retailers, with large store footprints and heavy inventories, in peril:

1. Amazon and other e-commerce retailers have changed the shopper's buying behaviors. Many items are now frequently purchased online instead of in the physical store.

2. These online retailers have decidedly logistical and financial advantages over bricks-and mortar-stores in terms of the cost of goods sold.

3. InstaCart, Peapod, and a host of other upstart delivery retailers are beginning to gain traction, especially with emerging urban-based affluent shoppers.

4. The emergence of a plethora of smaller bricks-and-mortar formats and stores offers the shopper the Big Head and limited portions of the Long Tail in hopes to capture the incremental sales.

5. Consequently, the shopper has more options and has greater mobility than ever before from which to source their needs.

"Nobody Goes There Anymore. It's Too Crowded"—Yogi Berra

The late, great Yankee catcher could have very well been thinking about shopping in large stores when he uttered this famous line. Stores crowded with thousands of items are off-putting to mission-driven shoppers who know what they want yet must navigate through long aisles filled with merchandise that is of no interest to them to get it.

Inevitably, physical stores as we know them today must change. Retailers who once believed bigger stores were the prerequisite for success are now scrambling to downsize. Other stores are experimenting with the concept of "stores within stores" to afford shoppers more organization and definition during their trip. A longer view of managing the Long Tail suggests that the store format of tomorrow *separates the Big Head from the Long Tail* (Figure 2.16).

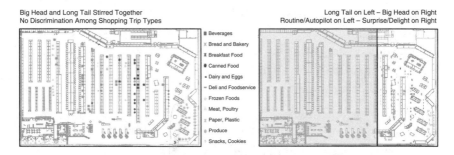

Figure 2.16 The store format of tomorrow separates the Big Head from the Long Tail, with a view toward moving the Long Tail progressively online.

Passive retailers everywhere will likely initially balk at this divided approach, given its counterintuitive approach to the precepts of traditional merchandising. However, when viewing the sales contribution of the bottom 50% of items, most retailers would agree that the status quo is not sustainable.

The evidence is compelling. Figure 2.17 tells a very depressing story about the productivity of the bottom 50% of items, collectively delivering only 5% of total sales.

Smartly assigning these items to a more productive role means reducing their store position and/or presence.

As we discussed previously, a significant number of these Long Tail items have affinities with Big Head items. Merchandising these items along with the Leader and Niche Big Head items on the Dominant Path surely will improve both the exposure and sales performance.

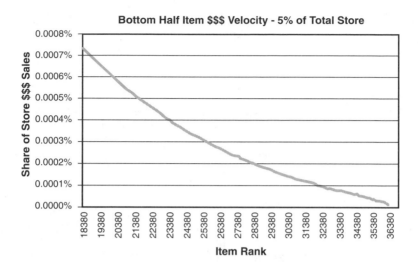

Figure 2.17 Many of these Long Tail items can be matched to specific Big Head items to enhance sales of both. Others will ultimately end up being sold online, within the bricks store itself. The pending "Long Tail Accelerator!" (Patent pending.)

Implications for Active Retailing

As a retailer, I see managing the Long Tail as a dynamic balancing act. Shopper behavioral science has firmly established that shoppers prefer and are accordingly migrating to a shopper-assisted experience. This movement is diametrically at odds with large stores with tens of thousands of items placed across tens of thousands of retail square footage.

Savvy retailers are talking about and executing plans that optimize item selection, but in most cases these exercises do not address the impact on the shopper and their new behavior in a digitally driven marketplace.

To address the vagaries of the Long Tail, an active retailer should consider both a short-term and long-term solution. Also, not all Long Tail items are alike, and we should not treat them as such. It is important to understand how the shopper views these items before we begin making decisions about their fate.

Table 2.1 shows a planned approach to identify and address the burgeoning item count in bricks-and-mortar stores. The strategies we propose here are viable, but retailers will need to make adjustments depending on their specific competitive environments, trade areas, demographics, and marketing positions.

Table 2.1 Long Tail Product Categories

Item Category	Characteristic	Short-Term Plan	Long-Term Plan
Surprise and Delight	Seasonal, special buys, in-and-out items	Merchandise early in trip progression.	Incorporate in Sequential Sales plan.
Scheduled Use	Commodity items that are consumed by house hold's on a predictable schedule	Monitor sales and test and offer in home delivery or in-store pick-up program.	Reduce store inventory. Access in-store kiosk for additional variety.
	Ethnic, international, foodie, exotic spices, and so on	Monitor sales, optimize offerings by specific store cluster.	Reduce store inventory and/or move to Auto Pilot side. Access in-store kiosk for additional variety.
Special Needs	Organic, gluten-free other nutritionally based items	Move to Auto Pilot side of store.	Reduce store inventory. Access in-store kiosk for additional variety.
Line Extensions	Flavors and sizes beyond the top sellers	Monitor sales and test and offer in home delivery or in-store pick-up program.	Reduce store inventory. Access in-store kiosk for additional variety.
Convenience	Hardware, cosmetics, travel	Move to Auto Pilot side of store.	Move to Auto Pilot side of store.
All Others	Slow movers	Cross-merchandise with co-affinity Big Head items and move to Auto Pilot side of store.	Reduce store inventory. Access in-store kiosk for additional variety.

Smartly segmenting items into manageable groups provides the retailer an opportunity to adjust store inventories down over time. In this process, many of the Long Tail retailers may continue stocking items on the shelf if they generate sufficient sales. These items may also warrant a secondary placement on the Dominant Path alongside Big Head items with which they have high co-affinity.

Other items may lend themselves to seasonal merchandising; still others may transition to availability only through e-commerce. Over time, as shoppers increasingly become comfortable with buying various items for in-store pick-up or home delivery, the number of items that a retailer can jettison off their shelves or into an e-commerce picking warehouse will grow.

In the interim, Long Tail item segmentation allows the retailer a systematic way forward to reduce inventories at store level, to improve exposure to selected Long Tail items, and ultimately to become a key tool in designing a dual-store design approach with Surprise/Delight and Auto Pilot/Routine areas of the store well defined.

Steps in Managing the Long Tail

A conceptual plan was offered in Chapter 1, to progressively migrate the Long Tail to online management. In Figure 2.17 reference was made to the pending Long Tail Accelerator, a device deployed by the retailer on the shelf, providing direct online access to product options no longer available on the bricks store shelves, but accessible either before the shopper leaves the store or by efficient delivery. No, all of this isn't foreseen in every detail. But meanwhile, guidance on what to do *right now* in the store is outlined here:

1. Understand numerically which Long Tail items represent the best opportunity for cross-merchandising in key secondary placement locations along the Dominant Path.

2. Develop Long Tail item segments, providing a role and specific longer-term strategy for each.

3. Begin the transitioning process of discontinuing the practice of using Big Head items as "magnets" to draw shoppers into remote areas of the store a way from the Dominant Path for the purpose of increasing exposure to Long Tail items.

4. Conversely, sprinkle Long Tail items that have *high co-affinities* with Big Head items along the Dominant Path to increase their exposure and sales conversion rates.

A Passing Thought about the Role of Displays in Active Retailing

In active retailing, measuring the performance of displays is integral to the ultimate success of bringing the product to the shopper in a more efficient manner. The performance dynamics of displays, whether it's an endcap, an in-aisle bump out, a free standing display, or a wing (side stack), must be more accurately and universally measured. For more information on special displays, refer to the Afterword.

Closing Thoughts

Practicing active retailing will not be intuitive for many seasoned merchandisers. It cuts across the grain of most everything retailers have considered standard practices for more than a century. For most of us, success was built upon huge stores, long aisles, and thousands of items, with signs and messages everywhere. We believed if we put the merchandise somewhere, the shopper would find it.

But as retailers struggle with declining sales, burgeoning inventory costs, and their customer's increasing adaptation to online shopping, it is clear that the old model of passive retailing is no longer working as well as it has in the past. Shoppers with many options and new technology have irrevocably altered the playing field.

In the new active retailing environment, physical stores and merchandising schemes will be concise, clear, efficient, and always customer-centric. The in-store experience will increasingly resemble the online environment and the two will work in lockstep to provide the shopper with what they want, when they want it. Retailers must take an active role in bringing the desired products more efficiently to the shopper in the physical store.

Active retailers will be poised to grow their business across channels and customer touch points. New metrics such as dollars/second, sales conversion rates, category exposure, and many more will enable retailers to continually fine tune their store designs, fixture placements, category presentations, and merchandising plans. It's a new day! The shopper is in charge and active retailing will become the new norm for reaching the shopper on their terms, not ours.

Review Questions

1. How have successful online retailers like Amazon change shopper expectations of modern retailing? What can bricks-and-mortar stores do to rise to such expectations?

2. What are the traditional (and false) assumptions of passive retailing regarding shopper time? Which metrics could a retailer use to reliably uncover how shoppers spend their time in-store?

3. Describe the concept of Big Head–Long Tail in merchandising. How do traditional passive retailers deal with these two groups of products? What is the assumption about shopper behavior that underpins that (traditional) strategy? What steps an active retailer could take to better manage the Big Head?

4. What is the most important factor in improving in-store navigation? What principles should be used in creating in-store environment and building displays?

5. Describe the Dominant Path in terms of shopper navigation and product assortment. How does assisted shopper navigation along the Dominant Path relate to sales?

6. Discuss the difference between a "clean aisle" and a "shouting aisle." Why are shouting aisles ineffective (consider shopper psychology and visual attention)?

7. What is the attraction of the Long Tail from the shopper perspective? How can a retailer manage the Long Tail more efficiently?

Endnotes

1. Phua, Peilin, Bill Page, and Svetlana Bogomolova. "Validating Bluetooth logging as metric for shopper behaviour studies." Journal of Retailing and Consumer Services 22 (2015): 158–163.

2. Bogomolova, S., Vorobyev, K., Page, B., and Bogomolov, T. (2016) "Socio-demographic differences in supermarket shopper efficiency", Australasian Marketing Journal.

3. Forrester's The State of Customer Experience, 2010.

4. Lee Resource, Inc.

5. Atlas is a Category Location tool that can be accessed at http://www.shopperscientist.com/atlas/. A description is available at: Suher, J and Sorensen, H (2010). The power of Atlas: why in-store shopping behavior matters, Journal of Advertising Research, 21, March, pp. 21–9.

6. Neale Martin, "Habit: The 95% of Behavior Marketers Ignore." (ISBN-13: 007-6092046561)

7. Continuities are merchandising programs that last for a number of weeks, like, "Spend $50 each week for the next 6 weeks and get $50 Off your next order" Or it could be a dishware or linen program where each week you get a new dish or towel for a great deal and complete the set at the end of the event period.

3

Selling Like Amazon Online and in Bricks Stores

S ince we published the first edition of this book, the march of technological progress has moved dramatically forward. Shoppers have become accustomed to the speed and efficiency of online retail, and Amazon has led the pack in developing online retail practices. Many of the techniques Amazon uses harken back to the era of personal selling in retail, when shop clerks guided shoppers through the process of identifying and selecting the products that best suited their desires and needs. Here, we examine how Amazon has returned personal selling to *self*-service retail, and how it and other online retailers are driving a new evolution in retail as groundbreaking as the development of self-service retail a century before.

There are three basic functions in retail, whether it occurs online or in traditional bricks and mortar stores: meeting of the minds, delivery of the goods, and payment of the money. (See Figure 3.1.) The importance of the delivery of the goods and payment of the money should be obvious. However, the essential element of the *meeting of the minds* is not so obvious. It's a legal concept that when a seller and buyer agree on the specifics of a transaction, their minds have met and a legally valid transaction, *the sale*, can occur. For our purposes here, we make a distinction between two kinds of mind meeting, *mediated sales* and *unmediated sales*. The mediated variety involves a clerk or salesman personally assisting the shopper. It is the clerk's job to guide the thinking of the customer by providing a selection of products, information, advice, experience, and knowledge until he achieves a meeting of the minds when the shopper says, "Yes, this is the product I want at the price I am willing to pay." This was the norm in retail until one hundred years ago when retailing began moving to the unmediated variety of sales through the *self*-service model. In unmediated sales, the shopper is left to explore their options, learn about the products, and to think their way through the purchase process on their own, unguided by a salesperson.

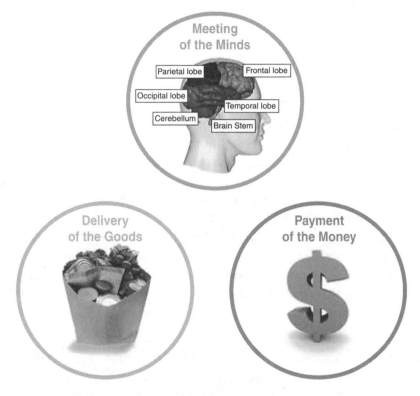

Figure 3.1 The three components of retailing.

Amazon's true advantage at retail is that they get to mediate the sale, like the store clerk of long ago; by guiding the shopper's thought process, step by step and click by click. Admittedly, they do this with the aid of a computer algorithm rather than through personal interaction with shoppers. The process is nonetheless as interactive as a real salesman interacting with the shopper in a bricks store. Thus, Amazon mediates self-service sales with their computer algorithm acting as *ghostly salesmen*.

In this chapter, we focus on how Amazon has slipped mediation back into self-service retailing online. We also show how the Amazonian techniques can be adapted to a wide variety of self-service bricks stores even without the benefit of Amazonian technology. The good news is that Amazon's *selling* advantage is not inherent to online retailing. Instead, it derives from the particular mental process through which Amazon guides its shoppers. It does not just passively stock merchandise and rely on shoppers to sell to themselves. The mental process a shopper goes through when making a purchase is remarkably similar in online and offline sales. This similarity was noted by Professor Peter Fader of Wharton:

> "I figured the process of someone standing at a shelf and deciding what juice to buy is going to be very different than someone sitting at the computer clicking through a bunch of different books or CDs—until I actually looked at the data, and it turned out that the patterns were remarkably similar."[1]

We will first identify *five specific points of focus* Amazon uses online: navigation, selection, immediate close, affinity, and crowd-social marketing, and reaching into the Long Tail. We will then see how these same five points can accelerate sales in bricks stores. Some are already doing it.

Amazon Selling Online

The mental process shoppers experience when making a purchase involves two steps. First, the retailer must make the offer. He accomplishes this by getting the customer and the merchandise together either by moving the customer or by moving the merchandise. Recall how we began this book by discussing the concept of bidirectional search, in which shoppers are looking for products whereas products, suppliers, and brands are looking for shoppers. We call the process of bringing shoppers and products together *navigation*. Second, to close the sale, the shopper must pick an option and accept the offer of the merchandise that she feels best meets her needs and desires at a price she is willing to pay. We call this part *selection*.

In the self-service bricks store, the retailer expects the shopper to move themselves, to navigate, to the merchandise. While online, conceptually, the retailer brings the merchandise to the shopper in response to the shopper's click-click-click navigation.

Amazon has an advantage in managing the shopper's navigation because they can deliver any offer to any shopper in a matter of a few key strokes, which only takes a few seconds. Bricks retailers, however, have a potential large advantage of their own with the much larger *screen* of the store. In the selling process, vision is the major connector between the shopper's mind and the merchant's mind.

Let's now examine through the Amazonian lens these two basic parts of a shopper's mental process, navigation and selection, by exploring five areas in which Amazon has a laser focus.

Amazon Point of Focus #1: Navigation—Simple and Fast

Greg Linden, former Amazon programmer commented, "We used to joke that the ideal Amazon site would not show a search box, navigation links, or lists of things you could buy. Instead, it would just display a giant picture of one book, the next book you want to buy."[2]

Amazon's mind is not on what they want to sell to the shopper. They make it easy for themselves by figuring out what is on the shopper's mind and sell that to them. This is a billion dollar tip for retailers. The goal is to sell as fast as possible, because the faster you sell, the more you will sell, whether online or offline.

To think about how Amazon helps shoppers navigate their sales program, let's imagine you are interested in buying a book on shopping science. From a conceptual point of view, selling books is not that different from selling "shoes and ships and sealing wax"—or anything else. Let's see how Amazon begins with rapid navigation to the shopper's probable purchase of a book about shopping science (Figure 3.2).

Exactly how Amazon's search algorithm works is not important. What is important is that in about two seconds Amazon delivered a list of 1,772 books. This is typical Amazon: with a Long Tail of millions of books Amazon wants to bring you what you want as quickly as possible. Crucially, the algorithm has ranked the selection beginning with the number-one bestseller. This is because statistically the bestseller is most likely to be the next one sold out of this selection of books.

Figure 3.2 A purchase always begins with some type of search, starting with navigation.

In fact, whatever you want to buy, Amazon will always take whatever clues it has and deliver you a ranked list. This is akin to the clerk in a bricks store showing you the product that most of his shoppers have found most satisfying. It is a prominent step in getting you to the book you want to buy and getting to the sale as quickly as possible. The book for you may not be number one in sales for the crowd. But the closer your book is to number one on Amazon's custom list for you, the more successful the algorithm.

Amazon Focus: Selection

We can illustrate the selection part of Amazon's sales program with a customer who has arrived at a single page representing a single book, which the customer *may* want to purchase. Let's suppose the shopper is not familiar with shopping science books. She notices that although fourth-ranked *Inside the Mind of the Shopper* is not the top-seller of the top books, it is the most highly rated of those top few. So the shopper curiously clicks on it, bringing up this page; we are now ready to explore the remaining four areas of Amazon focus (Figure 3.3).

Figure 3.3 A search leads to an *offer*, and "tentative" selection.

Amazon Focus #2: Immediate Close

A few specific features of this page teach us how Amazon handles this customer. First, Amazon offers an *immediate* close of the sale with subsequent delivery of the physical merchandise. Notice that the instant there is a meeting of the minds. (Amazon agrees to sell; shopper agrees to buy.) Amazon wants to consummate the sale with the immediate convenience of the 1-Click option (Figure 3.4). This follows the supreme dictum of personal selling, which states "Close early and close often."

Figure 3.4 A *real* salesman immediately seeks to complete the sale, not as a matter of pressure, but as a *convenience*!

Notice the *urgency* of Amazon in securing the sale. This kind of urgency demonstrates what Greg Linden noted above. This is the next book you want to buy. This issue is of such importance to Amazon that they patented their 1-Click purchase method. Rather than just putting the book in the cart, Amazon encourages the shopper to buy it immediately. Lots of sales are lost online through the abandoned shopping cart. In the bricks store, products do not even make it to the shopping cart. Shoppers simply abandon any consideration of the product.

Amazon Focus #3: Affinity Sales and Crowd-Social Marketing

Summarizing to this point, the shopper entered a search (first click), clicked on the likely desired book (second click), and purchased the book with another click (third click). 1-2-3, the deal is done! But Amazon is not done. It will, subsequent to the close, or if the shopper did not purchase, attempt to make another sale immediately on the heels of the first or as an alternate to the first offer.

Figure 3.5 And a *real* salesman never stops selling: If a sale is made, maybe an add-on; if not, still seek to fill the need with something related.

Moving down the page, on the left, as the eye naturally moves, Amazon introduces books closely related to *Inside the Mind of the Shopper*. With this effort, Amazon is still trying to sell the original offer because the shopper continues to have an interest in the book on which they initially clicked. But the shopper is not yet ready to close the sale (Figure 3.5).

So Amazon leverages two powerful selling strategies: *affinity marketing* (what goes well with this) and *crowd-social marketing* (what other shoppers have done).

These two techniques are closely related but with alternate motivations. For example, you might not think of purchasing ham and eggs together. But the reality is that large numbers of people do buy them together. So a good salesman could employ affinity marketing and suggest that you buy them together based on their inherent, complimentary properties. Ham goes well with eggs. Or she might use crowd-social marketing and suggest you purchase them together because lots of other shoppers have bought both ham and eggs and were happy with the results.

Robert Cialdini refers to this as the Principle of Social Proof: "We determine what is correct by finding out what other people think is correct."[3] In this case, the people who buy Paco Underhill's book[4] and Robin Lewis's book[5] also buy Sorensen's book. Therefore, the correct thing for the shopper to do is to buy Sorensen's book. This very clever use of crowd-social marketing is also nudging sales of Underhill's and Lewis's books, too, if the shopper hasn't already bought them.

Amazon Focus #4: Reaching into the Long Tail

Let's return to your initial search while shopping science books. You have not added *Inside the Mind of the Shopper* to your shopping cart or clicked the instant-purchase option. Just because the close hasn't happened yet is no reason to give up on the sale. Amazon is leading your mind into deeper and deeper consideration of the offer. Of course, Amazon would have liked to close the sale immediately, but you may be a maximizer. Barry Schwartz in *The Paradox of Choice*, points out that people tend to fall into one of two camps. The maximizer is always concerned that there may be a better choice, and is willing to spend considerable effort in maximizing their selection. The satisficer, on the other hand, operates with some, possibly subconscious, measure of suitability, and when that is achieved, is happy to buy without second thoughts about whether there might have been some better alternate choice.[6]

Ideally, the shopper would have closed with the first *1-2-3* offer, but we can afford to be patient, especially because this is Amazon and "we" are really an algorithm, mediating the sale to the shopper. We can afford to be patient, matching the shopper's every time expenditure with additional appropriate selling. In this case of a maximizer, the appropriate selling is a multiplication of choices, a reaching into the Long Tail (Figure 3.6).

I placed a Big Head/Long Tail graph over this Amazon web page to show you how, after the search, immediate offer, and social offer, the next step is to dip a bit further into the Long Tail. This is illustrated by a sliding scale of about 100 books, shown eight at a time, that "Customers Who Bought This Item Also Bought." This puts the book that the shopper is still considering and has on their screen (top-left corner), in the expanded affinity and social context of other items that they might be interested in.

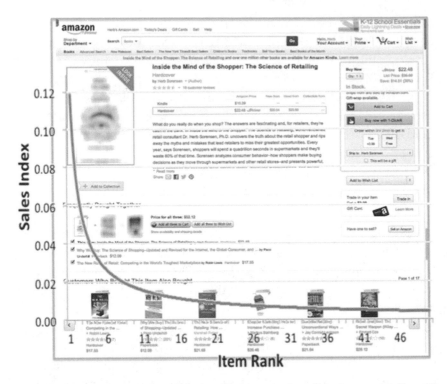

Figure 3.6 A large number of "related" items can be offered sequentially—all the way into a very long tail!

Amazon Focus #5: Info, Info, Info

From this point on down the Amazon page, the dominant theme is reviews, further rankings, biographical information, and links to other material that may be useful to the shopper. In fact, Amazon is one encyclopedic source of curated information about published knowledge, insight, and opinion that can be scanned at high or low levels to assess what leaders in any field are thinking about, and how other readers react to that thinking. People actually use bricks stores in this same way, to a limited extent.

The five selection foci listed above have direct counterparts, though perhaps not as obvious, in the bricks stores. But these five points define how Amazon meets the minds of its shoppers. Combine this with Amazonian delivery (logistics) and payment (money) and you have the winning global retailer in bricks stores a decade or two hence. But recognizing the store as a communal pantry, or bookshelf, or closet, or whatever, *the winning global retailer will be a bricks retailer*, possibly an Amazonian hybrid.

Amazonian Selling in Bricks Stores

A couple of concepts are essential in applying Amazonian techniques to bricks selling. The first of these concepts is that there is a lot less diversity in the shopping crowd than is on exhibit in the offers of self-service retail stores. Out of the 40,000 SKUs in the typical supermarket, most families buy only 150–200 different SKUs on a regular basis. We might then call the first principle "The focus of the individual."

The second principle is that the purchases of any randomly selected crowd of 10,000 people will have an amazing similarity to the purchases of any other 10,000 people. We might call this second principle "The constancy of the crowd." This is what makes it possible for a store with 2,000 SKUs to achieve $100 million in annual sales. Relating individual behavior to the crowd and the crowd's behavior to the individual is the key principle that allows intelligent relation of Amazonian selling (knowledge of the individual) to bricks-and-mortar selling (crowd knowledge—without smart phones).

But notice how Amazon's 50 million books attract shoppers who want to buy only one, in the same way the 40,000 SKUs in a supermarket attract shoppers who are most likely wanting to buy *five*. This attractive property is why any store with 40,000 SKUs should sell at least as much as the store with 2,000 SKUs. Amazon would use those extra 38,000 SKUs to attract more shoppers. But in fact, most stores have the advantage of that attractiveness and then unwittingly squander it by impeding the shopping inside their stores. Burying what the shopper wants in an indiscriminate sea of attractiveness is a great sales suppressing device that developed naturally as a consequence of self-service 100 years ago.

Let's think about how Amazon might manage the two basic issues of selling in a bricks store. Remember, these are *navigation*, getting the customer and the merchandise together; and *selection*, closing the sale by getting the shopper to accept the offer.

Amazonian Bricks Focus #1: Navigation—Simple and Fast

Before discussing how to assist shoppers in quickly selecting their desired purchase, let's first discuss how to best impede them in that task. This helps us understand how sales suppression occurs in store aisles. Knowing this will make more obvious what we need to do to remove the impediment.

Of course, Amazon has an advantage in that a targeted search online can lead to the desired location in a click or two. But the Amazon shopper can also flee their store in a click or two, so it isn't all advantage Amazon.

Another advantage of the bricks store is the visual advantage. Recall that in the selling process a major connector between the retailer and the shopper is vision. The bricks store has visual advantages with the shopper's eye taking in the store's offerings in more than 1,000 distinct points of focus over a mammoth screen, 25% of the whole store in a 10 minute shopping trip. Ten minutes online represent a comparable number of points of focus, with a far more narrow, more focused, field of vision. The bricks store has a much longer tail of visual experience, whereas the online store has a longer tail of merchandise. But therein lies the rub: that rich visual experience in the bricks store invites a lack of focus that is far more easily managed on a computer screen. But, it is possible for the bricks store to have a far richer, more varied field of vision and still retain essential focus and targeting.

So, how to impede shopper navigation? Let's begin with perhaps the worst possible navigational system (Figure 3.7):

Maze　　　　**Store**　　　　**Top Sellers**

Figure 3.7 The *worst* possible navigation system: today's typical store!

On the left, you have the extreme design of the maze, the worst possible navigation system. This is not an absurd approximation of an actual bricks store (center). Then, on the right, you see the actual locations the top 80 items that shoppers want most out of the tens of thousands of items on the store's shelves. These 80 items are the tip of the Big Head, so called because it generates big sales and profits. On the other hand, half of those tens of thousands of items, 20,000, generate about 5% of the store's sales. These 20,000 are the tailing end of the Long Tail. Large numbers of these items don't sell a single copy in a month, and quite a few, not in an entire year. The top 300 items constitute about 25% of total store sales. To really sell a lot, we need to understand the factors that drive not selling a lot (Figure 3.8).

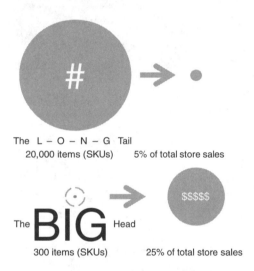

Figure 3.8 A tiny number of products are mostly what shoppers want; most other products do attract shoppers to the store—where they mostly buy from the few!

Large numbers of those items, like Amazon's 50 million books, do a great job of attracting shoppers to the store. But those items present a challenge to both navigation and selection. For navigation, the large selection virtually requires that a substantial amount of the store be devoted to a maze like, quasi-warehouse structure where shoppers serve themselves as stock-pickers (Figure 3.9).

To achieve Amazonian navigation in the bricks stores, the retailer must make lots of choices for the shopper, beginning with where they go in the store. The need for focus demands that the shopper's path be limited. It may be possible for the retailer to create two or three intuitive, instinctive, and distinctive paths. But designing the store with a single, Dominant Path, which the majority of shoppers in the store use, is the retailer's way of guiding the shoppers on an efficient path.

Figure 3.9 The rapidly growing number-two global retailer uses the *convenient* dominant U-turn path for most of its selling. (The struggling number-one retailer sticks with the maze, "warehouse" design.)

The Costco path really is intuitive, instinctive, and distinctive. I didn't notice it myself until I actually measured shoppers' experiences in the store. Costco also has a substantial Long Tail, which is visible to shoppers in the warehouse shelves on the outer perimeter of the store, or low table displays across the interior of the U-turn. Both are readily visible from the single dominant U-turn path, with plenty of opportunities for the shopper to listen to the siren call of the Long Tail (Figure 3.10). Any shopper, at any time, may turn off the Dominant Path to sate their interest in Long Tail.

Figure 3.10 Shoppers are not *forced* into the dominant U-turn, but enter on the front of the store at the right, and are naturally attracted to the convenience of the W – I – D – E aisle around the store!

An important consequence of the single Dominant Path is that it allows Costco to deal with the shopping trip as a process. It creates an orderly series of offers and acceptances, just as if personal salesmen were meeting the shoppers at strategic points along their trip and selling to them. It is not the merchant warehouseman's system of stacking the products on shelves and hoping the shopper can find what they want and need. This plays a role in the Amazonian selection assistance, too. Simple in-store navigation is part of the reason Costco is a growing international player, now number two globally[7] behind Walmart.

You don't have to rebuild the store in order to provide a dominant single path. Nearly any maze-like store can introduce a Dominant Path with minimal fixture alteration. Most stores already have a wide aisle to the back and a wide aisle across the back. Lower one gondola from the back to the front of the store to a height of four or five feet, and put one or two cut-throughs in it. This creates a close enough facsimile of a single aisle about 20 feet wide, given usual aisle and gondola widths. It has the advantage of adding two or more endcaps and a large increase of visual exposure to all the merchandise displayed in what is effectively a compound aisle (Figure 3.11). More cut-throughs equal more endcaps, an important tool for focus.

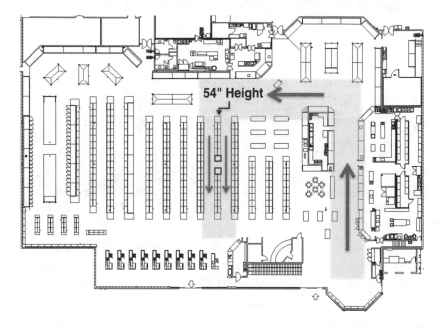

Figure 3.11 It's not hard to retrofit nearly any store to a dominant *wide* U-turn aisle.

In the example here, the store already had a wide aisle past floral and through the bakery and deli departments, leading to produce and then the fresh meat/poultry/seafood across from fine wines. This gets us to the return to the front, usually at the first checkouts to be seen from the back on the shopper's left. This is how you get Amazonian navigation into the supermarket—or any other store.

Summarizing the Amazonian navigation principles in bricks stores:

1. Provide a single Dominant Path to, and past, the merchandise most desired by the shoppers—the Big Head.

2. Maintain visual openness to the rest of the store, and specifically to the large array of merchandise that is attracting shoppers to the store, even if sales of those Long Tail items are more limited.

Admittedly, Amazonian navigation seems a bit more complex in a bricks store than it does using the bits and bytes of online navigation. But the principle is the same in both: get the shopper to the merchandise they are most likely to buy quickly and expeditiously, emphasis on the *most likely to buy*. Meanwhile, provide ready access to the Long Tail, without muddying the efficient choices from the Big Head.

Amazonian Bricks Focus: Selection

Previously we addressed the issue of getting the shoppers to the merchandise they want. Now, we address how the bricks Amazonian personal salesman, acting as a *ghost in the aisle*, assists the shopper in selecting the product they want, focusing on small numbers of options, mostly from the Big Head. The proper strategy is to use *crowd* statistics to relate to every shopper in the store *individually*. At each point on the trip, ask yourself "What will the crowd want?" The answer will be found in the transaction logs for the store.

Amazonian Bricks Focus #2: Immediate Close

We turn our attention first to the single Dominant Path, where most of the sales occur. Begin with a guiding principle set forth by Joe Girard, the world's greatest salesman, according to the *Guinness Book of World Records*. In his own words:

> "Over the years, I have discovered that the more choices presented to prospects [shoppers], the more difficult it becomes for them to make up their minds. While I don't have concrete evidence backed by formal research, I have observed that when people have to choose from more than three choices, they have a hard time determining which to pick . . . I recommend offering a maximum of three."[8]

Recall how our navigation of Amazon began in the previous section. We entered a search term and it showed us a ranked list of everything matching that search beginning with the top sellers. Your first step in navigation is to select one thing from that list of greatest interest to you. And moving from navigation to selection, if you don't immediately buy the item on which you first clicked, it offers you two or three options.

In the bricks store, the Amazonian salesman, as a ghost in the aisle, offers you the item you are most likely to buy in the immediate area wherever you happen to be in the store. For the vast majority of purchases, that should be on the Dominant Path. Now, where in the supermarket do you expect to find choices of three? The only places to consistently offer only a few items for choice are the endcap displays. And what does Costco have lining the right side of that single dominant aisle? Of course, it is a series of 37 endcaps, most with one, two, or maybe a few items.

The "top seller" is always in the context of what is being sold. Amazon has top sellers in thousands of categories. But it only touts the ones in the category where the shopper is browsing right now, as indicated by their click stream leading up to the current screen. Translating this to the bricks store means that some type of distinctive *Top Seller* tag for specific items in each department is probably appropriate. Although I have ideas on this subject, at the time of publication I have not conducted conclusive research in this area.

Amazon is not trying to sell the shopper what Amazon has in stock; it sells the shopper what the shopper wants. We repeat this distinction because it is so crucial. Amazon does not care what you buy, they will sell you anything they have that you want. This is true customer-centricity.

For the supermarket, think about the 300 items that will constitute 25% of store sales. It is a lot easier to figure out how to sell 300 items to the shopper rather than the 40,000 in the store. Let's begin by putting those 300 items on the Dominant Path, instead of scattering them around the store and burying them among the remaining 39,700 items of little to no interest to the shopper. Just as Amazon focuses the shopper by offering a small selection of its millions of products based on the shopper's search and ranking that selection according to which ones the shopper is most likely to buy, the bricks Amazonian retailer helps the shopper focus by placing the 300 items they are most likely to purchase on the single, wide, navigable, visible Dominant Path.

Two Closing Techniques

The immediate close in the supermarket is heavily focused on two techniques, the first of which is endcaps. That is because endcaps often have only three items on them, automatically creating Joe Girard's offering of three. Figure 3.12 shows some examples of top category performers on endcaps:

Category	Total Purchases (count)	End Cap Displays (share of category)	End Cap Purchases (share of category)
Carbonated Beverages	20%	47%	70%
Salty Snacks	15%	59%	73%
Crackers	11%	56%	66%
Breakfast Cereal	10%	23%	34%
Paper Products	10%	26%	43%
Bottled Water	8%	63%	85%
Cookies	7%	50%	70%

Figure 3.12 The major impact of endcap displays on total category sales.

The *Total Purchases* column is based not on dollars, but on the number of purchase events in the category—essentially distinct items purchased, by count, not by dollar. The second column, *End Cap Displays*, shows the share of promotional displays for that category, typically endcaps, but also freestanding aisle displays and others, across 13 stores for over a million shoppers. The third column, *End Cap Purchases*, shows the share of category purchases, by count, on the endcaps. Across these significant endcap performers, the average sales per display is 1.4 times the average purchases, 40% more than from main aisle displays counting each 4-foot aisle section as one display.

This average 40% lift is not due to price discounting. Glenn Terbeek[9] showed that only 25% of shoppers from a price discounted endcap were actually influenced by the price. Endcaps are an excellent sales tool, and their selling is primarily due to their focus on a limited selection.[10] Note that some top-tier global retailers regularly use promotional endcaps without any reduction in price. This does not mean that a low price image is not of any value. But the efficiency gains from everyday low prices (EDLP) can be passed on to shoppers for genuine savings.

All 300 Big Head items should be represented in the Dominant Path that we illustrate above. This does not mean that entire categories need to be moved here. For example, it is highly effective to use one of the refrigerated cases on this path to display a small selection of the best quality, highest margin dairy items. Do not lower the prices. The promotion is the location, not the price, and shoppers will gladly give you the extra margin for meeting their needs more efficiently. The full dairy department located elsewhere in the store will meet Long Tail needs.

The second technique involves not just making it convenient to reach the top seller items, but calling out and focusing attention on the single highest top seller. This is not a matter of selling that designation to the highest bidder amongst the brand suppliers. There are plenty of well justified opportunities for that, but not mixed and confounded with the shoppers' own choices. By highlighting the top seller, you leverage the same kind of crowd-social marketing that Amazon utilizes when it shows its shoppers the number one best seller. In the sense that you are calling attention to what most of the crowd buys from the options on display. Note that Amazon's online selling strategy would crumble if they allowed suppliers to buy the top ranking. They might make some short term profit gains, but if consistently practiced, they would erode a huge advantage they have against bricks retailers: Customers have come to trust Amazon's rankings.

Amazonian Bricks Focus #3: Affinity Sales/Crowd-Social Marketing

There is nothing wrong with offering a second or third option beside the top seller. There are several types of products that you can use to encourage purchase of the top seller. The first of these is affinity sales. What goes well with this item? The answer to that question requires no special culinary insight or marketing genius. When shoppers buy this specific item, what other items do they buy associated with it? Recall our discussion on ham and eggs earlier in this chapter.

The answer to this question requires a careful statistical analysis of the transaction log to verify that if shoppers buy item A, they are most likely to also buy item N. Sometimes the reason for the affinity is obvious. This is why can openers are often sold in canned pet food aisles. But we have to be realistic about the ability of bricks retailers to move items around, which is not virtually effortless as it is in Amazon's case. This means that affinities are more appropriately dealt with as adjacencies in bricks stores, and are better handled by categories than by individual items.

However, there is one affinity strategy that may be especially appropriate for store brand products. Consider the pie crust example in Figure 3.13.

Figure 3.13 Creating a "value" image for the store, while still selling more of high dollar product!

Notice that the store brand, Shoppers' Savings $, is priced 40% less at $2.49 versus $4.19 for the Shoppers' Choice, #1. In this case, we are calling the shopper's attention to the fact that there is a way to save significant money here. There is no reason to expect to divert shoppers from the proven number-one choice. The purpose is to tell the shopper, "Hey, if you are squeezing every penny, look no further, the best price is right here." The strategy is not to sell the alternate but to represent that this store has got your back, if you really need to save money. But it's not surprising that people will spend the extra $1.70 for the Pillsbury product. Amazon uses this same strategy at a much lower level by giving you the opportunity to rank a selection of products by price rather than by bestsellers.

Remember, the price tells you two things: *how much you will have to pay for this item,* and also, *how much this item is worth.* Studies have shown that shoppers will buy more of the exact same item if you raise the price. I know that seems counterintuitive, but the shopper's intuition is that maybe it's cheaper because it isn't as good. The image of price fairness is more important than the price. And maybe a pie that you are going to bake yourself is worth the extra $1.70 for a premium crust.

In a store with 40,000 SKUs, calling out the 50 or100 true top sellers selected from the top few hundred SKUs will generate significant lift for the entire store. Backing this up with affinity sales, carefully considered category adjacencies, sharpens shopper focus and provides a one-two punch for the most productive part of the store: the Dominant Path.

Amazonian Bricks Focus #4: Reaching into the Long Tail

As attractive as the Long Tail is, it should be seen and not heard. The challenge is to maintain the pull of the Long Tail without dampening the natural push of the Big Head. Remember, the Big Head consists of what the shoppers want to buy. Don't let the Long Tail get in the way.

Conceptually, we can solve this problem by maintaining the Big Head in a selling space while keeping the Long Tail in a warehouse space. Most retailers already have approximated these two spaces by designing stores with a wide open perimeter surrounding a narrow-aisled center-of-store warehouse. Unfortunately, many Big Head items are buried in that center-of-store warehouse and there are plenty of Long Tail items on display around the perimeter selling area. The bigger problem of the two is burying Big Head items anywhere.

The key then is making the warehouse space visually present in a maximum way. Costco has done this by leaving a very large warehouse space that rises to the ceiling all around the outer wall of the building. They knocked the center-of-store space, also a lot of Long Tail area, down to under four feet in height, giving great visual access even to the far wall of perimeter merchandise and visual openness comparable to the top-selling produce areas in typical supermarkets. Costco has an off-the-path, large, bazaar-like fresh food and produce area in a far corner of the store, but it maintains the openness through a very large percentage of the store. This combines two attractive properties for maximum use: the Long Tail attracts, somewhat indiscriminately; open space attracts, again somewhat indiscriminately.

Amazonian Bricks Focus #5: Info, Info, Info

Notice where Amazon puts the great bulk of their product information: at the bottom of the page, out of sight and out of mind, unless you scroll down to see it. You can think of information like the Long Tail, to be seen but not heard, unless you need it. The vast majority of information available to shoppers in the stores is already on the package. Providing information kiosks, brochures, short video clips, and other informative media can be helpful if it doesn't get in the way of Big Head sales. Nothing should distract the shopper from the convenience and efficiency of speedy selection from the Big Head.

Post Script: Visiting an Amazon Bricks Store in Seattle

Earlier this year Amazon opened its first bricks and mortar store in Seattle, only a few hours drive from my home in Portland, Oregon. As a great admirer of Amazon's online personal selling program, I was anxious to see for myself how the world's number-one online retailer translated its genius selling skills from online to the bricks retail world.

Knowing that successfully employing some online selling techniques in the bricks world might not be as easy as it may seem, my plan was to grade each of the five techniques outlined in this chapter, as deployed in Amazon's bricks store. Grading is on the familiar A – B – C – D or F. Since I used Costco in this chapter to favorably illustrate Amazon's technique in a bricks store, it seemed reasonable to assign the same type of grade to Costco, on a point-by-point comparison: online vs. bricks!

The purpose, then, is to provide a judgment comparison of two top quality retailers, in terms of *selling* technique, with Amazon presuming to move onto the turf of Costco, at least in a small, introductory way.

Principle 1: Navigation: On arrival at the new Amazon bricks store, it was obvious that the basic store layout was something like the typical, inferior maze-style store design. The basic bookstore is a cramped, narrow, high-walled facility with rows of intimidating aisles filled with thousands of books. To be fair, Costco also has a perimeter of narrow aisles reaching for the sky. However, the Costco shopper is naturally guided by a wide, dominant U-turn path, central to the store, that navigates all around the store. In fact, Costco has a substantial book section, too, but that is deployed on easily scanned tables across the wide, low, center-of-store.

For The Amazon store there was no easily recognizable Dominant Path. In fact, it would be hard to say that Amazon has a plan for the shopper to move through the store, therefore the "rat-maze" design earns at best a "D," while Costco gets an "A" for navigation.

Principle 2: Selection—Immediate Close: In comparing to Costco on the second principle, Selection-Immediate close, we may as well recognize at the outset that Costco makes no effort to "close" the sale (checkout,) immediately. In fact, Jim Senegal of Costco, explained the reason for NOT having any *express* checkout lanes is that they do not want to encourage checkout with one, or a few items. Costco's giant baskets do encourage immediately putting things in, so I generously score Costco a "C" on immediate selection, but maybe a "D" or "F" on the close—payment at checkout.

Taking into account Amazon's attempt at crowd-social marketing in its bricks store, I suggest a grade of "C" for selection and immediate close, no better than the thousands of mediocre competitors they face. To achieve the kind of focus we are driving for, and to improve its score, Amazon should consider focusing only on the Big Head in the store and have a smaller, supportive role for the Long Tail.

For Costco I assign a generous "C" as well—primarily based on the reality that bricks stores are not yet geared toward immediate checkout, although there are shopper apps that allow the shopper to scan their selections as they procede through their trip, running up their basket total as they go. Amazon, if they get serious about moving their online expertise into their bricks stores, will need to give serious thought about how to adapt "1-Click" purchasing for the bricks store.

It is my opinion that Amazon should be electronically recognizing the shoppers coming in the door of their stores, and responding with guidance and suggestions for purchases, just as they do online. It is also my opinion that shopping apps are a stunted opportunity, given their limited *acceptance* by the vast majority of shoppers. Perhaps the proper deployment of online in the bricks store, is the store's *own* tablet-type devices on the shelves. In fact, I have a patent pending on just such a device I refer to as the "Long Tail Accelerator." But note also the relevance of this to "The Webby Store" discussed in chapter 5 of this book.

Principle 3: Selection—Affinity Sales and Crowd-Social Marketing: In Amazon's bricks store there is a sea of books, each shouting, "I am highly rated by readers that have bought me!" Amazon has tagged every item on every shelf in every aisle with recommendations from previous buyers. But which one should I consider? As the Guinness World Record Holder for greatest salesman, Joe Girard, taught us, never offer more than three options to the customer you *are focusing on.* We can adapt that advice to a bricks store display by perhaps calling out and focusing the shopper's attention on three books in a single display, with perhaps a series of displays of various subcategories,

One of the first fixes Amazon could make in its bricks store is to provide prominent identification of the books that earned the top three slots of total sales in each category or subcategory. This can be finessed in terms of their first quarter sales or other metrics. Each of those three books might also have one or two *buddy-books* that shoppers most often purchased with each respective title. Shoppers will have an easier time selecting a book if clear displays tell them, "If you buy this book, your fellow shoppers who bought it also bought this one with it!"

Given a 3-foot wide shelf-fixture, perhaps one or two shelves in the 40–60-inch height range could really *sell* the top book of the category, with #2 and #3 situated beside or below #1. The idea is illustrated here in Figure 3.14.

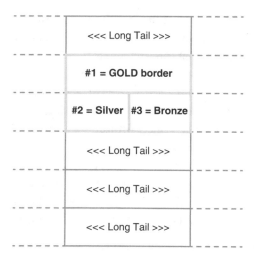

Figure 3.14 A schematic shelf offering/promoting the top 3 sellers, without "hiding" the Long Tail.

The three called out here are the "Big Head" for the specific subcategory. With shelves outside the main area of focus, above and below, displaying more of the "Long Tail" for that subcategory, with the balance of that in the warehouse/back room.

To Amazon's credit, it is attempting to connect with shoppers through crowd-social marketing, albeit in a haphazard manner. Crowd-social marketing, in this context, means creating a link between me as the shopper and my fellow readers, trusted peers who provided their own reviews of books in which I am most likely to be interested. Amazon accomplishes this well online but has lost something in the translation to its bricks store. In applying this technique to all of the books it offers, it only managed to overwhelm.

Amazon's Bricks Store Score for Selection—Affinity Sales and Crowd-Social Marketing: We expect better from Amazon when they exhibit such a marvelous understanding of these techniques online. Again, taking their haphazard crowd-social marketing attempt into consideration, as we did for their score in immediate closing, we generously give the Amazon bricks store a "B" for affinity sales and crowd-social marketing. I will not rate Costco on this point because they are quite successful with the approach they are using, particularly supplier demos to engage shoppers moving around their wide U-turn aisle. (There is no apparent "social" aspect to their selling.)

Principle 4: Selection—Reaching into the Long Tail: If Amazon had followed its own online personal selling program, I would have encountered a Dominant Path upon first entering the store, with books attractively and invitingly displayed according to the most purchased products. This path would have been wide, with low displays and a long field of view, allowing me to take in many different focal points with an initial glance. The Dominant Path would have been lined with endcap displays, each featuring about three different offerings and related affinity or crowd-social marketing offerings. The shopper would have been drawn along this Dominant Path and at strategic points along the way we would have encountered offers, displays, and crowd-social and affinity marketing related to the subject matter and products typically purchased in those areas.

Online, Amazon would provide a listing of Long Tail offerings based on the initial search and click. This is not as easily accomplished in the bricks world, but it's not impossible. As we have discussed elsewhere,

Costco approximates this quite well. Radiating from the Dominant Path, Costco's store design features aisles filled with Long Tail merchandise. These aisles do not interfere with the shopper's navigation of the Dominant Path, but they are very visible and accessible to any shopper who might have an interest in the products stored/displayed there.

If Amazon utilized its own online, personal selling principle of Reaching into the Long Tail in its bricks store, then at some point along the (nonexistent) Dominant Path, one would have been able to readily find categories and subcategories of interest, offered in a Long Tail, warehouse-style aisle that could easily be accessed from the Dominant Path.

Amazon's Bricks Store Score for Selection—Reaching into the Long Tail: Based on the fact that Amazon fell into the trap of indiscriminately mixing its Big Head items among the thousands of Long Tail items it offered at its bricks store and that it made no attempt to help us navigate either the Big Head or Long Tail, I give it a grade of "C" on this fourth point of retail expertise and practice. Again, Amazon could easily improve this score by establishing a Dominant Path and assisting its shoppers in navigating that path, and if they do not find what they are looking for along that path, providing corresponding assistance in accessing the Long Tail.

Principle 5: Info, Info, Info: It is actually ideal to use packaging for signaling, branding, and billboard functions, with textual communication kept to a minimum. The introduction of an integrated tablet on the shelf would more fully execute the convergence of online, mobile, and bricks retail. (Possibly the "Long Tail Accelerator" mentioned above.)

Conclusion: As shoppers become more accustomed to the personal selling techniques they encounter in their online shopping trips, they will become increasingly intolerant of bricks retailers who fail to provide the same algorithmic personal assistance, attention to their interests, and consideration of their time their online rivals offer.

Likewise, online retailers who attempt and fail to successfully translate their online selling principles to the bricks world will encounter similar displeasure from their customers.

As stated before, as society incorporates and adapts to new technologies, the retail landscape will shift, just as it did 100 years ago when the Industrial Revolution ushered in the age of the self-service retailer. But as a communal pantry, bricks will always have an edge over online. And the self-service, bricks "store of the future" is still out there somewhere. It's just not the Amazon Bookstore in Seattle.

Retrospective: It would perhaps be unfair to not include at least a passing comparison of Amazon's bricks store to an Apple store. In fact, a substantial central area of the store is dedicated to Amazon's technology products. No effort is made here to judge the value of this, since Apple is largely featuring high-dollar, high-margin products in their stores; where a very large service staff is available. This is the virtual antithesis of the *self*-service retailing this book is about. However, if Amazon is thinking of emulating the Apple store, bear in mind that the Apple store is not terribly relevant to the wider world of *retail*.

Review Questions

1. Describe the function in retail called *meeting of the minds*. How does this function usually occur in self-service retail? How does Amazon facilitate this function through its online store? What advantage do online stores have? What about bricks stores?

2. How does Amazon assist shopper navigation? What is their mechanism replacing the salesperson service? How can self-service bricks retailers apply these techniques?

3. Describe how Amazon uses affinity sales. How do these techniques relate to the concept of *personal selling* or *mediated sales*? How can self-service bricks retailers utilize these tools (think of the challenge of Long Tail)? How can a retailer decide what goes with what on a shelf?

4. How does Amazon manage the Long Tail in their bricks store? How does this compare to the concepts of the *Dominant Path* and the *Dark Store*?

5. Describe how individual shopper behavior relates to crowd behavior and how the use of numbers, metrics, and crowd statistics makes it possible to predict future sales for the majority of shoppers.

6. Consider Costco's layout. What makes its layout a good example of a store with clear Dominant Path? How do shoppers access the Long Tail in a Costco store?

7. What simple changes in a typical bricks store could deliver visual openness to the Dominant Path and the merchandise?

8. The paradox of choice suggests that too much choice might confuse shoppers. Which shelf spaces and displays in a bricks store could be used for a limited selection offer? Why would they be suitable for this task?

Endnotes

1. Fader, Peter, Moe, Wendy, "Integrating Online and Offline Retailing," Chapter 4 of *Inside the Mind of the Shopper* (Sorensen) 2nd Edition.

2. Brandt, Richard L. (2011). One Click: Jeff Bezos and the Rise of Amazon.com. New York, New York: Penguin Group.

3. *Influence: Science and Practice* (http://www.amazon.com/Influence-Practice-Robert-B-Cialdini/dp/0205609996?ie=UTF8&keywords=cialdini%20influence&qid=1376787837&ref_=sr_1_2&s=books&sr=1-2)

4. *Why We Buy: The Science of Shopping—Updated and Revised for the Internet, the Global Consumer, and Beyond* (http://www.amazon.com/Why-We-Buy-Shopping-Updated-Internet/dp/1416595244?ie=UTF8&ref_=pd_bxgy_b_text_y)

5. *The New Rules of Retail: Competing in the World's Toughest Marketplace* (http://www.amazon.com/New-Rules-Retail-Competing-Marketplace/dp/0230105726?ie= UTF8&ref_=pd_bxgy_b_text_z)

6. Schwartz, Barry (2009). The Paradox of Choice. New York, New York. HarperCollins.

7. Gaul, Ray, "Top 50 Global Retailers," Chain Store Age magazine, vol. 89, no. 6, October 2013.

8. See: "Choices of Three" in "How to Close Every Sale" (Commentary on Joe Girard's book) http://www.shopperscientist.com/2011-10-06.html

9. Terbeek, Glen A. (1999). Agentry Agenda: *Selling Food in a Frictionless Marketplace*. Chesterfield, VA: American Book Company.

10. See also, Anderson, Eric and Duncan Simester, "Mind Your Pricing Cues," (http://classes.bus.oregonstate.edu/winter-06/ba499/elton/Articles/Mind%20Your%20Pricing%20Cues.pdf) and "No, the Customer is *NOT* Always Right!." http://www.shopperscientist.com/2009-07-23.html

4

Integrating Online and Offline Retailing: *An Interview with Peter Fader and Wendy Moe*

AUTHOR'S NOTE

In the seven years since we first published this book, online retailers have firmly and inextricably established their dominance in the retail industry. No longer just a distant cousin to bricks retail, online retail is driving an evolution of the industry that rivals the emergence of the self-service retail concept. As we have shown in previous chapters, online retail employs *personal selling* techniques and tools that not only are rapidly propelling them to the front of the global market, but also are changing the way shoppers shop in the bricks world. That's why, seven years later, this chapter is even more relevant and prescient than before. Fader and Moe's study of shopper behavior presents profound implications for any retailer, whether online or in bricks stores.

Although I have spent most of my career studying the *click-click-click* of shopping carts in physical retail stores, the *click-click-click* of online retailing has emerged as an important new window on shopper behavior. With new technologies moving into retail stores, and with the increasing integration of online and offline commerce, studying online retailing also provides insight into how shopping might evolve in the future. I had long been aware of Wharton School professor Peter Fader's shopper modeling studies in physical retail stores, and I had a chance to collaborate with him in studying the in-store shopping process. In the late 1980s and early 1990s, he and other researchers used a growing avalanche of point-of-sale scanner data to analyze what people buy. Their models could help us understand, for example, why shoppers bought one brand of orange juice over another. Although linking sales data to specific customers was a leap forward, it still offered limited insight into the behavior of shoppers in the store. Our work initially helped fill that gap in the physical retail space, by carefully observing and analyzing how shoppers shop.

But then came the Internet. In addition to his studies and his modeling of physical retailing, Fader, along with his colleague Wendy Moe, an associate professor of marketing at the University of Maryland, conducted path-breaking studies of online behavior. In studying their work on online shopping, I saw that the core principles bore a striking resemblance to what we see in physical stores. The point-by-point clickstreams of online shoppers are similar to the point-by-point visiting, shopping, and purchasing behavior of in-store shoppers. Although I focused more on "crowd" statistics in my work, looking for descriptive insights for all shoppers or major groups, Fader and Moe (along with other colleagues) looked at patterns of individual shopper behavior as a means of assessing the drivers of individual behavior. The picture is richer from both perspectives than from either alone, and each confirms the other. In this interview, they share some of the insights from their research.

How Did the Internet Change the Study of Shopping Behavior?

Fader: For my first ten years or so here at Wharton, I was looking strictly at point-of-sale scanner data, just analyzing what people buy and completely ignoring the context around it. Not that I wasn't interested in the context, but there was just no data. So, we had all these models trying to help us understand why people buy this brand of orange juice instead of that. The models worked great and people applied them to very different areas such as pharmaceuticals and financial services. Then everything changed with the dot.com revolution. As everyone was jumping into these uncharted waters, I initially wanted no part of it. I figured the process of someone standing at a shelf and deciding what juice to buy is going to be very different than someone sitting at the computer clicking through a bunch of different books or CDs—until I actually looked at the data, and it turned out that the patterns were remarkably similar. The same types of patterns were apparent in both purchasing *processes*. It was really fascinating. I never expected it.

Moe: I focused on online research from the beginning. My early research looked at online shopping behavior, how frequently people come to the store, how much they visit it, and what kind of search activities they use in comparison to other stores. That can give us an idea of how much they purchase. Then we can forecast their purchasing. We looked at patterns across visits and repeat visits to predict what they might buy in the future. I realized, however, that for some categories of products, consumers are not necessarily going to make repeat visits before they buy, so I focused on page-to-page behaviors within a single store visit. I looked at issues involving the focus of search behavior: Does one look at a specific brand or jump around across categories? Within a category? Is the consumer buying or just browsing? What do these patterns mean for purchase behavior?

E-commerce marketers have an abundance of data that most offline retailers don't have access to. They use this for better diagnostics and more accurate forecasting. They also can experiment with product layout and promotional messages. In the physical world, customer data have been focused mainly on when, what, and how much people buy. What researchers in physical stores haven't been able to measure as well are activities such as comparison-shopping and information gathering, which often have a strong influence on the final choice. Insights from online data might help offline retailers better understand shopping behavior.

> *"I figured the process of someone standing at a shelf and deciding what juice to buy is going to be very different than someone sitting at the computer clicking through a bunch of different books or CDs—until I actually looked at the data, and it turned out that the patterns were remarkably similar." —Peter Fader*

In What Way Are the Online and Offline Patterns Similar?

Fader: We found that people's tendencies to do something and decide whether or when to do it again—and how many more times to do it— were similar. The mathematical models describing the behavior could be applied in almost a "cookie cutter" way to a variety of products, from cans of baked beans on the shelf at the Safeway to books online at Amazon.com. I threw myself into e-commerce because there we could see not only what people buy, but also the process leading up to it. We began looking at the interplay between visits and purchases online. There were all these patterns, that we could never see before, that were consistent with what we had been seeing. Then we came across your PathTracker studies in bricks-and-mortar stores, using RFID tags on shopping carts, and this allowed us to integrate these two areas of research, measuring shopper behavior with a variety of different tools (see the sidebar, "Studying the Same Shoppers on Different Paths"). We could take the rich context that we were able to see in the online world and marry it with our deep understanding of what happens in the grocery world. It allowed us to address questions such as: Which zone will you visit next? Are you just passing through or are you really shopping there? And if you're shopping there, what things, if any, are you going to buy?

Studying the Same Shoppers on Different Paths

The same shoppers move through a path and decision process in finding and buying, whether online or offline. Different research tools are used to track and compare the behaviors of these shoppers in these different environments, including the following:

- **Retail shopping:** Radio frequency identification (RFID) tags underneath shopping carts track consumers' in-store movements.

- **Eye tracking:** Researchers ask subjects to view print advertisements and capture the subjects' eye movements using infrared corneal reflection technology, or use the same technology in the store.

- **Web browsing clickstreams:** Consumers' web-browsing patterns are tracked by recording the sequence of web pages visited in a session.

- **Information acceleration:** Researchers immerse subjects in a multimedia environment to understand how they collect information and make decisions about a radically new product or service.[1]

How Are Paths in the Supermarket Similar to Paths Online?

Fader: Online and offline marketing both have path-type data associated with them, yet very few people consider the path aspects. They simply look at outcomes. Look at some of the e-commerce work on how people click from page to page and whether they are buying. I tended to think, like most people, that there's nothing else like it in the physical world. The Internet is brand new, right? But clicking through an online site is a lot like someone pushing a cart up and down the aisles. Turning left or right in the grocery store is a lot like clicking on this link or that link, even though the physical movements are quite different. The decision process, when you get down deep, appears to be pretty similar. A path is a path, whether it's online or offline, people or birds.

Can Online Retailers Learn from Offline Shopper Behavior?

Fader: Take a small example: Herb, your in-store research has found that shoppers tend to look to the left and move to the left, counterclockwise, as they move through the store. Where is the shopping cart located on just about every online site? On the right. You've got people who will experiment with absolutely everything in designing their website—different content, different colors, different everything. But the shopping cart is always on the right. They have no idea why. Should they test the cart on the left?

We should no longer be surprised when we see these online/offline analogies. We should expect them. But a lot of people don't buy it. They say, oh no, come on, looking at a screen is totally different than pushing a cart in a store. There's very little evidence to suggest that it's really different. On the other hand, offline retailers, who have spent all this time laying out the aisles and getting the merchandise at the right height, don't think they could learn something from online. But I believe they can. The ultimate irony is that bricks-and-mortar retailers are outsourcing their online business to online firms. They say: Make our website as efficient as possible and just tell us how much money we are making. These online companies are running thousands of different experiments every day. But they tend to be two completely different species of people, and they are not taking any of these learnings back to the offline store.

Some of the areas that we have studied that have implications for both online and offline retailing are crowding and herding, sequencing or licensing (buying "vice" products such as chocolate after "virtue" products such as vegetables, for example), shoppers speeding up as they move toward their goals, shopping momentum, the impact of variety, and hedonic shopping behavior.[2]

Tell Me about What You've Found Out about Crowd Behavior?

Fader: Studies online and offline show similarities in crowding and herding. It boils down to this: If I'm in a store and I see a big crowd of people down an aisle, does it attract me or repel me? There are two schools of thought. One says that a crowd attracts people, the other that it repels. But it's not that straightforward. People tend to go where there is a crowd—but they won't necessarily shop there. I see a crowd in a store, so I am going to push my cart down there to see what is going on; however, it might just be too crowded to engage with products on the shelf, so I'm going to move on. What we found is that it doesn't just depend on the individual but also on the type of behavior. We have some insights, but there is still a question about how these two forces counterbalance each other. This is an excellent example of why we need a statistical model.

It is also worth mentioning the connection here with GRPs (gross rating points) and their constituent components, reach and frequency. The question is: Do we want to get people staring at the shelf often, or do we want to get *a lot* of people to stare at the shelf? You might get a lot of reach but repel people at the same time because of the crowding.

What Have You Learned about Licensing and Sequencing—Such as the Purchase of Vice Items After Virtue Items?

Fader: There is a sequence in how people buy things. One important driver of this sequencing may be "licensing" behavior. If shoppers buy a virtue product—something good for them—then it gives them license to buy a vice product—something that they might enjoy but is probably not good for them. If they pick up broccoli or tofu in the produce section, they can buy the ice cream or chocolate cake or cigarettes. It has tremendous implications for the placement of products on the path through the retail store or online. This is one of the reasons why sequence matters. The chocolate cake at the beginning of the shopping trip might be viewed differently than at the end, when the shopper has accumulated some virtue products and now might be more willing to indulge in a vice.

We see this in the laboratory, but it has yet to be validated in the real world. We sit people down and show them a list of things and ask them to indicate which ones they would buy. But for certain people, you prime them by saying you've already bought a certain product (virtue or vice), and then see if they buy the vice product after the virtue. There is some variation across people in how attractive the vice products become after the virtue ones.

> *"If shoppers buy a virtue product—something good for them— then it gives them license to buy a vice product." —Peter Fader*

What Have You Found Out about the Pace of the Shopping Trip?

Fader: Research has shown that the closer you get to your goal, the more you speed toward it. This is called the "goal-gradient hypothesis." We see this in the context of loyalty programs, where people buy ten and get one free. A number of researchers have noticed that as you get closer to the goal, you speed up purchasing. This is consistent with what you've seen in the store, the concept of the "checkout magnet," where shoppers move more quickly as they get closer to the checkout. We could extend the goal gradient hypothesis beyond the checkout, to look at other goals that occur as you shop. They might be items on your shopping list, parts of the store that you go to on every visit—for example, to see if meat is on sale each week. This is difficult to study because, other than the checkout, shoppers have different goals. But we believe we will see evidence that this goal-gradient hypothesis applies to intermediate goals as well as the final checkout.

What Have You Learned about Shopping Momentum?

Fader: The idea here is that as more purchases are made, everything in the store becomes more attractive. Once shoppers pick up a number of items, it gives them the momentum to buy more. Once you have two or three items in your cart, you start really rolling and then pick up a lot of stuff. The more you buy, the more you buy. As your studies have shown, the most common number of items purchased in a grocery store is one. That means many shoppers never really get rolling. They may get that one item and, before they can be enticed to buying a second or third, they leave. If they do build momentum, they buy a lot more.

Just as with the other forces in play in the store, the impact of the forces at play such as shopping momentum will vary across individuals. That, again, is why we need a proper statistical model to measure the effect of these forces on individuals.

What Have You Learned about the Role of Variety in Shopping?

Fader: There are some people who say that people like variety. If there's greater variety, then you're meeting people's needs in a better way and, therefore, the category as a whole becomes more attractive. On the other hand, if you have too many forms and flavors, as Barry Schwartz points out in *The Paradox of Choice*,[3] people are actually put off by too much choice.

We've only tested this so far in an indirect way—across categories, which is not the best way. We looked at categories that have high variety and those with low variety to see how attractiveness varies across them. What we see is that high variety is more attractive.

This doesn't necessarily refute your perspective or Barry Schwartz's that offering more limited selections can increase sales. We're looking across categories within stores, rather than the same category across stores, and there is tremendous opportunity for reverse causality here. It could be that if a category is more attractive, people really like it, and then retailers are going to want to stock more SKUs in it. That could explain why greater variety in a category is associated with greater attractiveness. There is a lot of testing that needs to be done.

What Have You Learned about Efficiency? Is It Better to Allow Shoppers to Get Quickly In and Out of the Store, or Should Retailers Try to Prolong the Trip?

Fader: Traveling salespeople are famously well organized. They have to be: They are always on the move, visiting a certain number of clients every day, so they need to find the most efficient route possible. Our studies of the paths taken by 1,000 grocery shoppers at a store in the western U.S. have found that shoppers, unlike traveling salespeople, are often quite inefficient.[4] They might choose the right order in which to travel to find the products they want, but they take too long and go further off course than they need to. Another interesting finding is that inefficient shoppers tend to have more in their carts than those who shop more efficiently, so this inefficiency within reason is not necessarily a problem for retailers.

This research has major implications for both store owners and brand manufacturers. Retailers want their customers to have as efficient an experience as possible. On the other hand, they want the shopper to stay longer and interact with more products in the hope that it will drive more impulse purchases and incremental revenue and build the relationship that will make shoppers want to return. If, however, they prolong the shopping trip through confusing store design and bad signage, customers will get annoyed and not return. More time spent shopping could be a good thing if it is a sign of increased engagement but might be negative if it reflects confusion and aggravation.

In the online world, measurement has taken a radical turn from looking at how many unique visitors are attracted to a website to measuring time spent per session. Again, there is the divergence between efficiency and engagement: To what extent should retailers, whether online or offline, help shoppers finish shopping as quickly as possible or try to hold them for as long as possible?

Moe: I conducted a study on the impact of pop-up promotions on people's online surfing behavior. People often complain that these advertisements are annoying. They don't like them. But actually they influence their behavior positively from the perspective of the retailer. People who are served pop-ups at the right moment actually stay on the website longer and shop and search a little bit more. If the pop-up itself has good content that matches their needs, visitors are encouraged to stay, search, and buy. If the pop-up is on a gateway page—a home page or category page—that visitors use to get to the products they want to see, a pop-up is stopping them from getting to their ultimate destination. These are received poorly.

> *"People often complain that these [pop-up] advertisements are annoying. They don't like them. But actually they influence their behavior positively from the perspective of the retailer." —Wendy Moe*

This Raises the Question of Whether Shoppers Are in the Store for Utilitarian Reasons Alone or If They Are Interested in an Experience. What Is the Difference?

Fader: Shopping can be for a utilitarian purpose—something that has to be done—or it can be done for a hedonic purpose—for the sheer enjoyment of it. Online grocery shopping has not caught on in the U.S. to the same extent as the U.K. This might be because larger U.S. bricks-and-mortar stores offer the hedonic experience that online shopping lacks. Many Americans live in large houses spaced farther apart than their European counterparts, which makes going to the store more of a social experience. Again, this is an area ripe for investigation in both the online and offline world. In the online world, you can watch the same individuals over a number of shopping trips and start to notice patterns. Offline, what is needed is to marry data from a series of PathTracker[5] studies over time with data from a shopper loyalty card to find out exactly who is doing the shopping. This would show how often they are shopping hedonically versus in a utilitarian fashion and whether there were patterns involved.

What Have You Learned so far about What Shoppers Are Looking for When They Go Online?

Moe: My research has looked at the underlying objectives of online shoppers and the expression of these objectives in purchases. I identified four distinct types of visits associated with different online behaviors, as follows:

- **Directed-purchase visits** are where the shopper enters the store with a clearly defined purpose of walking out with a specific purchase.

- **Search/deliberation visits** are utilitarian visits where a future purchase is being considered, and the store visit is designed to gather relevant information before buying.

- **Hedonic browsing visits** are more about enjoyment, where shoppers browse without looking for anything specific but might make an impulse buy.

- **Knowledge-building visits** are also enjoyable but are more geared toward collecting information for possible future purchases.[6]

It is important for online retailers to understand this to target their marketing activities effectively to the right people. Shoppers come into bricks-and-mortar stores for some of the same reasons.

How Do Online Retailers Use These Insights about Shopper Visits?

Moe: The next stage of research looks at differentiating between online shoppers not just according to what pages they are looking at, but by also actually examining the products they are interested in.[7] In other words, what are the characteristics of the products they are searching for and interested in? And what are their ideal products? Building a model based on data from this research enables the retailer to estimate the probability of purchasing. For example, if someone looks only at a series of black shoes, you can infer that she has a clear preference for this color shoe. Someone else might be looking only at shoes in a certain price range. The sequence of pages tells the researcher something about what a person's preferences are. This helps predict not only *whether* they will buy, but also *what*.

By understanding better what shoppers are looking for, retailers can, in theory, create a virtual smart salesperson to help. This assistant might be compared to the salesperson in a physical store who, through observation and experience, can help shoppers find products they prefer while carefully screening out items they feel the shopper is uninterested in buying. A model of purchase expression could help create a virtual assistant that could do the same thing.

This Captures the Whole Point of What We've Called "Active Retailing." Online Is Leading Offline in This Area. How Does This Come into the Physical Store?

Fader: This has obvious implications for online retailing, but as more interactive technology comes into offline retail stores, through cell phones, PDAs, or other devices, it could also be done in the bricks-and-mortar world. To offer this kind of assistance, you need to understand shopper behavior and how it relates to purchases.

How Do Some of the Complex Forces of Shopping Behavior Play Out? Why Is There a Need for Better Modeling?

Fader: As we've discussed, there are sometimes countervailing forces in shopping. Crowds attract shoppers but might make them less likely to actually shop. (This is similar to the attraction of the Long Tail discussed earlier, which attracts shoppers to the store because they know they can get anything they need—although they may only buy from the Big Head.) The checkout serves as a magnet to draw shoppers to the end of their journey, the goal gradient, but at the same time, shopping momentum makes shoppers absorbed in the process of shopping the more they shop, spending more time in the store. Efficiency is another area of balance. On the one hand, you want the trip to be as efficient as possible, so the shopper finds what he or she needs and leaves. On the other hand, you want to create engagement, to make the shopper stay longer and interact to drive more impulse purchases and form some kind of relationship. You also want variety, but not too much.

These forces counterbalance each other, which is why we need a statistical model to understand behavior. There is no way we can just look at the observed data and figure this out. These effects vary across people, and their interactions also vary across people. We need a proper statistical model that lets each person have his own momentum effect and each person have his own checkout attraction and to see if we can pull him out from the data.

What Topics Are You Studying Now?

Fader: A big issue we are looking at is edge detection in the "stores within stores" in what you call a "compound store." Since the edges of these stores are not always formally delineated, we are defining the way shoppers see different parts of the store. Where are the invisible walls? For example, if people tend to circulate within one area, it could be a self-enclosed zone. Why is that? How do they move beyond the borders of that area? Is it tied to products, or is there a psychological reason? We can study this through eye tracking and through models drawn from disease mapping, which look for clusters of diseases. There is a lot of scattered literature about how we can do this kind of boundary definition or edge detection, and we're just now starting to apply that to the grocery store.

Moe: I'm trying to refine the model for a virtual salesperson, as we discussed, and also looking at the role of online reviews. There is a lot of research that shows reviews have a significant impact on sales. If you have more positive reviews, or even just a higher volume, you get more sales. But the process of posting is something that we don't understand very well, and lots of managers and marketers and some researchers have speculated that there are biases in those reviews. Posted reviews tend to present more extreme views, so they don't really reflect the true quality of the product. I'm trying to separate the effect of that bias from the effect of true product quality. The purpose of doing that is that some marketers have started to seed some of these chat rooms and product reviews with their own comments to try and get the ball rolling. So the question is: Do these fake marketing posts have the same effect as an organic consumer-posted review?

Review Questions

1. In what way are the online and offline shopper behavior patterns similar? What are the similarities between online and offline shoppers' patterns?

2. Describe *licensing* and *sequencing*. How are these concepts related to *navigation* both online and in bricks stores?

3. Consider the issues of variety and range. What have you learned throughout this book about different perspectives on these issues?

4. Discuss the concept of shopper efficiency. To what extent should retailers (online or offline) help shoppers finish shopping as quickly as possible or try to hold on to them for as long as possible? What are potential drawbacks of having too efficient or too inefficient shoppers?

5. Describe how the four types of online shopping visits Moe identified relate to the four shopping states discussed in Chapter 1.

6. What are the next big things in researching online and offline retailing, according to our experts?

Endnotes

1. Hui, Sam K., Peter S. Fader, and Eric T. Bradlow (2009), "Path Data in Marketing: An Integrative Framework and Prospectus for Model-Building," *Marketing Science*, 28(2), pp. 320–335.

2. Hui, Sam K., Eric T. Bradlow, and Peter S. Fader (2009), "Testing Behavioral Hypotheses Using an Integrated Model of Grocery Store Shopping Path and Purchase Behavior," *Journal of Consumer Research*, Vol. 36(3), p. 478–493.

3. Schwartz, Barry. (2005), *The Paradox of Choice: Why More Is Less*, New York: Harper Perennial.

4. Hui, Sam K., Peter S. Fader, and Eric T. Bradlow (2009), "The Traveling Salesman Goes Shopping: The Systematic Deviations of Grocery Paths from TSPOptimality," *Marketing Science*. See also (2006) "The 'Traveling Salesman' Goes Shopping: The Efficiency of Purchasing Patterns in the Grocery Store," http://knowledge.wharton.upenn.edu/article.cfm?articleid=1608.

5. Moe, Wendy (2006), "A Field Experiment Assessing the Interruption Effect of Pop-Up Promotions," *Journal of Interactive Marketing*, 20 (1), 34–44.

6. Moe, Wendy W. (2003), "Buying, Searching, or Browsing: Differentiating between Online Shoppers Using In-Store Navigational Clickstream," *Journal of Consumer Psychology*, 13 (1 and 2), 29–40.

7. Moe, Wendy (2006), "An Empirical Two-Stage Choice Model with Decision Rules Applied to Internet Clickstream Data," *Journal of Marketing Research*, 43 (4), 680–692.

5

The Coming Webby Store

T he *webby store*, a store in which every display is visually managed just as an online web page, has been an increasing focus of my research for the past few years. Here I share a bit of the progress and describe where the convergence of online and bricks retailing is leading us. I always caution that as long as people are living in bricks-and-mortar houses, they will be shopping in bricks-and-mortar stores. But bricks retailing is quickly learning the advantages achieved by online shopping, *within the four walls of their bricks stores*. Buy-online-pick-up-in-store (BOPIS), or click-and-collect, is an example of this convergence and a natural response to the success of online retailers like Amazon. The webby store is the next logical advance that will lead bricks retailers to manage every display inside the store as if it were a web-page. Conceptually, it already is. (See Figure 5.1.)

We illustrate here that no matter whether the shopper is online or offline, the path to the sale is mostly through the eyes. Some details of this are measured and reported in my blog post "From Opportunity to Final Purchase."[1]

On the left, we see the *actual* Amazon display of salty snacks, with one major adjustment to what is actually a fairly large web page if you scroll from top to bottom. But here we removed everything from the "shelf" except the packages on display—much like a comparable display in the supermarket. We discarded all the non-package printing and collapsed the product images into the remaining blank space. Notice that Amazon has a lot more products in a comparable space, and this is a direct consequence of the fact that their warehousing is elsewhere, whereas the bricks retailer does most of their warehousing on their own store shelves.

Figure 5.1 Supermarkets can spotlight a few top sellers, just as Amazon does!

I have enlarged Amazon's social marketing tool, the *#1 Best Seller* tag, as well as our own comparable *Top Seller* tag to make them more visible in the photos. On the actual Amazon web page, the two tags are actually far removed from one another with one near the top of the page and the other near the bottom, so the shopper doesn't see them both at the same time. That's a tip for the bricks retailer, too.

Now that you can see something of the foundation of a webby store, Figure 5.2 shows some early results for one of the several hundred displays in this store:

The bubbles on the left accurately reflect, by area, the sales of the actual item under the bubble. This lets you see at a glance, for single displays or whole aisles, what is moving and what is not. You'll notice that the largest bubble falls onto a product called out by the *Top Seller* social marketing tag. Across the store, 80 such items enjoyed an average 40% lift compared to total store sales movement. This specific item enjoyed a 25% lift. It's a lot easier to sell shoppers what they want to buy than what suppliers and retailers typically want to sell. In the tug-of-war between sellers and buyers, give up and come around to their side, and sell them what they most want to buy. What shoppers buy the most of—that's what you can sell them even more of!

Your top product becomes your top product because it scratches an itch that the shopper has, and it does that better than any other of your products. The shopper is really number one, not you or your top seller.

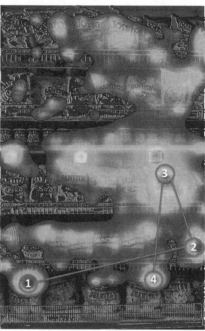

Figure 5.2 What the crowd of shoppers actually purchased (on the left); and the mathematically modeled attention and path of their eyes (on the right).

Some marketers assume that whatever they are selling a lot of is approaching some limit. Was Robert Woodward wrong in 1923 when he set the goal for Coke that his product should be "always within an arm's reach of desire?"[2] Forrest Mars promoted the same "arms reach" philosophy within his candy company. Don't limit shoppers, your products, or yourself.

The eye track on the same display, illustrated on the right, shows you the density of the eye's focus. That is, a mathematically modeled representation of just how long the eye can be expected to stare at that exact point. The labels 1,2,3,4 show the modeled order in which the eye is expected to look at each item.

Notice that in this instance, the eye first looks at the bright red-orange package on the bottom shelf, then glances to the far right of the second shelf at the contrasting, distinctive blue package, and then to the third shelf at another orange package before ending back on the bottom shelf, where most purchases are made from this particular display. Notice the three intense areas of focus on the edge of the fourth shelf, where three different salsas are being offered. But the focus is mostly on the price tags, not on the product itself, possibly suggesting particular price sensitivity about these items. This representation does not totally represent the actual shelf, because the current modeling program uses a photograph rather than the actual shelf. We expect to improve this technology to conform distortions in the photo process to the real world of the store shelf.

Charles Schwab Used the Suggestive Power of Metrics to Double Production

Not only do most shoppers really want to buy more, most employees, from the bottom to the top, really want to be more productive and efficient. I have come to see that true creativity is a bottom-up process. The top will be most successful when recognizing and enabling bottom-up creativity without unleashing chaos.

This is relevant to our webby store initiative. We aim to create an engine that provides intelligent and limited reporting appropriate to each level in the retail enterprise, enabling them to direct their own energy and creativity to better serve number one, the shopper.

This story from Dale Carnegie illustrates the principle. In one of Charles Schwab's steel mills, the management could not increase shift production above three heats, or smelting cycles, per shift:

Just before the night shift came on, Schwab asked the manager for a piece of chalk, then, turning to the nearest man, asked: "How many heats did your shift make today?"

"Six."

Without another word, Schwab chalked a big figure six on the floor, and walked away.

When the night shift came in, they saw the "6" and asked what it meant. "The big boss was in here today," the day people said. "He asked us how many heats we made, and we told him six. He chalked it down on the floor."

The next morning Schwab walked through the mill again. The night shift had rubbed out "6" and replaced it with a big "7."

> *When the day shift reported for work the next morning, they saw a big "7" chalked on the floor. So the night shift thought they were better than the day shift, did they? Well, they would show the night shift a thing or two. The crew pitched in with enthusiasm, and when they quit that night, they left behind them an enormous, swaggering "10." Things were stepping up.*
>
> *Shortly this mill, which had been lagging way behind in production, was turning out more work than any other mill in the plant.*
>
> The principle? Let Charles Schwab say it in his own words: "The way to get things done," says Schwab, "is to stimulate competition. I do not mean in a sordid, money-getting way, but in the desire to excel."
>
> "The desire to excel! The challenge! Throwing down the gauntlet! An infallible way of appealing to people of spirit."[3]

In some ways, this mathematical modeling of visual images parallels our own mathematical modeling of category performance across stores. The Atlas[4] tool allows modeling of store layouts with rather detailed reports of performance of *all* of the categories, depending on the placement of categories of interest, as well as all the rest of the store. One derivative of this work is the discovery of the geographic impact of in-store location. We divided categories into five performance groups, listed at the bottom of Figure 5.3.

We are working toward a long-term goal of mathematically modeling all shopper behavior in stores, both their physical movement around stores, and what their eyes are doing while making those movements— ultimately leading them to make individual purchases.

All these detailed spatial metrics in bricks stores open the way for those stores to enjoy the same merchandising advantages as online stores have in managing their web pages. "Web" metrics of bricks displays can facilitate the same detail and flexibility that online retailers enjoy inside the four walls of the bricks store. However, more detailed visual metrics in the bricks store will return the favor to online operators. The total visual experience in bricks stores is often superior to the total online experience.

This development of metrics is *not* an academic interest. It is vitally important to move the efficiency/productivity of stores. Metrics *can* move

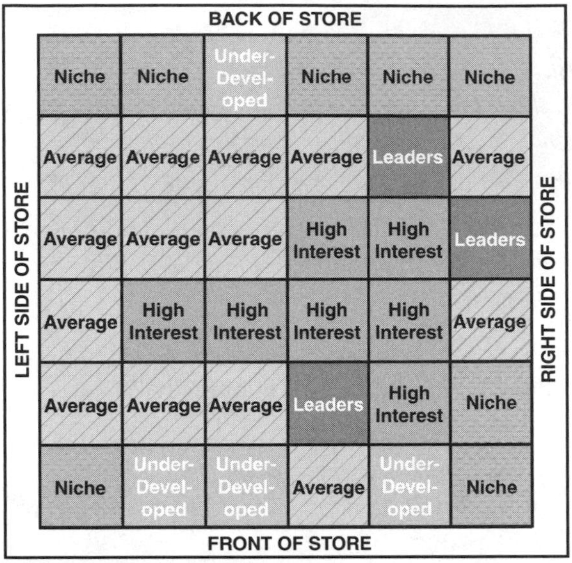

BACK OF STORE

Niche	Niche	Under-Developed	Niche	Niche	Niche
Average	Average	Average	Average	Leaders	Average
Average	Average	Average	High Interest	High Interest	Leaders
Average	High Interest	High Interest	High Interest	High Interest	Average
Average	Average	Average	Leaders	High Interest	Niche
Niche	Under-Developed	Under-Developed	Average	Under-Developed	Niche

LEFT SIDE OF STORE (left) · RIGHT SIDE OF STORE (right)

FRONT OF STORE

LEADERS: Good at stopping the traffic; as well as closing the sale.
NICHE: Not good at stopping traffic; but good at closing the sale.
AVERAGE: Moderate stopping power; moderate closing power.
HIGH INTEREST: Good stopping power; poor closing power.
UNDERDEVELOPED: Poor stopping power; poor closing power.

Figure 5.3 The geographic locations in a store have a major impact on how shoppers shop it. Same is true of location on a web page. (Suher, J and Sorensen, H (2010) The power of Atlas: why in-store shopping behavior matters, Journal of Advertising Research, 21, March, pp. 21–9.)

performance—see the sidebar, "Charles Schwab Used the Suggestive Power of Metrics to Double Production."

I always try to represent the best interest of the shopper. And that true interest, expressed through their behavior, is in acquiring their wants and needs more efficiently and conveniently. Whatever is done efficiently will be done in greater quantity. And the webby store is the ultimate in efficiency for the bricks store, just as a "bricky" website, one informed by bricks store learnings, may be the most efficient web store. What works best for the shopper is what works best for me and you.

As long as bricks-and-mortar retailers rely on the kind of operations and product-oriented reports that they have in order to survive and thrive, they will be sitting ducks for retailers with reports that give a picture of shopper behavior, reports which make obvious even to a stock clerk how to be more helpful to the shoppers in exactly the right way. Again, see the sidebar on Schwab's use of a simple metric to effortlessly lead to massive production increases.

Just as I have spent years getting to this point, I don't expect an entire transformation in a short time. But I do expect immediate increases in sales and profits for the retailer as a consequence of greater convenience (and efficiency) for the shopper. We're putting the shopper in the driver's seat to the benefit of all involved!

The "Ideal" Sized Store

Understanding the concept of the webby store, in which web services are the norm within the bricks store, gives us a glimpse into how retailers of the future might manage the Long Tail. Remember, Amazon is the "Everything Store." Conceptually, there is no limit to the number of items in such a store. Just as the Industrial Revolution felled many barriers that once seemed natural at the beginning of the twentieth century, the Internet is currently shaping a world without the barriers we now consider unyielding.

Here we use the scientific principles of human behavior and the potential role of technology in expanding and making that behavior more efficient and pleasant to assess how large a bricks store should be to most efficiently serve the shopping crowd. (See Figure 5.4.) Now, the retail industry is slowly embracing online selling techniques mostly as a pasting together of two distinct forms of retailing. (Further thoughts on this can be found in my blog post, "Retail 'Spoons.'"[5])

Apply this to the large spectrum of bricks retailing, illustrated here. Bear in mind, our science of shopping is built from studies across hundreds of stores, not just those illustrated here, but including electronics stores, building centers, auto parts stores, clothing stores, gift stores, and more.

This focus has led to the recognition that every supermarket is essentially a convenience store with a big long floppy tail. That is, regardless of your class of trade, your total range of merchandise, and whether the range is hundreds, thousands, or hundreds of thousands of items, the vast majority of your shoppers still leave the store with only a few items

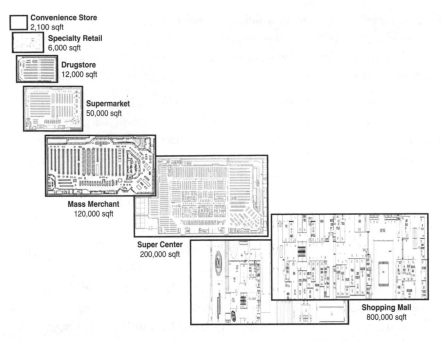

Figure 5.4 Married to an online engine served from a shelf device, the ideal size for a webby-bricks store is probably in the range of 10–20 thousand square feet: more stores, closer to the shoppers.

purchased, most likely in single digits, and rarely in the dozens. And the more of those items purchased, the less likely that those items will be needed in the next few hours or even days.

This means that even though the Long Tail is a powerful, attractive force bringing shoppers to the store, most of it can be served by pick-up or delivery later. Hence the assertion that every bricks store is a *convenience* store. However, the attractive property of the bricks store needs to be served by offering the entire online Long Tail from within the bricks store, not as a pasted-on addition.

Most thinking about online selling within bricks stores has settled on shoppers having a personal device, such as a smart phone, tablet, or the like, to actually bring the Long Tail within the store. This concept pits stores that rely on shoppers to BYOD (bring-your-own device) against stores that utilize the shelf edge not only to display prices but also to display—through the store's own devices—a range of products beyond those available on the shelf. These devices can also facilitate the purchase of those items *at the shelf,* transforming the shelf from an immediate delivery device into a sales device that opens access to hundreds or thousands of additional products that might be picked up later on this shopping trip, delivered within hours to the home, or picked up at the same store on another convenient day. Now, we are talking about a *real* convenience store, servicing more than the gas-and-snacks model! However, this means that even a current-model convenience store might increase their offering from a few hundred items to millions.

Review Questions

1. What is a *webby store* and why should bricks self-service retailers consider utilizing this concept?

2. How are *crowd social marketing* and *affinity marketing* utilized in a webby store? What implications does this have for managing the Long Tail?

3. Ponder on the phrase "every supermarket is essentially a convenience store with a big long floppy tail." What does this realization mean for grocery retail competition? Can online ordering, click-and-collect, and delivery services bring convenient stores closer to traditional supermarket formats?

4. Consider the paradox of the Long Tail—it—is a powerful force that attracts shoppers to the store, but the sheer volume of this "parked capital" can detract shoppers from getting what they need in a store. How can the Long Tail be managed in a convenience store and in a traditional supermarket?

Endnotes

1. http://www.shopperscientist.com/2014-03-24.html

2. http://businesscasestudies.co.uk/coca-cola-great-britain/within -an-arms-reach-of-desire/introduction.html#axzz3vwEnBRFR and https://www.youtube.com/user/3MVisualAttention

3. Carnegie, Dale (2010-08-24). *How to Win Friends and Influence People* (pp. 209–210). Simon & Schuster.

4. http://www.shopperscientist.com/atlas/ or Suher, J and Sorensen, H (2010). The power of Atlas: why in-store shopping behavior matters, Journal of Advertising Research, 21, March, pp. 21–9.

5. http://www.shopperscientist.com/2014-01-26.html

PART II

Going Deeper into the Shopper's Mind

6

Long-Cycle Purchasing

By James Sorensen

I n this book, we focus mostly on fast-moving, frequently-purchased
goods: products like cereal, carbonated soft drinks, laundry detergent, and cleaning supplies. These are routine purchases in which
shoppers do not usually invest a lot of thought or effort. We discussed
how the shopping and decision-making process shoppers go through
when buying such items is highly habitual. We usually shop for these
items on autopilot. In this chapter, however, I discuss the purchases that
often require a much more engaged process: things like automobiles,
apparel, computers, tablets, and home appliances. We call these *long-
cycle* purchase items.

Shoppers purchase long-cycle items infrequently, and many things can
change in the time between purchases. Since their last purchase, shoppers
may no longer be familiar with the latest features or benefits of the items
currently available. They may not be familiar with the brands at all. Take
automobiles, for example: As the commercial famously told us, "It's not
your father's Oldsmobile." The features available on an automobile today
have changed dramatically from just five years ago.

I recently purchased a new car for my wife. The last new car I purchased
was just about 10 years ago. At that time, I focused on hot topics and
new features such as safety bags, repair records, and cup holders. This
time, I spent weeks researching various makes and models, reviewing
Consumer Reports and other online review sites, walking the floor of the
dealership, talking to friends and coworkers to learn about the must-
have and nice-to-have features. I learned that rather than cup holders
and safety bags, the features to study and carefully consider these days
involved connectivity: onboard navigation, linking to mobile devices,
onboard entertainment systems, sensing systems for safety, and other

technologies that were not widely available the last time I was in the market for an automobile.

Let's look at home appliances. The average shopper buys a home appliance such as a refrigerator or a washer and dryer set once every 10 years. The features available on a washing machine today are totally different than those available 10 years ago. Shoppers entering the market for a refrigerator for the first time in 10 years need to focus on more than in-door ice makers. They must also consider all new features such as high efficiency models, smart technology, and even indoor soda dispensers. Two of the top brands for home appliances did not even exist 10 years ago. Samsung and LG entered the home appliance market and brought new features with them.

Perhaps no consumer good experiences change more rapidly than computers. The last time you bought a new PC, you may have had only a laptop, a desktop, and two or three processor levels to choose from. Today, you must choose from a tablet, two-in-one convertibles, all-in-one devices, Chromebooks, and even smart TVs. You must choose among five or six different processors and decide whether you need or want a diversity of new features, including voice recognition, gesture control, competing operating systems, and platforms.

Higher Cost Leads to Anxiety and Indecision

Most long-cycle items are also higher-cost items. Higher cost serves as a barrier to purchase because it adds to the risk, the anxiety, and ultimately to the potential deferment of the purchase. When deciding what to buy, shoppers are constantly weighing the cost benefit not just of various features, but whether they should buy at all. The calculation of cost versus need can lead many shoppers to decide they don't really need the item. They may decide to continue to make do with the older version they already have or they may decide they don't need it at all.

A consumer may decide he doesn't need a full-feature electric razor that costs more than $100. Instead, he will continue to use much cheaper disposables. Another consumer may decide to get his old washing machine fixed rather than go through the time, energy, and expense of evaluating the myriad of new features offered with newer models. A shopper looking at tablets may decide that a tablet may be convenient for emails and web surfing, but she'd probably just spend most of her time on it playing games. Therefore, the tablet is a discretionary luxury and she should spend her money on something more productive.

Longer Shopping Process

The complexity and the higher cost of long-cycle purchases can make shoppers delay the decision to start shopping and make the shopping process lengthy.

My family needs to buy a new washer and dryer. My current machines are at least 15 years old and are on their last legs. They do the job, but not very effectively. My wife and I have been casually studying various makes and models of machines for several years. We searched the web and read online reviews. We even on occasion seriously discussed buying a new set of machines, but the need for a new set just hasn't quite overcome the time, cost, effort, and complexity of the shopping process we would have to undergo to actually purchase a new washer and dryer. So, we remain on the sidelines.

Some categories may require weeks or even months of exploration before the shopper is ready to make a purchase. In the PC category, rarely does a computer literally stop working. Shoppers normally do not have to fill an immediate need for a new computer. Therefore, they can spend weeks reviewing websites, visiting stores, talking to friends and family, and evaluating their options before they finally put the coin on the counter and make their purchase.

Role of Time and Building Desire for Long-Cycle Purchasing

Time remains a critical dimension for long-cycle purchasing, but in ways different from Routine/Autopilot purchases. Although it is still important for retailers to make good use of the shopper's time while making a long-cycle purchase, there are two additional time factors for the retailer to consider:

- Reducing the time between purchases by triggering—or inspiring—the need for the item at an earlier point in the cycle.

- Compressing the time from trigger to purchase.

A Word about Building Desire

A traditional view of retail and shopper marketing is focused on facilitating the purchase, but retail levers must also be harnessed to build desire. In a truly integrated world, inspiring desire is not just the job of the brand marketer. As marketers and merchandisers, it is our job to build desire and help the consumer and shopper move from *wish* to *want*, from *want* to *need*, and finally from *need* to *got*.

- **Wish**—We need to plant the seed and inspire the consumer to see what might be possible.

- **Want**—We need to help consumers envision how the product could benefit their lives.

- **Need**—We need to show the consumer how the product will solve a pain point in her life.

- **Got**—We need to help the consumer decide on a specific purchase and easily facilitate the transaction.

Romancing the Sale

From the shopper's first awareness of the opportunity of the product or service to the point at which the opportunity is translated into reality—a crescendo is achieved, the "close" of the sale. To emotionalize the process, we might refer to it as "romancing the sale." Simply illustrated in Figure 6.1.

Figure 6.1 The long purchase cycle can be thought of as "romancing the sale," A process that progresses from first attraction to the culmination of the sale. (From left to right: © Kurhan/Fotolia, © Phrase4Photography/Fotolia, © gstockstudio/Fotolia, © Monkey Business/Fotolia)

It all begins with simple recognition, with a positive impression, leading progressively to the completed sale!

Wish

Retail's role in building desire is largely driven by visual presence. The old adage, "out of sight, out of mind" is largely true. Retail's job is creating circumstances where we can visually demonstrate the benefits of the product so that the consumer progresses along the *wish* to *need* to *got* continuum.

Herb used to listen to a motivational speaker who told his audience to put pictures of the things they wanted on their refrigerator. These pictures serve as constant, visual reminders and help progress the consumer along the desire continuum. This is a major part of retail's role in the early stages of building desire. Be present and be a constant reminder of the benefits of the product.

Want

We can use retail stores and websites to plant the seeds of desire. Endcap displays near major traffic areas are great tools for both creating the *wish* and advancing it to the *want*. Store circulars remain one of the most-read media, so they are also great tools for utilizing the power of suggestion. Much like an endcap display in the store, an online retail site can offer compelling images of new and inspiring product uses. Even social media sites can serve opportunities to plant and germinate the seed.

Need

Although digital and broadcast media can and should appeal to consumer needs and build demand, retail touchpoints are increasingly more critical influencers.

The saturation of TV, print, and even digital media have made these channels less effective. Consumers often overlook or ignore messages delivered via these media. Conversely, consumers are more responsive to in-context and relevant messaging. This is where retail touchpoints, both in-store and online, play an important role.

While at a home improvement retailer shopping for shelving for their laundry room, a shopper will walk past the home appliances and spend a few minutes admiring the new features on the washing machine endcap display. The shopper notices that the machine's drying time is twice as fast as their current machine and she realizes how much time this would save her each week, getting her one step closer to *needing* a new machine.

While shopping online at Amazon.com where he is buying a new video game, a shopper might see a popular new computer advertised and click on the link to see a video of its latest features. The new gesture control feature adds an amazing new dimension to gaming that gets him one step closer to wanting a new PC.

Even driving past the car dealership and seeing the elegantly displayed vehicles out front can serve as a demand builder.

All of these examples inspire and educate consumers about the benefits and features of these products, which can take them from "I don't want it" to "I wish I had that" to "I want it," and from "I want it" to "I need it."

Got

After establishing the need, we must push them through to the *got*. We must maintain many of the principles of the wish/want/need by maintaining desire so we can be sure we don't lose them back down the ladder, but we must step it up and begin to speed the shopper along the process so they get to the *got* as quickly as possible.

Understanding the shoppers' path to purchase is important for all types of products, but it is imperative for long-cycle purchasing. But the focus should be less about general path-to-purchase learning and more about how to influence shoppers at each touch point. In particular, we will focus on in-store and online.

Store plays a broad role throughout the journey. Many think that the store is primarily focused on influencing shoppers late in the shopping process and closing the sale. Most stores are merchandised and set up to address these shoppers' needs. But *the store is a top method for inspiring desire prior to the trigger*; it is a primary information source early in the shopping process and it is also critical to closing the sale.

Online plays an important role early and late in the journey. Early, it informs and educates about available options and helps shoppers narrow down their choices. But late in the process, it is either a convenient way to buy, or at a minimum, it serves as a way for shoppers to do a final check to confirm their purchase via reviews, ratings, and price checking.

Omnichannel is the buzzword of the day in our industry. Pure-play retailing is becoming *passé* and those that play only on one side will eventually lose out to the retailers that more effectively serve the customer across both in-store and online. For example, Macy's and Nordstrom are very effective at serving the customer in both channels in a seamless way. The goal should be to deliver the shopper the same products and pricing regardless of channel, but leverage the strengths of each channel. Tactics such as click-and-collect, or the ability to return goods purchased from online to the store are things shoppers are beginning to expect.

The Shopper Engagement Spectrum

Let's now discuss the specific strengths and weaknesses of each channel and how they are working to address the needs being met by the other. To do this, I will use the shopper engagement spectrum framework:

In this framework, we categorize all purchases into one of three groups:

- **Grab and go:** Whether it's a long-cycle product or a frequently purchased one, an item in this category requires little thought or consideration and is purchased quickly. The shopper's desire is to simply find a product that meets his needs. The shopper purchases quickly and moves on.

- **Information seeking:** These are purchases that require considerable thought and education. The shopper wants relevant and trustworthy information.

- **Immersive experience:** The shopper wants to learn something new and to be inspired.

Each channel delivers unique strengths for each group, as shown in Table 6.1.

Table 6.1   Three Long-Cycle Purchases: Relative Strengths, In-Store vs. Online

	Strengths of In-Store	Strengths of Online
Grab and go	Immediate need—get what you want right now.	Auto replenishment—online has begun to transition shoppers into an auto-replenishment mode for frequently purchased items.

(continued)

Table 6.1 *(continued)*

	Strengths of In-Store	Strengths of Online
Information seeking	Advice—talk to a store associate or sales rep.	Interactive and reviews—the ability to see what others think, to be served up relevant content, and to watch videos.
Immersive experience	Tactile—ability to pick up and touch.	Personalization—customized content that is personalized based on prior purchase behaviors.

And each channel is experimenting with changes to improve and better address the strengths of the other, as shown in Table 6.2.

Table 6.2 3 Long-Cycle Purchases: Trends, In-Store vs. Online

	Things In-Store Is Doing	Things Online Is Doing
Grab and go	Stores are getting smaller and are being introduced into smaller neighborhoods to get closer and closer to the customer.	Faster delivery—some services are offering delivery of the goods in hours, rather than days.
Information seeking	Stores are bringing interactive technology into the store and working to link this to past purchase behavior so information and offers can be customized.	Personalized service—services such as Stitch Fix and Trunk Club are offering personalized service and advice.
Immersive experience	In-store retailers are using store space to introduce shoppers to new information, to educate them and to provide them a better overall experience.	Pure-play online retailers are beginning to open bricks-and-mortar stores—like, for example, Amazon Book Store.

Speeding the Shopper along the Path-to-Purchase: First Build Desire and Facilitate the Tipping Point

As discussed earlier, our goal in this stage is to move shoppers from want to a need. We have found that one single trigger or need rarely tips the consumer into the *need* mode. Rather, needs build up one by one, until the consumer reaches a tipping point where they are finally ready to make the purchase.

A tipping point for a new refrigerator might simply be a broken refrigerator. If you have a fridge full of food but your refrigerator doesn't work, you will tip to making a purchase immediately. But this is a relatively rare example. More often, a series of factors involving life changes, product benefits, and ability to pay form the tipping point. Understanding these three types of factors that lead to the tipping point, helps drive desire through communication and marketing efforts.

The Intel Experience—Creating the Tipping Point

An example of one of the most innovative retail tactics for inspiring the need is The Intel Experience[1], a unique store within a store display within Best Buy[2]. Intel designed the display to introduce shoppers to new technology, not just specifically to sell. Every three or four months, the display introduces new sets of experiences featuring unique and innovative technologies:

- 3D printing
- Augmented reality via Intel-based tablets
- Gesture control through RealSense
- Wearable devices
- Ultimate video gaming
- And more

The experiences are cutting-edge, fun, and simple. The experience is staffed with a well-informed sales representative who is trained to

---

educate and inspire shoppers in the store, many of whom aren't even planning to buy a new computer right away. The experiences engage the hurried shopper. Ultimately, the experiences inspire shoppers to want more from their technology and buy higher value, unique technology devices sooner rather than later.

Life Changes

I might need to buy a new refrigerator because I move to a new home, or I might have a larger family so my needs have changed. As my children get older, I might begin to need an additional PC because the kids need a computer to do their homework. Or I might need a different type of automobile because I got a new job and need to drive across state, rather than just across town. All of these, and many other, life changes will play into building up to create a tipping point.

Product Benefits

As technology evolves and products improve, a consumer may find that a new product will meet a need that their current product does not. I might want a new dryer because the drying time is 2 times faster. I might want a new car because I believe an electric engine will help save the planet. I might want a new PC because I want to use gesture control to play the latest, hottest video game. All of these and more can build and lead to a tipping point.

Ability to Pay

Because many long-cycle purchases are often big ticket purchases, a shopper's ability to pay is always an important factor. Improvement in ability to pay could be a big price discount on the item or a change in personal income. If I get an unexpected tax refund, or an unexpected bonus I may make a purchase I couldn't make before. Holidays, birthdays or even back to school events often trigger additional disposable cash that can improve shoppers' ability to pay. Or I might sit and wait until end of year sales hit and I can get a big discount.

The Shopper's Journey

The goal of this stage is to speed the shopper's journey. Even after having the need and getting to the tipping point, shoppers can take weeks or even months to finally progress through the education process and complete the transaction in some categories. If we can help the shopper quickly learn early in the process and then help them complete the sale late in the process, we can shave days or weeks off the purchase time, which will increase sales and profits all along the value chain.

Early in the Shopping Journey

Our goal is to first help educate the shopper about the benefits and to educate ourselves about their needs. But then retailers need to be bold and provide the shopper with a limited number of choices that meet their needs so they can quickly and easily make a decision. For example, a shopper looking for a new leaf blower will typically first go to an online retailer site and begin reading reviews and watching videos so she can see how each of the top blowers work and their unique features. She will quickly want to narrow her choices down to the two or three leaf blowers that fit within her acceptable price range and do the tasks she needs done.

Educate

Online is frequently the first step. Shoppers often visit a retailer's website, check out the available brands and features, read reviews, and begin to narrow down their choices. Online outlets can help speed this process by providing the most relevant information and delivering it in a short, concise way. Videos are a great tool for helping the shopper quickly gather information.

One of the biggest shopper challenges in this process is an encounter with conflicting reviews. One site recommends one brand and feature and another site recommends a different brand and a different feature. Limiting this type of conflicting information by keeping the shopper focused on a single information source is ideal.

Retailers can speed the process by making bold recommendations to the shopper. As any good sales person knows, we need to narrow down the selection to just a few items and help the shopper choose. Ideally, we can mine customer data or use smart "triage" to make informed recommendations, as Amazon does with its recommendation pages. But in-store we need to get more creative with smart questions by the sales staff, interactive kiosks, or even sensing technology to tailor messaging and product offerings to the shopper.

In-store the sales associate is often the secret to success in this early stage, but most sales associates are not equipped to succeed here. Most sales associates are incentivized and trained to *close the sale*, meaning to push sales and try to get the shopper to commit. This tactic can kill the deal for a shopper who comes to the store looking for trusted advice and education. Sales associates need to first take the time to educate the shopper and then pivot to narrowing down the choices to help the shopper make her selection.

Late in the Shopping Journey

Our goal needs to be to facilitate the transaction, which includes providing a competitive price and an easy transaction and fulfillment/delivery process. Example: After learning about the various options and features, the leaf blower shopper might quickly revert to going to Costco where she expects to find two to three good/better/best options so she can quickly make her decision. She is trying to complete her lawn project this weekend, so she needs to get the product quickly and at a good price. Costco, then, is an easy option. Additionally, high-touch customer service, installation, and warranties are less important, so the lower service levels of a Costco are just fine.

Validating Choice

By the time shoppers approach the conclusion of their long-cycle purchase processes, they have become very savvy. At this stage, they are looking to gain validation of their choice and want to do one last check to be sure they didn't miss anything. As any good sales person knows, now is not the time to introduce doubt or raise additional questions. If the shopper is ready to buy, then it is important to validate their choice and close the sale.

Complete the Transaction

Price plays a critical role as the shopper begins to narrow down his choices. Some shoppers will do extensive price comparing and simply go with the lowest. Others will weigh intangibles such as service levels, installation, warranties, and convenience. Price sensitivity and value is a very complex topic that is out of the scope of this discussion. Although price is important, it is not usually the defining factor in the purchase decision. Shoppers are generally well informed on price through their extensive research; many will easily trade up to higher cost options to achieve higher value features. We find that retailers and brands put too great of a focus on competing on price, rather than on increasing value to the shopper by helping narrow down solutions, highlighting the most attractive features, and offering superior service.

Mobile

Mobile is increasingly playing a more important role in retail. It can play a role in early stages, but it is most commonly used as a resource in-store as a last-second price comparison or as a check to ensure something isn't missed.

Again, the Sales Associate Is Key to Closing the Sale and Completing the Transaction

This tends to be where sales associates are most experienced, but many can also improve in carrying the service level through to the point of delivery, and even in some cases installation. Best Buy was able to actually identify an opportunity and business with Geek Squad to take service levels all the way through the post-purchase. (The post-purchase process can be a strong key to teeing up the *next* purchase.) These steps are critical for more complex purchases such as an automobile or computer purchases, but less so for more transactional products such as a leaf blower or clothing.

Conclusion

Long-cycle purchasing is an increasingly dynamic and less linear shopping process. Through the shopping process, the consumer often becomes an expert on the category, the product features, and pricing. The retailer must up their game to meet these expert shoppers where they are and use their retail and merchandising tools and expertise both to drive desire and to close the sale. By doing both of these things well, the purchase cycle can be compressed, which saves the consumer time, and is also a critical path for growth for long-cycle products.

Review Questions

1. Describe a long-cycle purchase process. What are the similarities and (separately) differences between this process and the purchasing of fast-moving consumer goods? Can you think of examples of products where the boundaries between these two are blurred?

2. What are the challenges faced by retailers (and manufacturers) of long-cycle products in terms of managing and influencing shoppers' time?

3. Discuss the four stages a shopper goes through during a long-cycle purchase. What is the role of online retailing and information at each stage?

4. Compare and contrast strengths and weaknesses of online and offline retailing across the three stages of shopper engagement spectrum. Think of what learning can each format take from the other to improve the shopper engagement and experience.

5. Why is the initial learning/information searching stage so important in long-cycle purchases? What can retailers and manufacturers do to speed up this stage?

6. Can a long-cycle product be purchased on impulse? What factors would drive such a process?

Endnotes

1. http://newsroom.intel.com/community/intel_newsroom/ blog/2014/10/15/the-intel-experience-opens-exclusively-in-50-best-buy-stores

2. http://www.bestbuy.com/site/computing-promotions/ regularcatpcmcat342300050006/pcmcat342300050006.c?id= pcmcat342300050006

The Quick-Trip Paradox:
An Interview with Mike Twitty

T he quick trip has become the most common unit of shopping, yet most retail stores are designed primarily for stock-up shoppers. We interviewed Mike Twitty when he served as shopper insights director of Unilever Americas in the U.S. Since then, he has opened his own company, First Light Insight (see sidebar). Throughout his career, he has conducted pioneering research on quick-trip shoppers. As he notes, although quick trips account for about two-thirds of shopping trips, shoppers buy many different types of products on these trips. This is the Quick-Trip Paradox. This means catering to the quick tripper is not as simple as defining a small set of "quick trip" products.

How Do You Define a Quick Trip?

Twitty: In Unilever's research, the term *quick trip* is a relative term that shoppers use to describe the amount of time, effort, and money they invest in a given trip to a retailer.[1] Shoppers spend an average of about $100 on major stock-ups, about twice what they spend on fill-in trips (about $50), and four to five times what they spend on quick trips (about $20). Because quick trips are relative, they vary in size, depending on the retail outlet visited. A quick trip to a club store is substantially longer and has a higher spend (about $44) than a quick trip taken to a convenience store (about $15). One way to think about the terms *quick trip*, *fill-in trip*, and *major stock-up trip* is that they represent three different sizes of trips: the small, medium, and large trips that most shoppers take to their retailers.

AN UPDATE FROM MIKE TWITTY

When we embarked on this type of research in 2004, we were asking questions to help us become better shopper marketers and retailers. At that time, our industry relied primarily on sales data for guidance, yet we needed a model of shopper behavior that helped to explain why shoppers did what they did. We hypothesized that understanding the shopper's motives on their different shopping trips, coupled with more detail on what they actually purchased on each of those trips, would result in real insight. It would enable us to understand which stores they were likely to choose for a given trip, how they were going to use that store, which items they were likely to need on that type of trip, etc. We created a shopper model which showed for the first time, the relationship between shoppers' motives and their behavior, identifying the items purchased on each type of trip to each of the major retail channels that sold food and consumer products.

Today's insight needs are much different. With the increasing fragmentation of broadcast media, the inexorable rise in consumers using shopping outlets, media outlets and sharing information on the internet, consumers and the internet play a more active and central role in the fortunes of brands and retailers. In response to this and the rapid evolution of new technology, manufacturers and retailers are retooling their relationships with consumers, in order to achieve their goals. My company, First Light Insight, LLC is a consultancy which specializes in helping manufacturers to develop communication strategies for their target consumers and shoppers. We do this by doing the research to identify the most important touchpoints for influencing consumers and shoppers of their brands, as well as the most important messaging for influencing the audience at those touch points. As we illuminate the key points along the consumer's journey or the shopper's path to purchase, we develop insight about the target audience's mindset … what they need, what they want and what works best to motivate them to take the actions our clients desire. You can reach me at: mike@firstlightinsight.com.

Three Shoppers: Quick Trip, Fill-In, and Stock-Up

Building on the work of Wharton Professor Peter Fader, we studied data collected on 75,000 shoppers across a series of three stores to develop behavioral segmentation of shoppers. By mathematically clustering a large number of shoppers by factors such as how fast they walk, how fast they spend money, how much of the store they visit, and how long their trips are, we found that shoppers group themselves into three basic segments or clusters, as shown here.[1]

Description	Clusters—Market Segments		
	Quick	Fill-in	Stock-up
Share of store visited	11.2%	21.1%	41.0%
Trip duration (in minutes)	13.4	18.5	25.3
Walking speed (feet per second)	0.52	0.66	0.98
Buy time (seconds to buy a single unit)	38.7	30.2	21
Spending speed(dollars per minute)	$1.88	$1.32	$1.23
Efficiency (seconds per dollar)	31.9	45.5	48.8

Each of the segments exhibits fairly distinctive shopping behavior, as follows:

- **Quick:** Short time, small area, slow walk, high-spending speed, very efficient.

- **Fill-in:** Medium time, medium area, slow walk, average-spending speed, modest efficiency.

- **Stock-up:** Long time, large area, fast walk, low-spending speed, lowest efficiency.

Very few supermarket retailers are aware that half of all shopping trips result in the purchase of five or fewer items (these numbers come from actual transaction logs from every continent except Africa and Antarctica). This ignorance is a consequence of the justified focus on the economics of the stock-up shopper, and a lack of attention to the behavior of the mass of individual shoppers in the store. This huge cohort of quick trippers is not a different breed of shoppers. They are simply stock-up shoppers on a different mission.

Any way you slice it; these quick trips are an important part of retailing. *Single item* purchases account for more than 16 percent of all shopping trips. Further, as noted, half of all shoppers walk out with five items or less, and the average purchase size is about 12 items. As shown in the figure, in addition to looking at the average, we also need to consider the "median," half of the distribution, and the "mode," the most common result.

The quick trip is different in frequency and purpose. In our research, we found that shoppers took an average of about 10 trips per month that resulted in a food purchase. Six of these were quick trips, and only one was a major stock-up trip. Fill-in and major stock-up trips both focus on buying items for the longer term or for restocking the household or pantry. Quick trips, in contrast, are focused on buying items that will be used shortly after purchase, usually the same day or the next.

If you spend enough time watching shoppers in most retail outlets, you will notice, among other things, that few of the shoppers actually shop the whole store. In addition, if you read the research that measures actual shopping behavior, rather than what shoppers *say* they do, you will see mountains of data showing that most consumer packaged goods (CPG)/ food shopping trips are composed of a small number of items per basket. Considering these two observations, one obvious question is "why?" This simple question has driven a whole body of research aimed at understanding shopping trips, the shopping decisions that take place outside of the store, and how they affect the behavior that takes place within.

Why Do Shoppers Make So Many Quick Trips?

Twitty: The simple answer is: because they can. Because we have easy, affordable access to so many retail outlets, shoppers often choose to get what they want as they discover they want it. Instead of having to organize their lives around the availability of the retailer, they develop strategies to use the abundance of available retail options, cherry-picking them to best serve their changing needs. Although shoppers use a variety of strategies, the important thing is this: Most shopping trips to buy CPG and food items are quick trips, and quick-trip shopping is a unique opportunity for manufacturers and retailers.

Quick trips are a byproduct of our affluence and its effect on both U.S. households and our retail space. If we flash back in time, to some 78 years ago, the first supermarkets appeared on the U.S. landscape, and shoppers of King Cullen and Ralph's delighted in taking advantage of two key benefits they offered: self-service and one-stop shopping. At that time, there were many fewer retail outlets, and shoppers had fewer opportunities to buy. In those days, shopping trips were infrequent, and planning before each trip was more important because running to a nearby store whenever you needed something was just not an option. Over the years, however, more and more retailers offered the items found in grocery stores and more and more retail space was built. Simultaneously, food and CPG items were also beginning to take smaller percentages of our growing incomes.

Looking over the course of time since the first grocery stores were created, we can see that as our household affluence increased and our retail options multiplied, the value of one-stop shopping declined. Today, we believe that with the great supply of retail alternatives available, when household money supplies expand or are in great supply, there is less of a need for one-stop shopping. When household money supplies contract or are in short supply, the value of one-stop shopping increases.

Although it is true that one-stop shopping and stocking-up are more economical ways to shop because they decrease the number of trips we take, our comparative affluence and easy access to retail has reduced our reliance on this practice. It follows, then, that quick trips are a convenience that has been enabled by easy, affordable access to retailers.

Another appeal of quick trips is that they enable shoppers to spend less time and effort planning. Quick trips make our lives more convenient by allowing shoppers to avoid the time and effort of planning before a shopping trip and by minimizing the need to live our lives limited by making sure that we have access to the resources available from our homes. Instead, shoppers can go more places and do more things because they can replenish their resources practically wherever they travel and whenever they choose. Regular stock-up shopping still takes place, usually on a weekly basis, and is vitally important in most households, but shoppers find themselves taking frequent, smaller trips to supplement their major stock-up trips. Although it's true that increasing costs of shopping trips can change this pattern of shopping, for now it appears that quick trips are still the way that the majority of CPG and food items are shopped for.

How Do Pre-store Decisions Affect the Quick Trip?

Twitty: Before they enter a store, buyers of food and packaged goods have a relatively clear idea of what they want, and this knowledge steers them to visit some parts of the store while avoiding others. Unilever research shows that about 70% of all category purchase decisions (the decision to buy a product category such as mayonnaise or shower gel) occur *before* shoppers get to the store. Recent research from Ogilvy*Action* found a similarly high percentage of such decisions were made outside of the store.[2] Such pre-store decisions also play a great role in determining how much shoppers will spend on that trip. For manufacturers, understanding and influencing shopping behavior outside the store is at least as important as understanding and influencing what happens within. For retailers, some argue that leveraging shopping behavior outside the store is even more important, because it often determines whether the shopper will visit their store on a given trip.

As soon as a consumer decides to get something they need or want, they become a shopper, and shoppers have lots of decisions to make. Two of the more important decisions they will make are which store or stores they will choose to visit to get the items they seek and what type of trip they will make. In this context, the words "type of trip" are a kind of shorthand that describes the shopper's objectives for a given trip and the personal resources they choose to invest in that excursion.

What Factors Do Consumers Consider in Deciding Where and How to Shop?

Twitty: For any given shopping trip we might choose to take, there are three primary considerations that shape the trip: 1) What do we need or want?; 2) How much money do we want to spend for what we need or want?; and 3) How much time and energy are we willing to devote to acquiring what we need or want?

Shoppers pit these considerations against their knowledge of the retail landscape to determine where their investment will take place. There are a host of other important considerations that follow these three, especially when focusing on shopping behavior within the store, but these three seem to be the most important considerations that determine the type of shopping trip they take and which store(s) will be visited.

How Do Consumers Think about Shopping Trips?

Twitty: Using our "trip management" research method, Unilever has studied over 20 million trips and years of household tracking with the general population and key subgroups, such as Hispanics and Baby Boomers. We pioneered the method in 2004, which enabled shoppers themselves to classify the types of trips they took, based on trip definitions determined from prior ethnography. Shoppers also indicated where the trips were taken and what was purchased. In addition, shoppers provided the researchers with their register receipts to validate the shoppers' claimed behavior. This research was the first time CPG shopping trips across all major retail channels in the U.S. were measured attitudinally and validated with actual purchase behavior. The result was a powerful look across the major retail channels and retailers, as well as most CPG categories. It provided new insight into how people shop for CPG/food categories and how they use retailers to achieve their shopping goals.

One important distinction from other shopper studies is that the trip classification in this research was done by the shoppers themselves, rather than inferring or guessing at the shopper's motive based on the items purchased. The way it was done was very simple. After each shopping trip that included a food item, shoppers were asked to answer two basic questions about the trip:

1. How would you best describe this trip?

   - Major stock-up trip
   - Fill-in trip

- Quick trip—to get a few items for a meal to be eaten within the next day or two

- Quick trip—to get a few items

2. What was the *main* reason for the trip?

- To restock the pantry or kitchen

- A routine grocery shopping trip to buy items for today

- A routine grocery shopping trip to buy items for the next day or two

- To get an urgently needed item or two, quickly

- To take advantage of a special offer

- Just to get out, to look around, or have fun

- To shop for a special occasion (for example, for guests, a party, or the holidays)

- To get "ready-to-eat" items to eat/drink right away or before I return home

- To purchase a nonfood item (but I eventually purchased a food item)

All household shopping trips that resulted in a food purchase were tracked over a two-week period, resulting in over 4,400 trips from about 900 households, across all major retail channels and most CPG/food categories. Since this first study, we have removed the limitation of looking only at trips that resulted in food purchases and now track households over the course of a year or more rather than just two weeks. Looking at all of these results has enabled insight into the basic patterns of CPG/food shopping.

What Did You Learn from This Research?

Twitty: Quick trips are the most common trip for consumer packaged goods or food shopping. Shoppers classify the majority of their trips to buy CPG or food items as quick trips. In Unilever's original research published in 2004, "Trip Management: The Next Big Thing," 62% of all trips were classified by shoppers as quick trips, as shown in Figure 7.1.

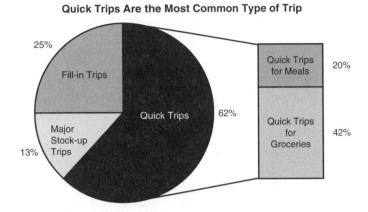

Figure 7.1 When shoppers define their shopping trips as either quick trips, fill-in trips, or major stock-up trips, quick trips are the most common trip they report when buying groceries.

In recent trip management research where 11 million Nielsen-measured trips to all retail channels were monitored over the course of 2007, and all CPG trips were included, we found that 64% of the trips to purchase CPG categories were quick trips.

That such a high percentage of trips were quick trips was eye-opening, but what was absolutely shocking was that quick trips were the most common type of trip to *every* major retail channel—warehouse clubs and supercenters included! This finding has been confirmed every time the study has been replicated.

Rise of the Small Store

When supermarkets failed to respond to the needs of half their shopping trips, others stepped into the vacuum. This led to the creation of the entire convenience store industry and encouraged the growth of competitors with small-store formats. In 2007, for the first time in two decades of expanding superstores, the average size of a grocery store fell slightly. It appears that large retailers are finally waking up to the power of the quick trip.

Many of these smaller stores such as Lidl and Aldi attribute their success to their low pricing. But in addition to offering discounts, they created streamlined stores that reduce navigational and choice angst. Many consumer studies show that pricing is not the primary factor that drives retail. Giving people money to buy things has to be the least creative way of selling something. As with Stew Leonard attributing his success to superior customer service, the success of retailers might not be for the reason they think. In the case of Lidl, Aldi, and others, our studies indicate that the reduction in SKUs and simpler navigation may play as great a role as pricing in their success.

At the same time that supermarkets were being attacked by the small stores from below, the big box outlets were taking a large slice of the stock-up shoppers. Winning retailers of the future will earn their top-tier status through clearly distinguishing shoppers into quick/fill-in versus stock-up, and serving the two groups distinctly, rather than dumping the whole store together and expecting the shoppers to sort it out. This does not mean, however, that it cannot all be done in the same building

How Could It Be that Even Warehouse Clubs and Supercenters—Whose Design so Strongly Encourages Stock-up Shopping—Receive More Quick Trips than Stock-up or Fill-in Trips?

Twitty: The answer is that on most trips, shoppers are using these stores in ways that make the most sense for their busy lives and in ways that are possible simply because they have the financial resources to do so.

Figure 7.2 provides a great deal of information about the way shoppers use retail channels. You can easily see how shoppers use the different retail channels and the relationship between the size of the retailer's box and the types of trips that shoppers take there.

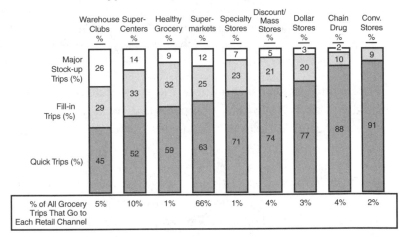

Types of Trips Taken to Each Retail Channel

	Warehouse Clubs %	Super-Centers %	Healthy Grocery %	Super-markets %	Specialty Stores %	Discount/ Mass Stores %	Dollar Stores %	Chain Drug %	Conv. Stores %
Major Stock-up Trips (%)	26	14	9	12	7	5	3	2	
Fill-in Trips (%)	29	33	32	25	23	21	20	10	9
Quick Trips (%)	45	52	59	63	71	74	77	88	91
% of All Grocery Trips That Go to Each Retail Channel	5%	10%	1%	66%	1%	4%	3%	4%	2%

Figure 7.2 Quick trips were the most common type of trip for every retail channel, even warehouse clubs and supercenters.

Given that Quick Trips Account for Two-thirds of Shopping Trips, How Can Retailers and Manufacturers Cater to these Shoppers?

Twitty: It would seem that all we have to do is understand what shoppers buy on quick trips and we would have the basis for serving them better. Unfortunately, this is where things begin to get difficult. Looking at the 2007 data (featuring Nielsen's Syndicated Category definitions and purchases from all outlets), we can see the troubling observation we call the "Quick-Trip Paradox."

What Is the Quick-trip Paradox?

Twitty: The paradox is that although most shopping trips are quick trips, these shoppers are not coming to the store for the same products each time. In fact, we found that the average CPG category is purchased on a quick trip just 38% of the time. Quick-trip shopping must be composed of a very broad and changing variety of CPG categories. In a single week, a household might make a quick trip for milk, chips, and beer on one day, whereas a day or two later they might take another quick trip seeking light bulbs and paper towels. The following week might see a quick trip for antiperspirant, shampoo, and mouthwash. There just isn't a concise set of related categories that would satisfy the range of shoppers' needs on quick trips.

There are a wide variety of products that draw quick-trip shoppers to the store. This is a substantial impediment for anyone hoping to capitalize on the quick trip by dedicating retail space to serve these trips efficiently.

> The Quick Trip Paradox: Although more than 60% of shopping trips are quick trips, the average consumer packaged good category is purchased on a quick trip only 38% of the time.

Given this Paradox, How Can Retailers and Manufacturers Capitalize on the Quick Trip?

Twitty: Trying to identify the ideal assortment to satisfy the quick trip is maddening. There are no simple answers. Some categories are purchased more often on quick trips than the other trips. Out of roughly 120 categories, just 27 product categories are purchased mostly on quick trips. Table 7.1 is a ranking of categories that are more likely to be purchased on a quick trip. The categories that have the highest percentage of their purchases occurring on quick trips are at the top of the list. The table below excludes infrequently purchased categories, categories that are purchased on less than 1.5% of all trips.

Table 7.1 Top Categories That Are Purchased Most Often on Quick Trips, After Removing Slow-Moving Categories

Category	% Times Item Purchased on Quick Trip	% of Trips That Include the Category
Computer/Electronic Products	70.9	3.5
Tobacco and Accessories	70.4	4.7
Housewares/Appliances	63.6	2.0
Office/School Supplies	62.9	6.1

Light Bulbs/Telephone	60.6	2.1
Misc. General Merchandise	59.7	3.8
Cosmetics	58.3	1.9
Battery/Flashlight/Charge	56.8	2.9
Cough and Cold Remedies	56.1	3.1
Beer	54.2	3.1
Medications/Remedies	53.3	5.6
Grooming Aids	53.2	1.7
Candy	52.1	14.6
Vitamins	50.4	3.6
Pain Remedies	49.6	2.4
Skin Care Preparations	49.4	2.5
Wine	48.7	2.1
First Aid	48.4	2.4
Kitchen Gadgets	48.2	3.0
Pet Care	48.2	3.9
Gum	47.4	2.8
Sanitary Protection	46.7	1.9
Hair Care	46.4	4.9
Oral Hygiene	42.5	5.3
Pet Food	42.1	9.5
Shaving Needs	42.1	1.8

Can you spot the link between these frequently purchased categories that are most likely to be purchased on quick trips? Is it clear what ties these items together? Can one understand what would be the best assortment and layout of a "quick trip retail space" by speculating on the underlying motivations of quick-trip shopping based on this list of categories? It's very difficult!

Could the Shoppers' Motives for Making the Trip Offer Insights into the Best Assortment to Offer?

Twitty: What is it that shoppers are seeking when on quick trips? Shoppers told us that when they were on quick trips, they usually wanted to accomplish their shopping quickly, and as we have already said, they were seeking items to be used or consumed in the very near future, meaning that day or the next. Unfortunately, the range of products that can be needed somewhat urgently, for that day or the next, is staggering because literally every product category qualifies. So, it seems that neither the shoppers' known motives for taking quick trips nor the list of quick-trip categories provides the necessary insight to define a workable retail space tailored to serve the quick trip efficiently.

How Can Retailers Best Meet the Needs of Quick-Trip Shoppers?

Twitty: If we chose to assemble a collection of the most frequently purchased categories, we would probably have a much greater likelihood of attracting and satisfying those valuable shoppers who are in a hurry to get items they expect to use that day or the next. Stocking the most frequently purchased categories in a convenient way assures that you have the assortment for the broadest array of quick-trip shoppers. See Table 7.2 for the most frequently purchased categories across all outlets, as compiled by the Nielsen Company.

Table 7.2   Most Frequently Purchased Items (All Trips)

Category	% Times Item Purchased on Quick Trip	% of Trips That Include the Category
Bread and Baked Goods	33.4	23.4
Milk	34.0	21.0
Fresh Produce	28.0	18.4
Snacks	34.6	18.4
Carbonated Beverages	40.7	17.3

Paper Products	32.1	14.7
Candy	52.1	14.6
Juice/Drinks—Can, Bottle, and so on	29.6	14.5
Cheese	23.2	13.3
Packaged Meat	24.1	13.3
Condiments, Gravy, and Sauces	22.4	11.3
Cereal	26.4	11.1
Prepared Foods—Frozen	23.0	10.0
Pet Food	42.1	9.5
Vegetables—Canned	21.1	8.6
Cookies	33.8	8.4
Eggs—Fresh	26.2	8.2
Prepared Food—Dry Mixes	21.7	7.8
Soup	22.3	7.7
Prepared Foods—Ready Serve	21.9	7.1
Vegetables—Frozen	20.6	6.8
Crackers	24.9	6.6
Dressing/Salad/Deli	24.8	6.5
Detergents	32.0	6.4
Butter and Margarine	19.2	6.2

A SLOW WALK ON A QUICK TRIP

It seems counter-intuitive that a quick-trip shopper would walk more slowly than a stock-up shopper. But bear in mind that this "walking speed" is an average based on their total shopping trip—total distance walked divided by total time. The trip itself is composed of time shoppers spend actually selecting merchandise for purchase *and* time they spend cruising from one purchase location to another. The greater the share of their time spent purchasing, the slower the average walking speed.

So, quick trippers have very slow average walking speeds due to their high focus on purchasing, whereas stock-up shoppers have very fast average walking speeds due to the high percentage of their time spent navigating around the store, with an occasional purchase. This is the kind of reality of shopping that is totally missed by researchers studying about shopping but not studying the phenomenon itself.

Bread, milk, produce, snacks, soft drinks... these familiar, high-frequency categories may provide a better basis for building a reasonably efficient "quick-trip retail space." It would be a good idea to supplement this list with categories identified by a basket analysis against each of the most frequently purchased items. (A basket analysis identifies those items that are most often in the basket when a given item is purchased.) This analysis will identify the items most likely to be purchased, along with these high-frequency winners. Although it is focused on the most frequently purchased items rather than just those purchased on quick trips, organizing a retail space around these items seems to be a better basis for serving quick-trip shoppers—and all shoppers.

What Are the Implications for Retailers and Manufacturers?

Twitty: Retailers seeking to satisfy quick-trip shoppers should focus on how they manage their most frequently purchased categories. This is because satisfying shoppers on quick trips is not a simple matter of identifying those categories that are purchased most often on quick trips and making them conveniently available in a retail space. Quick trips do not center around a limited number of items that are always purchased on quick trips. Quick trips are composed of an impossibly broad array of items that are purchased on quick trips simply because they are needed for use or consumption on that day or the next. Such items range from soft drinks for immediate consumption all the way to items that are usually stocked-up on, such as light bulbs or batteries that, on this occasion, happen to be needed "right away" or for use in the near term.

Similarly, manufacturers should not be aiming to engineer products or "solutions" to be purchased on quick trips. Instead, they should focus on creating offerings that have high purchase frequency so that they have a greater likelihood of being purchased on any trip.

Review Questions

1. Describe the quick trip and how common they are. How do quick trips vary from other types of trips based on time, money, travel speed and store coverage? Which trip type is more economical?

2. Why do shoppers make so many quick trips? How would prevalence of quick trips differ: (a) in rural versus metro areas, and (b) at times of economic prosperity or downturn?

3. Why does Mike Twitty say that quick trips are a convenience? What do consumers "save" by doing quick trips, if those trips are less economical?

4. What purchasing state(s) discussed in Chapter 1 best describes the quick-trip shopper? How does this help retailers to better serve quick-trip shoppers?

5. What percentage of purchase decisions do shoppers make before arriving to the store? What are those decisions? What implication does this preplanning have for the concepts such as navigation, selection, affinity, and crowd social marketing discussed in previous chapters?

6. What is the Quick-Trip Paradox? What types of products do shoppers purchase most on quick trips? What does this knowledge mean for how retailers should plan their efforts to satisfy quick-trip shopper? What other analysis could be used to deal with the Quick-Trip Paradox?

7. What is the biggest difference between the broad range of "Quick Trips" that Mike Twitty describes, across all retail, and the typical "Convenience Store" trip?

8. Which is more likely to be "the store of the future," the convenience store, or the super-center? Explain why each might be the store of the future; and also why each might not be the store of the future.

Endnotes

1. The terms "Quick Trip," "Major Stock-Up Trip," and "Fill-in Trip" have specific meanings in Unilever research so they are capitalized as proper names when used to refer to these definitions.

2. Ogilvy*Action*, Shopper Decisions Made in Store, 2008.

8

Three Moments of Truth and Three Currencies

"If we will not buy, we cannot sell."
—U.S. President William McKinley

A woman in her 30s moves through the aisles of a Stop & Shop outside of Boston. She was selected for our study because she planned to purchase dish detergent, one of the types of products of interest to our client. We fitted her with specially designed glasses connected to a device that records her field of vision every 3/25ths of a second and relays it to a computer (see Figure 8.1). The glasses also reflect the corneal image of her eyes so we can track exactly what she is looking at in her field of vision as she moves through the supermarket aisles. Instead of merely watching shoppers, the glasses allow us to actually see what they see and focus on.

After the images are overlaid with crosshairs that indicate where her gaze is focused, they are analyzed by technicians in India (see Figure 8.2). We know where she went, what she looked at, and what she did as a result. We are not asking her what she did after the fact. We are not just observing her. We are seeing through her eyes. Short of crawling inside her head (and we are actually beginning to do this), this is as close as anyone has ever gotten to understanding the complexity of the shopping experience and what shoppers actually do in their natural habitat. Given that 90% of all sensory input comes through vision, understanding what shoppers see offers a pretty good view of their thinking.

Figure 8.1 Specially designed glasses record the eye movements of the shopper as she walks through the store.

Point of Focus

Figure 8.2 The images from the glasses show the field of vision, and cross-hairs indicate the shopper's point of focus at each step, second by second, along the route through the store.

In this one-minute journey (images from the first 30 seconds are shown in Figure 8.3), our subject moves quickly past shelves of paper towels, tissues, and napkins, scanning left and right without stopping. She is on a mission. At mid-aisle, she looks at the endcap display on the left. Then, she looks all the way to the end of the aisle, perhaps to get her bearings, scanning the very bottom shelf of the left side of the aisle. She swings her gaze across the aisle to the bottom shelf of the right side, and then moves up along the second shelf. Her gaze zigzags to the top and then to the bottom. She hits a display of brushes and other cleaning products and that breaks her path, so she goes to the left side again. She reaches rows of detergents and stops her cart, scanning rapidly up and down the shelves. Just before she grabs the detergent, she looks down at her cart where a store circular sits on the seat. Could she be checking on the brand in the circular before grabbing the product? She leans a bottle of green detergent forward just before taking it off the shelf. Then, she puts back the green bottle, looks up to the top shelf, and pulls down a pink bottle to put into her cart.

Figure 8.3 Images from a 30-second segment of a shopping trip show the shopper checking the end cap, entering the aisle, scanning right and left, and making a purchase. The diagrams below each figure indicate the way the shopper is facing between the two aisles.

This video clip of her passage down one aisle of paper goods and detergents lasts just half a minute. In thirty seconds, her gaze has passed over hundreds of products; she has considered a few and selected one. She has evolved from a visitor to a shopper to a buyer.

A few years ago, Guinness worked with ID Magasin, one of Britain's leading retail research and design companies, to improve its sales. They created in-store displays designed to stop customers and get them to buy. To analyze behavior, researchers filmed thousands of customers visiting the beer, wine, and spirits aisles, and interviewed a large sample afterward. Selected participants wore point-of-focus/eye-mark recorders, which record the precise point-of-focus of the eyes. This provided quantitative data on penetration and conversion rates and the nature and duration of consumer interaction with the category. It also enabled understanding of the search and selection process and established the draw of the various elements of the displays.

Exhaustive analysis of the findings indicated principles to improve in-store visibility. Based on these, Guinness created a prototype fixture and installed it in test stores, as shown in Figure 8.4. The extruding fins were highly visible, ensuring that the offer would reach shoppers at the end of the aisle. The fins also broke the linear nature of the aisle, helping to stop shoppers by the display. Product layout was clear and authoritative. All these elements were within the cone of vision. Strong brand block and the use of signpost products reduced visual "noise," strengthened impact, and acted as guides around the fixture.

Figure 8.4 This Guinness display, using fins to break the aisle, helped stop shoppers and increase sales dramatically.

Guinness monitored checkout scanner data in the test stores. It then modified the design in response to these findings and installed the display in various retail sites. Guinness then installed the new display in ten sites and identified another ten control sites for a formal test.

The new fixture increased sales dramatically. Why? The new display was able to pull customers through the three moments of truth: reaching, stopping, and closing the sale. The fixture made stout easier to find in this busy category, so the display *reached* out to shoppers. The time until the first customer interaction decreased from an average of 38 seconds to 11 seconds. The majority of stout purchasers went straight to the fixture, so it did a better job *stopping* them in front of the display. The total average visit time was reduced from 2.08 minutes to 1.53 minutes, indicating that the new fixture was easier to shop from. U-turning in the middle of the aisle halved, to only 24%. More customers were now shopping the whole aisle. And, finally, these customers *bought* Guinness in much higher numbers. In the test stores, Guinness draught sales increased by 25% in value and 24% in volume. Total stout sales grew by 10% and total beer sales by 4%.

Moments of Truth

Each shopper second is a moment of truth—an opportunity to sell something. Unfortunately, many of these seconds are lost. As noted in Chapter 7, "The Quick-Trip Paradox," in the typical retail store, 80% of these seconds are wasted in commuting between shopping points. Shoppers would like to spend more money in retail stores. But as long as retailers approach retailing with the attitude that it is a tussle between the store and the shopper about money, and just how to relieve shoppers of a bit more of it, stores will get only their minimum allowance. Shoppers come into stores with the express purpose of getting stuff they want, and they have no compunction about wanting more. Of course, they would like to spend as little as possible, but that's not because they want to get as little as possible. Focus on delivering what they want, and amazing things can happen. To make a sale, however, retailers need to take shoppers through three moments of truth.

Table 8.1 shows the three moments of truth in the shopping process. As indicated, there are parallels between these three moments of truth and the concepts of exposures, impressions, and sales in advertising. The retail experience is similar to an advertising-rich environment. Note that this table includes both shopper "presence" and shopper "vision." This is because the eye has a crucial and parallel role in what happens in the store. Indeed, vision is the immediate motivating force behind shopper behavior, as discussed next.

Table 8.1   The Three Moments of Truth in the Shopping Process

First Moment	Second Moment	Third Moment
Reach	**Stop/Hold**	**Close**
Visits (V)	Shops (S)	Purchases (P)
Exposures	Impressions	Sales
Offer	Engagement	Persuasion
Appearance	Attention	Action
Presence	Interaction	Consummation
Place	Time	Money
Navigate	Find	Decide
Location	Scans	Follow through
Paths and counts	Observation and interviewing	Scan data and observation

Seeing the Truth: Eyes Are Windows to the Shopper

We shop with our eyes first, so vision is at the center of the three moments of truth, as illustrated in Figure 8.5. There are three general stages of eye activity in shopping. First, the eye serves as the pilot that steers shoppers around the store. Next, it serves as a rapid scanner of a category or section to home in on prime candidates for purchase. Finally, it feeds the sales communication to the brain, thereby closing the sale. Just as no sale can occur without the juxtaposition of the merchandise to the shopper, nothing will be bought that does not first fall into the field of vision of the shopper, and it is that field of vision that leads to the shopper coming into juxtaposition with the products.

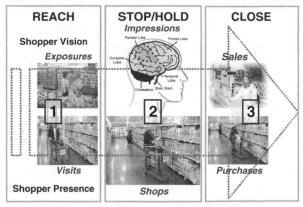

Figure 8.5 The three in-store moments of truth: reach, stop, and close.

Vision research offers insights into this process. Distilling what we have learned from two point-of-focus methodologies, mobile and fixed, some general principles emerge that describe the purchase process, as follows:

- It is really fast!

- Category complexity leads to visual blindness.

- If the shopper can't find or see the products, they are unavailable.

- Poor merchandising and communication make it difficult to find products.

- Shoppers navigate using signpost brands.

- Eye-focus level is three to five feet.

- Shoppers rarely do the math in the store; price does *not* register.

- Shoppers have been trained to shop on deal.

- Gondola ends increase sales, but the opportunities are rarely maximized—a strong "call to action" is needed.

- Most in-store communication, both promotional and corporate, is not seen by shoppers.

- Shoppers will read very little while shopping; instead they respond to colors, shapes, and images.

- Shelf edge is the most powerful location for communication.

Finally, research has shown that shoppers scan horizontally more than vertically (two-thirds of our eye muscles are designed for horizontal movement) and that when standing at a fixture, we work horizontally within a vision cone of about 5 feet (1.5 meters). However, visual attention is drawn by vertical strips when we are traveling (which is why fins such as those used by Guinness work), because this attracts peripheral attention. Most research tests show that horizontal is stronger than vertical blocking unless the vertical blocks are of a sensible width (that is, 3 feet or about 1 meter).

Not everything the shopper sees in the store is for sale. This is a mixed blessing because although shoppers need a break from solid commercial activity, time spent in these areas is definitely not spent shopping. A typical supermarket that accrues a total of 20 million exposures from all shoppers, per week, averages out to about 300 exposures per item per week across a total of 10,000 to 20,000 shoppers per week in the store.

There is a bigger waste factor, as we have discussed—the time shoppers spend traveling through the store. This is where vision becomes critical. Shoppers do not wander around the store with closed eyes and then open them to see where they have arrived. They do not teleport to their new location. The eye leads the body like a pilot. In fact, to understand shopping, it is helpful to think of the shopper as a pair of eyes mounted in a head, with the rest of the body acting as a servant to work the will of the brain. Because 90% of the sensory nerves entering the brain come from the eyes, the eyes not only rule the shopping process, but they also, in reality, rule life.

This has profound implications when trying to understand shopping by measuring bodies around the store. Whereas the body passing through an aisle may come within "reach" of all the categories in the aisle, at any given point the eyes are exposed to only about one-fourth of what is within reach (an elliptical cone, as shown in the left side of Figure 8.6)— unless our shoppers have eyes in the backs of their heads. That is why we always give consideration not just to counting shoppers, but also to taking note of their orientation and direction in the store, as well as the amount of time being spent. Again, at any give time, shoppers have the *potential* for 360-degree orientation, but at any given instant, they only realize about a quarter of that potential.

The right side of Figure 8.6 illustrates the relationship between physical reach and exposure to vision. The parallel dashed lines represent a typical seven-foot-wide store aisle. The six-foot radius sphere (labeled "reach sphere") represents the physical reach of the shopper, whose eye is in the center of these spheres, facing up the dashed-line aisle. Most people's peripheral vision extends to about 180 degrees, but the far edges of that peripheral vision best detect things like color and movement, not detail. The resolution of images occurs more accurately in a 90-degree range centering around the line of sight. For comparative purposes, the 20-foot radius sphere (labeled "vision sphere") is a fairly convenient scanning radius for the eyes. To understand the shopper, we use eye tracking to learn more about the shopper's vision (see the sidebar, "How Eye Tracking Works"). We have analyzed these moments of the sales and purchase process in minute detail, ultimately in fractions of seconds, to understand how quadrillions of shopper seconds add up to $15 trillion of annual retail sales.

How Eye Tracking Works

Eye tracking is an unobtrusive method for measuring what the shopper looks at every tenth of a second. Proprietary software analyzes the focal point information, providing valuable insights into how a shopper navigates a category, responds to POS, or reads packaging.

Here's how it works:

- Eye tracking uses specialist technology to track the cornea of the human eye, thus recording exactly what the eye is looking at (fixating on).

- The technology has been adapted to form a pair of glasses.

- Respondents are recruited to shop a store while wearing the glasses.

- The output includes a recording of shopper fixations (what has been looked at).

- A minimal fixation lasts a tenth of a second. This is the amount of time for the brain to register a single piece of information.

- The average respondent will have around 600 fixations per minute.

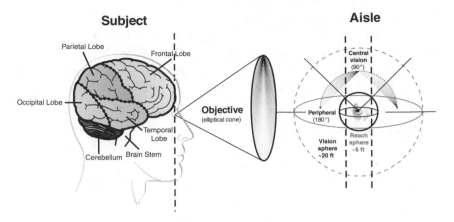

Figure 8.6 Cone of vision: The eyes are exposed to only about one-fourth of the items in the total sphere of vision.

Reach: Impressions and Exposures

Reach is the first essential step in the shopping process: It's when the shopper and the merchandise are in the same place at the same time. In other words, the product *reaches* the shopper. This is the same process that media mavens go for when they seek *reach and frequency* for their advertising material. (See the sidebar, "In-Store Media," for further comparison of advertising and in-store media.) It is fair to say that no offer to sell has been made simply because both the product and the potential buyer are in the same building.

Everywhere the shopper turns, there are commercial messages—typically packages—competing for attention. Even in a short trip, the shopper is going to be "offered" thousands of different items. The actual selection of an item for purchase, including the shopping part, often requires just a few seconds per item. So, actual shopping and purchasing happens at blazing speed.

In-Store Media

Thinking of shoppers in a store as an "audience" in the traditional media sense can offer some intriguing possibilities. Gross rating points (GRPs) are used in advertising to measure reach and frequency, and this is the appropriate convention in-store as well. GRPs combine exposures and frequency, meaning that as much weight was given to showing one advertisement to 100,000 people one time as was given to showing the same advert to 50,000 people two times. However, in-store, many purchases occur in less than five seconds. We consider both exposures and seconds. For example, even though only about one of five shoppers in a particular store carried the weekly circular with them, their frequent references to it, though brief, accumulated enough exposures to make it one of the forms of media with the highest GRPs. Sales are preceded by exposures. Any exposure that creates an impression that leads to a sale is a worthwhile exposure. Consider that in the typical supermarket, there are a large number of items that sell one or fewer copies *per week!*

It is relatively easy to establish a common opportunity to see (OTS) measurement for all media of a *single type*, because the relationship of actual exposures to opportunities for exposure is likely to be relatively constant within a single media type. However, any distortion is unlikely to be comparable across disparate media: television, radio, print, outdoor, Internet, in-store, and so on. The drive to achieve common metrics across all media must lead to a more careful assessment of actual exposures in each of the media types, as opposed to simply opportunities for exposure. The use of such in-store metrics does create the opportunity to take a broader view of exposures and impressions across diverse types of media.

The point of focus is the prime mover for engagement of the shopper, but the point of focus is *selected* from the entire field of vision, large parts of which never come into specific focus, but are nevertheless received and processed by the brain. And, of course, the point of focus shifts around quite freely as the observer scans and takes note of this or that. We need to make a clear distinction between exposures and impressions. Exposure is what happens in front of the eyes, and an impression is something that goes on in the brain—or to put it more succinctly, exposure is what you *see* and impression is what you *look at*. In that sense, everything in the field of vision is *exposed* to the shopper, but only the point of focus makes an *impression*. This line of thinking is very important when one begins to make a distinction between the shopper's entire field of vision—what they had an opportunity to focus on or were exposed to—versus what the shopper *looked at*—which items actually made an impression.

Beginning with a purchase, we can back up to what the shopper focused on at the exact point when they selected the item for purchase, and back up further than that, asking what they focused on before that, and before that. When we are thinking this way, and when we recognize that all those points of focus were selected from the field of vision, it becomes increasingly valuable to ask what did the shopper *not* look at, which they *might* have.

Table 8.2 is a direct tabulation of various media that appeared in shoppers' fields of vision in a specific store—without any consideration of the specific points of focus. For the store represented here, we report not only the share of shoppers being reached by each media point, but also the number of seconds the average exposed shopper sees the media during their full shopping trip. Notice that they are *seeing* the media (because it appears in their field of vision), but that does not mean they are looking at it, which would require tracking their point of focus. So, these are *exposures*, not impressions.

This table reveals exactly which visual media (including store staff) are actually being seen by shoppers as they proceed through the full shopping trip. *Reach* is simply the percentage of shoppers who at any point in their trip "see" the designated media by having it appear in their field of vision. For *frequency*, we used the total number of seconds that "reached" shoppers see the media. In terms of measuring impact, the total seconds per shopper are almost certainly a better measure than how many times they see it.

Table 8.2 Shoppers' Exposure to In-Store Visual Media

Stimulus Exposed	Share Exposed	Times/ Trip	Seconds/ Exposure	Seconds/ Shopper	% Reach x Frequency
End aisle displays	100%	15.5	5.8	90.1	90.1
Free-standing product display racks	100%	9.0	4.0	36.3	36.3
Display bins	97%	4.2	3.3	13.9	13.5
Floor ads	91%	2.9	2.4	7.0	6.4
Free-standing ads, cutouts, inflatables	88%	3.8	3.4	13.0	11.5

Pallet of featured product	85%	2.1	4.9	10.6	9.0
Navigational signs (aisle directories, product markers)	74%	5.7	3.3	19.0	14.0
Shelf ads	62%	4.9	2.5	12.3	7.6
Coupon dispensers/ tear-off pads	50%	3.9	3.0	11.5	5.7
In-store flyers	21%	14.0	5.6	79.0	16.3
Refrigerator/ freezer door ads	21%	4.4	3.8	16.9	3.5
Store staff	6%	1.5	45.0	67.5	4.0
Video or interactive displays or kiosks	3%	8.0	2.5	20.0	0.6
Shopping cart ads	0%	—	—	—	—

Based on these data, you can see that there are nine different media that are seen by at least half of the shoppers, with the lion's share of that exposure going to end-aisle displays and the free-standing product display racks. Possibly surprising is the impact of the in-store flyer and the staff, both of which get a lot of attention in terms of the total seconds/shopper. For the flyers, even though only one in five shoppers carry them around the store, their frequent, short references to the flyer add up to a lot of exposure. For the staff (not including checkers), few shoppers are exposed, but the staff tend to be in view for a long time—presumably during interactions.

There is no point in thinking about media in the store without considering the package. All media competes with all other media in the store, and not only does the package feature in two of the top three areas of greatest impression—end aisle displays and free-standing product display racks—but also in center-of-store aisles, 80% of visual impressions are packaging.

In addition to measuring individual exposures, we can *compute* the probable field of vision from the path that shoppers walk. The head usually faces the same way as the body, and the eyes almost invariably face the same way as the head. It would obviously be more desirable to measure the point of focus and field of vision of shoppers, but the practical reality is that we can measure full-trip points of focus for only a few shoppers in any given study, and can measure the fields of vision for a few hundred. By contrast, we can measure the locations and orientations of tens of thousands and have, in fact, measured the full trips of millions. This means that we can use path and shopper position data to compute reliable estimates of actual exposures.

One practical application of this is determining the relative exposures that every endcap (end-of-aisle display), or other types of displays in the store, receives. Often this analysis is confused with simply counting the shoppers who pass by. But it is so much more than this, taking into account as it does the position and orientation of all the thousands of shoppers who come within eyesight of the display, their distance from the display, and the amount of time they are there. Figure 8.7 shows the exposure all the endcaps in this store received. The bigger the circle, the higher the exposure. The endcaps at the back of the store (top of diagram) receive little exposure, whereas the largest exposure is at the back of the produce section.

A study of breakfast cereal purchases illustrates the difference between exposure and impression. The results for nine stores in the study (see Figure 8.8) show that in one store (B), 73% of shoppers were exposed to breakfast cereals, the highest exposure rate of any of the nine stores in the sample. Yet only 8% of all the shoppers in that store purchased a breakfast cereal, nearly the lowest share across all of the stores. The shoppers in the store saw but did not *look*. They had more exposures but fewer impressions that led to purchases.

Although there is variability from store to store in terms of share of baskets purchasing a given category—cereal, in our example—the reality is that the share of baskets with category purchases is *relatively* constant across stores. In this case, about 9% of baskets contain a cereal purchase across this series of stores, across the United States, across chains. To be sure, some sell more and some sell less, *per basket*, but the relative constancy of category sales is a reflection of the constancy of crowds.

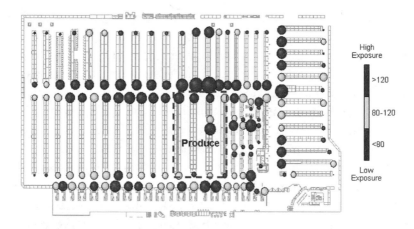

Figure 8.7 Exposures at endcaps: Endcaps at the end of produce receive the most exposure (largest circles).

Category: Breakfast Cereal

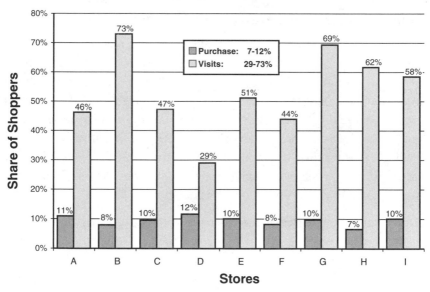

Figure 8.8 Exposures and sales of breakfast cereals for nine stores: Although 73% of shoppers were exposed to cereals in Store B, only 8% purchased them.

Although there will be differences, any 100,000 people will behave pretty much as any other 100,000 people will, at least in terms of cereal purchases (and for most other categories, for most of the time).

In Store B, many people were exposed to cereal, but this did not affect the percentage that made purchases. As any magazine advertiser knows, the opportunity to see (OTS), while easier to measure, is quite different from actually seeing. Magazine buyers have the opportunity to see every ad in the issue, but will typically only see a few, and pay attention to ("look at") an even smaller subset. David Polinchock, chairman of Brand Experience Lab, comments about the Wal-MartTV network: Although they claim to have 140 million viewers a week in their stores, "What if this study showed that they really only have 2 million *engaged* [italics added] viewers?"[1] There is a big difference between 140 million exposures and 2 million impressions. End-aisle-displays, other free-standing product displays, and the in-store flyers (weekly circulars) receive the most exposure in the store. It is not surprising that 30% of all store sales come off end-aisle displays. On the other hand, we have found that even very limited exposures can be highly effective in producing sales.

Stopping Power (and Holding Power)

Stopping power is the second crucial element of the process—translating these many exposures into impressions that lead to arresting the shopper's forward movement through the store. It begins with some change in the shopper's behavior. Because shoppers navigate the store by walking around, "shopping" may begin with them starting to walk more slowly, increasing their time within an orbit of products. The initial impact of a category or product causes them to halt their nonshopping behavior (cruising) and switch to shopping mode. It might be a very slight or weak interaction, but it alters the shopper's behavior.

Admittedly, the line between reach and stopping can be hazy. At what point does a person go from being exposed to something, to being engaged with it? If you want to decide this from a scientific, analytic point of view—which we do—then *time* is what distinguishes visiting from shopping, because if you take a visit and add time, you have shopping. Time converts a visit to a shop, whatever other behavior may occur. Looked at from the point of view of the product, stopping power is what converts a "visitor" to a "shopper."

This transition is again a matter of degree. Stopping can mean a "California stop," as when motorists roll through stop signs slowly, or a full stop. A momentary pause may indicate that some element of "shopping" has occurred. But is a momentary pause adequate? Before addressing that question, let us recognize that measuring the amount of the time involved here is measuring "holding power." As in *Goldilocks and the Three Bears*, too much holding power is not good, and likewise for too little. It needs to be "just right." We can also divide holding power into two subcategories: "buy time," which is the holding power, however long that may be, which results in purchase, and "dwell time," which includes the time that both purchasers and nonpurchasers spend on the products, display, or category.

Closing Power

Capturing the shopper's time is only effective inasmuch as it leads to *closing power*. Holding a shopper at a product is a mixed blessing because reach and stopping power, if they don't lead to a sale (or display closing power), become a wasted exercise. Excessive time that does not lead to a sale probably creates angst and burns through shopper time in the store, resulting in lower profitability. The third moment of truth is closing the sale.

In this context, the array of choices presented to shoppers is critical. The typical retailers have no conception of what it costs them in lost opportunity when they jam up their stores with tens of thousands of "choices" that are largely irrelevant to their shoppers. Stew Leonard's chain cuts the Gordian knot by eliminating all but *2,000 items* in his supersized store. That may seem radical, but it is eminently reasonable from the shopper's perspective. Remember, the shopper is only going to buy up to 400 different items in an entire year. This means that Stew Leonard is giving the typical shopper, on average, *five options for every item they buy*. This represents a massive reduction in selection angst for the shopper.

For some people, this selection angst may not be too large of an issue. But as Swarthmore College professor Barry Schwartz points out in his book, *The Paradox of Choice*, there are two kinds of people—maximizers and satisficers. *Satisficers* have some level of performance that they require when they make a choice, and as long as the product meets their expectation, they are satisfied, without spending a lot of time worrying about whether something else might be better.

Maximizers, on the other hand, always want to make the best choice. Giving them lots of choices can overwhelm their decision system and lead them to either not make a decision, or fret with dissatisfaction over whatever decision they have made, on the grounds that, with all these choices, there must have been a better option. This is not theoretical: Shoppers have been shown, under parallel test conditions, to buy ten times more from a limited selection than from a large variety. Dr. Schwartz describes an experiment involving product demonstrations at matched stores: "In one condition of the study, 6 varieties of the jam were available for tasting. In another, 24 varieties were available. In either case, the entire set of 24 varieties was available for purchase. The large array of jams attracted more people to the table than the small array, though in both cases, people tasted about the same number of jams on average. When it came to buying, however, a huge difference became evident. Of the people exposed to the small array of jams, 30% actually bought a jar; only 3% of those exposed to the large array of jams did so."[2]

As Dr. Schwartz observes, "A large array of options may discourage consumers because it forces an increase in the effort that goes into making a decision. So consumers decide not to decide, and don't buy the product." In this case, fewer choices led to ten times as much purchase! This surprising result confirms what we have seen in the aisles of store after store: Fewer choices lead to higher sales. A passive retailer simply waits for each of these moments of truth to happen, whereas the active retailer understands all three and works with the shopper to expedite them. While the abundance of the long tail may attract customers to the store, this experiment demonstrates how the presence of the long tail in the aisle may impede sales. The retailer that can identify the right six products to sell, rather than burying them in the entire set of 24, can sell significantly more of the products.

Three Currencies of Shopping: Money, Time, and Angst

So far, we have focused primarily on shopper time in examining these moments of truth. But shoppers are not just expending time; they are also expending money and angst as they move through the retail store. Money, time, and angst are the inputs that shoppers invest in shopping. There are two outputs: purchases and satisfaction. At any point in this journey, the shopper is balancing the inputs and outputs. Effective retailing means minimizing the inputs to generate higher outputs.

Most retailers focus a great deal of attention on the money part of this equation, ignoring the other two currencies. Many observers see the retail transaction as, simply, the shopper gives money and receives a product. Given this view, it is not surprising how retailers used the data from electronic checkout scanners in the 1970s, which opened the way for massive and relatively accurate measurement of the money and items exchanged, the two most obvious of the shopper's inputs/outputs. In fact, two of the largest research organizations in the world, IRI and Nielsen, are founded on the business of compiling the counts of these two variables and metering them out to both retailers and suppliers, for a healthy stream of profits.

For many years, great numbers of retailers used scanner data for little more than totaling up the shopper's payment at the checkout and for inventory control: monitoring the flow of goods through the store. It is especially significant that this data is summed up at the store level and compiled *on a weekly basis*. Weekly totals are hardly the kind of detail that might be required in terms of understanding actual shopper behavior in the store.

To understand the moments of truth, we need to look beyond collective data to the individual experience of a single shopper. Individual data for this purpose does not even exist in the weekly roll-ups that are provided by Nielsen and IRI. It is not just shopper identity that is required, but also the detailed log of those shoppers' every single shopping trip and every single item purchased on those trips, which delivers the value. (Better to have all the detailed data for a few shoppers, than all the *pooled* data for *all* shoppers.)

Although some stores are measuring customer satisfaction through surveys outside the store, this recalled experience does not always equate with the actual experience in the store.

Because we know quite a bit about the money side of this equation, we will focus on insights about time and angst.

Time

Think about it: If you are a supplier who wants to move merchandise through a retail establishment, having shoppers in the store isn't what brings you sales; it is having shoppers in the aisle or location where *your* merchandise is. More than this, it is not the shoppers who are hurrying past your location on their way to somewhere else, but shoppers who are spending at least a modicum of time considering your (and your competitors') offerings. *Traffic in itself never buys anything; it is traffic investing time that becomes shopping.*

Time is an opportunity to sell, but not a sale in and of itself. As we saw in the previous example of breakfast cereals, there is a difference between time spent moving around and looking versus time spent buying. Based on a variety of research studies, it is apparent that it takes about a second for a shopper to actually take note of a stimulus, whether of a package, a product display, or some other media. This means that one second of one shopper's time is a pretty good basis for measuring how much shopping is going on. Hence, as noted earlier, shopper-seconds are the basic unit of shopping. Retailers commonly compute the turnover of cash per square foot or meter. This is certainly a useful and valid measure of the productivity of the real estate. Why wouldn't we want something to tell us the productivity of their use of an asset of far greater value: the shoppers' time? In fact, it is not too great a stretch to say that many retailers know a good deal more about the management of real estate (and inventory) than they do about the management of shoppers. One can succeed in retailing with this situation because it is *self*-service, and shoppers are expected to manage their own shopping experience.

To become actively engaged with the shopper, it is necessary to understand how shoppers are spending their time in the store—or, perhaps more accurately, understand *where* shoppers are spending their time in the store. The reason for this is so that, rather than waiting passively for shoppers to find their way to the merchandise they need, we can actively understand their needs and make relevant offers to them to expedite their purchases.

This is a crucial concept. Instead of frustrating shoppers by trying to "build basket size" by holding them in the store longer and hoping they will buy something more, we will build basket size by getting more merchandise into their baskets more quickly. The simple fact is that, in the long run, holding them in the store longer will mean that they won't be coming here so often. Because, in the long run, whether they put words to it, they will come to realize that *you* are not being as helpful as your competition.

But there is a very important point to add: Most shopper behavior is *not* driven by the location or arrangement of merchandise! In fact, a very large share of shopper behavior in the store is not driven by the merchandise. As we noted before, only a minority of the shopper's time is actually spent in the direct acquisition of merchandise. The role of active retailing is to identify this economically unproductive time and to do more selling during that time. Simply attempting to increase shopper time in the store has counter-productively led to fewer shopping trips, of shorter duration.

Another way to look at this is that, instead of trying to lure shoppers to where they are not, learn where they are (and where they are going) and merchandise to that, as we discuss in Chapter 9, "In-Store Migration Patterns: Where Shoppers Go and What They Do." But of course this active retailing will begin with knowledge of just where the shoppers are spending their time. It is shopper knowledge rather than product knowledge, the latter being the specialty of most retailers and their suppliers.

The Versatility of Time as a Measure

We have noted that time is one of the three currencies of shopping, second only to money in terms of importance. We also say that time is the proper metric of shopping. It does, however, play an even greater role than simply counting the seconds a shopper spends in this or that activity, including the full trip. In fact, a good deal of our in-depth knowledge of shoppers derives from connecting precise *clock time* with just a few other data inputs: the exact geographic location (xy) of the shopper, the exact location (xyz) of every product in the store, and the list of exactly what the shopper purchased (T-logs). Some of the distinct uses of time include the following:

- **Elapsed time:** This is used to assess the magnitude of the shoppers' involvement, whether from the trip length (for the full store), or any portion of the store (department, category, brand, or single items). The elapsed time can be evaluated for all shoppers, for some specific group (such as purchasers versus non-purchasers), or for individual shoppers.

- **Serial time:** In what order did events occur? This should begin with the shoppers' path, its progression, and the location where any designated event occurs. Once all shoppers' trips are catalogued, the trip progression—the first 20% of the trip, for example—can be examined for individual shoppers or grouped by cohort.

- **Clock-calendar time:** This is the basic time stamp that is placed on every event or series of events. Events can then be related by identity, location, and time. For example, the items purchased on a trip can be identified by the exact time that trip passed through exactly which checkout lane, and exactly which products were scanned at checkout. This time is also the key to analysis by hour, day-part, day of week, week, month, and so on.

- **Time-derived measures:** Dividing the distance between two points in the shopping trip by the elapsed time between those two points gives the *speed* of the shopper. Derived measures like this can give important insight into whether the shopper is dawdling, engaged, or just speeding by displays. Other insightful measures, like seconds per dollar spent, measure the efficiency of the shopping trip, and indeed, of the entire store, chain, channel, country, and so on.

Angst: A Vague and Unpleasant Emotion

Angst is driven by time and money, but it also arises from excess choice or difficulty in navigating the store. The third currency of shopping is easy to understand but difficult to measure. Shopper's angst is a psychological, emotional deficit that can involve anything from a long checkout line to an out-of-stock item. Although it may be difficult to measure, this does not mean that the effects are slight or inconsequential. Although angst is clearly affected by time and money, here we want to focus on two other major drivers of angst, both of which are related to the matter of choice. As noted previously, a smaller selection of products sometimes can actually *increase* purchases, primarily because a smaller set reduces the angst involved in the purchase decision.

Retailers are driving sales to new heights by moderating choice angst, offering a more limited selection of items. But there is a related angst issue in most stores: "Where is the ...?" We refer to this as *navigational* angst. And there is no question that navigation can create significant frustration, whether it is navigating the shelf visually or finding one's way around the store. There are at least five ways to reduce navigational angst, as follows:

- Design the store and lay out the merchandise in a logical and intuitive way.

- Provide signage or other navigational aids to assist the shopper.

- Reduce the size of the store to reduce the need for navigation.

- Remove visual barriers so shoppers can see the whole store.

- Eliminate or reduce path options.

The first two of these seem reasonable, but are sometimes violated with a deliberate strategy to cost the shopper time, in hopes of translating that into sales. Making shoppers spend more time looking for merchandise and less time buying is never a good idea. It reduces overall sales for the store and significantly increases navigational angst on the part of the shopper.

A Complex Optimization

In summary, the three currencies that the shopper pays in the store are money, time, and angst. The key to retailer profits—and massive customer satisfaction to go with massive amounts of merchandise bought from the store—is to deliver goods and satisfaction while reducing the expense in time, angst, and money. This is the crux of the matter—what is the optimum? The reality is that money, time, and angst are themselves interrelated, so there is not a single optimum.

This brings us to a criticism of a great deal of shopper and retail research. It is simplistic, depending on data and tools readily at hand; consequently, the focus is on the easy, not the important. Paraphrasing a professor's criticism of a student paper: "The parts of shopping research that are easy are not important, and the parts that are important are not easy." Understanding the money part of the shopping experience and the products sold is as easy as tallying up register receipts and tracking inventory. But understanding other currencies, and how the three moments of truth lead to sales, is a more complicated proposition. We need to observe and study shoppers to understand their true behaviors in the store, where they are experiencing angst from choice or navigation, where they are investing their time, and whether that time is leading to sales. This approach can also help in improving sales forecasts. To understand how they spend their time, we need to understand the difference between time spent in the three moments of truth: reach, stopping, and closing. We can then look for opportunities for encouraging shoppers to spend more time buying and less time getting to the sale. This requires hard data on shopper behavior—each of the moments of truth and the three currencies—but gives us a much more accurate assessment of what is going on in the stores and the strategies that lead to profits.

Review Questions

1. What are the three moments of truth in retail? How can each moment be observed in shopper behavior?

2. What is the role of vision in shopper behavior? What is commonly known from vision in-store research about how consumers make purchase decisions?

3. What is the difference between *exposure* and *impression*? How does this relate to the concepts of navigation and selection discussed in previous chapters?

4. What are the most effective visual stimuli in the store that achieve the most exposures? What does this knowledge mean for retailers and brand managers?

5. Describe the difference between *maximizers* and *satificers*. What implications do these different traits have for the purchase process in the store?

6. Name the three currencies shoppers bring to the store. Why does the author consider time to be an important currency? What information can a retailer learn about shopper behavior in-store by using time measures?

7. Describe the *currency of angst*. How can retailers reduce *navigational angst*?

Endnotes

1. *Advertising Age*, June 12, 2006.

2. Schwartz, Barry. *The Paradox of Choice: Why More Is Less*, pp. 19–20, New York: Harper Perennial, 2005.

9

In-Store Migration Patterns: Where Shoppers Go and What They Do

"There is no path. You make the path when you walk."
—Antonio Machado, poet

AUTHOR'S NOTE

We began this second edition of *Inside the Mind of the Shopper* with a discussion on navigation, getting shoppers to the products they want. Throughout the book, we have closely examined the elements of navigation: bidirectional search, the single Dominant Path, open spaces that create open visual fields and how each of these elements is critical to accomplishing the first step of the shopping process: bringing the product and the shopper together. We have also discussed how each of these elements is mirrored in both the online and bricks retail worlds, and the inherent advantages and disadvantages in each. As online retail becomes an ever more dominant force in twenty-first century society, shoppers are growing more and more accustomed to the ease and speed of navigating an online store and less tolerant of the navigational impediments typical of the bricks store. Understanding shopper behavior in bricks stores by understanding where in the store they go and how they get there is vital to matching the efficiency of the online shopping experience.

An award-winning store in the Philadelphia area was designed with a dual entry—one entrance on the left and one on the right. It was arranged by the designer in such a way as to make the right entry inconvenient to reach, creating what was expected to be a dominant left entry. Customers were expected to move from the parking lot into the left entry and then proceed around the store starting from the left. Of course, shoppers did enter from the left, but this is where the plan broke down. The designer knew a lot about design, given that the store won industry awards, but not as much about shoppers. When the store opened, shoppers were so determined to make a right entry that they entered through the left door, and then crossed the entire front of the store to shop in the natural direction, starting at the right and moving counterclockwise.

Managers deemed this unacceptable shopper behavior, so they positioned several pallet displays to impede efforts to execute a counterclockwise shopping trip. Given these obstacles, they thought shoppers would come to their senses and start from the left. Instead of accepting the flow of the shoppers, the managers tried to change shopping behavior. The managers, of course, were wrong. It was with real sympathy that we observed shoppers struggling to maneuver their carts around these pallets, as determined as salmon swimming upstream. Because this store won awards, it reveals a weakness in understanding shoppers not only by the store itself but also across the industry.

Retailers who understand the natural migration patterns of shoppers can design stores that fit with shopper behavior, rather than trying to change behavior to fit the store. Sociologist William Whyte reflects this understanding when he writes about the virtues of a good entrance: "A good entrance draws people—not just those who mean to go in, but those who do so out of impulse. It draws them not by forcing a decision, but by making a decision unnecessary." To illustrate, he describes the entrance of Paley Park in Manhattan, which has been cited as one of the finest urban spaces in the United States. "Its attractive paving and trees extend out to the curb. There is no clear line between the park and the street, and because that entry space is so broad, there is a full view of the activity within. Passers-by look at it. Some will pause. Some will move a few steps closer, then a few steps more, and they are in, without having decided to be ... Store doorways should be similarly inducing."[1] Contrast this view with the image of store managers throwing obstacles in the path of hapless shoppers.

The experience of many shoppers and many stores shows that changing such basic shopping behavior is like trying to convince a dog not to spin around several times before settling in for a rest. Understanding and aligning with this behavior can lead to higher sales and profits. In fact, one retailer we worked with increased sales by 7% simply by moving the left entrance to the store to a more natural position. This is a huge increase in sales just from a better understanding of shoppers, and perhaps more valuable to a retailer than a design award.

If You Stock It, They Will Come

Retailers are quite expert at where to locate stores. They put stores at major expressway interchanges and other high-traffic areas. (In fact, it was traffic studies that inspired, in a way, our in-store studies of shopper traffic patterns; see the sidebar, "A Time-Lapse Photograph.") Retailers study demographics and traffic patterns to place retail in the path of consumers. Except for Wal-Mart's counterintuitive early strategy, retailers don't locate their stores in the hinterlands hoping that customers will make a pilgrimage. This may work for religion, but few retailers have that kind of draw, even among their most passionate zealots. Retailers take the stores to places where they are likely to find customers.

A Time-Lapse Photograph

PathTracker began conceptually 40 years ago when I was stretched out on the living room carpet with my kids, looking at a *Time-Life* book that showed a time-lapse photo of night-time automobile traffic passing through an intersection. If people could look at the traffic on a road over time, why not do the same thing in a supermarket?

That way of looking at, and thinking about, traffic stayed with me for my first 30 years of studying shoppers in stores, although I had done very limited shopper tracking studies to that point, mostly focusing on observing shoppers at-the-shelf, and interviewing them about their experiences and opinions. I was certainly not the first to study shopper paths. Farley had done shopper tracking in the '60s, the Marsh super-study in the '90s did extensive shopper tracking, and Paco Underhill and Siemon Scammell-Katz both included shopper tracking in their practices. However, when I began serious tracking in 2001, it was with the express goal of generating an electronic stream of behavioral data from the sales floor that might provide helpful understanding of the electronic scan data of sales, recording the final delivery from the store.

PathTracker is designed to produce massive amounts of shopper data (millions of trips) to match the massive amounts of sales data available. PathTracker has evolved into a sophisticated tool integrating data about shopper paths (often measured with cart tags and antennas in the store, as illustrated), sales data, product locations in the store, and shopper demographics, psychographics, and attitude data.

Yet when shoppers arrive at the entrance to one of these stores, this logic and science tend to disappear. Retailers may have an entire department dedicated to studying what happens before shoppers arrive, understanding the traffic that will bring shoppers into the store. But the locational focus is lost once the shopper is inside.

One reason for this state of affairs is that retailers and brand suppliers alike believe that the location of the products in the store determines where shoppers will go once they are inside. So, if retailers put the products in certain places, the shoppers will "find" them—a *Field of Dreams* logic: If you stock it, they will come. This is the model that retailers have followed for years. In their minds, the relationship between people and products represents the most important aspect of shopping. This is an illusion of knowledge and is a consequence of being intimately involved with stores without actually *measuring* what shoppers do there.

The traditional view is that people come to the store to buy goods, and travel from one product to another, rationally working their way through their supposed shopping list. As discussed in Chapter 7, "The Quick-Trip Paradox: An Interview with Mike Twitty," the quick-trippers who dominate retail may not even *have* a list. And, as we saw in Chapter 8, "Three Moments of Truth and Three Currencies," exchanging products for money is not the only concern in the shopping experience. Shoppers are spending time and angst along with their money, and they are receiving experience along with hard goods. The approach of letting shoppers find their way to products focuses on the exchange of products for money but does not place a very high value on shopper time or angst. Whereas money is the proper metric of the outcome of shopping, time is the proper metric of the process of *shopping*. Money measures sales, and time measures shopping. So, if shopping is our subject, time is our focus.

A passive retailer relies upon gross measures—sales, margins, inventory, and square feet or meters—which offer a pretty good picture of the relationship of the store's assets to profit. But between the time the shopper walks through the entrance and reaches the checkout, a great deal has happened. In this period, our passive retailer has left the shopper to do all the work in finding products in the store. How has the shopper spent time during this shopping trip? Did the shopper earn a decent return for this time? What kind of debt of angst has the shopper racked up? Could the retailer have reduced this angst and time, while realizing opportunities along the way to make additional sales? The data on shopper time and angst never appear on the retailer's balance sheet, but you can bet they are top of mind, at least in qualitative form, for the shopper.

A more active retailer plans to pursue the sale by making offers to *where the shopper actually is*, including where they are facing, and for how long. The questions are: Where are shoppers to be found in the store? And what is the most efficient way to make offers to them?

Understanding Shopper Behavior

To understand shopper behavior in stores, we need to look at where and how shoppers are spending their time in stores. These measures are similar to the studies of frequency and reach in advertising (see the sidebar, "Three Measures: Counting Shoppers, Time, and Direction"). As with studies of vehicle traffic used to locate stores, looking at traffic volume, speed, and direction, in the store we need to measure where the shoppers are, how long they stay there (in time or speed), and where they are heading. With these measures, we can create distribution maps that show the high-traffic and low-traffic areas of a given store, as illustrated in Figure 9.1 (which we presented in the Introduction). The checkout stands typically are centrally located across the front of the store. For the most part, the retailer has absolute control over only two points in the shoppers' trip—where they enter the store and where they check out and exit. We consider three insights from these studies: the importance of the entrance, shopper direction, and the role of products in dictating shopper traffic.

Shopper Asymmetry

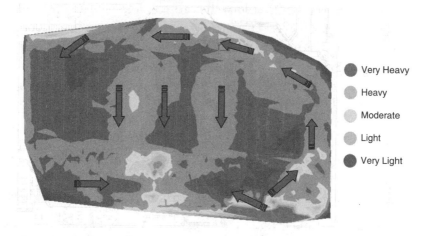

Figure 9.1 Shopper movement through a store.

Three Measures: Counting Shoppers, Time, and Direction

Advertisers have long used reach and frequency (gross rating points) as a standard metrics for advertising exposure. It was Wharton Professor Peter Fader who first pointed out to us years ago the relationship between the metrics we were developing and advertising metrics. *Frequency* and *time* are closely related. Just as one person viewing a single advertisement five times results in the same five gross rating points (GRPs) that five people seeing the advert once does, so 50 people visiting an aisle for an average of 20 seconds each results in the same 1,000 shopper seconds (gross rating points) that 20 people for 50 seconds would. And just as with advertising's GRPs, it is the total shopper seconds that are the proper accounting of the opportunity of shoppers to buy—or the opportunity to sell, if we take a more active view.

First Impressions: The Entrance

As with stage acting, a strong entrance sets the tone of the entire trip. First, we notice that there are a lot of shopper seconds being invested just inside the entry. This is because nearly 100% of shoppers visit this area, and a very large number of them stop at the cart corral to pick up a shopping cart. But this "landing area" plays another role: Here is where shoppers can stop to get their bearings as to where they are going to head and to check their shopping list, if they have one. For the active retailer, *this is an important opportunity to begin the sales process.* For many supermarkets, this opportunity is taken to establish a "fresh, attractive" ambiance by featuring prominently such items as produce, fresh deli, and possibly the in-store bakery. As we discussed in Chapter 1, this would also be the location for the *convergence depot*, in the ideal self-service store of the future where shoppers would pick-up their preordered, Autopilot purchases before proceeding into the rest of the store for Surprise/Delight purchases.

This, however, definitely doesn't happen in every case. Our purpose here is not to consider the pros and cons of all the different ways of handling the immediate entry, but just to call attention to its extreme importance. And this is *not* simply for grocery operations, but for any type of store. As William Whyte notes in the previous comment, a good entrance finds visitors "in, without having decided to be." Whyte suggests minimizing the demarcation between inside and outside and widening the entrance (extending the welcome) to the extent practical. Personally, I prefer air curtains, even in fairly harsh climates, rather than doors of any kind. It takes shoppers three to four times longer to buy a frozen food item than another grocery item, as we will consider next. This is almost certainly— or at least partially—because of the door that you have to go through to retrieve what you want.

Of course, the second area with a great concentration of shopper seconds is the checkout area. Nearly all shoppers must pass through here, as with the entry. Otherwise, one sees a band of high density of shopper seconds most of the way around the perimeter of the store, with two bands of heavy concentration linking the back of the store with the front of the store. In fact, one or the other of those two bands represents the heavy flow of the traffic from the back of the store to its front.

Some retailers have experimented with left-entry and center-entry stores, in addition to the more traditional right entrance. With center-entry stores, most shoppers turn to the left when they get to the back of the store. The entry is the last place you want to have a choke point. McDonald's realized this years ago when they replaced their small windows for taking orders with a storewide counter. It removed a choke point right at the entry. Center-entrance stores have a choke point at entry. This nearly always leaves such stores with under-shopped areas to the right of the entry. Again, the dominant back to front traffic is the first aisle leading to the checkout, and again in this example, the wide frozen food aisles, which have in this case been arrayed at the beginning of the left third of the store. Almost certainly it is the continuation of the wide perimeter aisle, here returning to the front along the left perimeter, that has encouraged a quite wide distribution of shopper seconds in this store.

For the left-entry store, we previously discussed the Philadelphia store that tried to force customers into the left-side pattern. Some shoppers make their way to the right side of the store so they can move in a counterclockwise pattern. What happens to the others? Some shoppers move directly back from the entrance through produce, as hoped. Others walk along the front of the store and then turn up one of the aisles, then resuming their counterclockwise progression from that point. If they turn up the middle aisle, for example, they will miss half the store on their right.

Shopper Direction: Establishing a Dominant Path for the Elephant Herds

In addition to finding out where shoppers spend the most time in the store, we can also discover the general direction of their movement, as shown by the arrows in Figure 9.1. (Just like vehicle traffic studies, the direction of travel has a significant impact as discussed in the sidebar, "Walgreens Finds Profits in Two Directions.") We see that not only do the shoppers enter at the right of the store, but that the dominant traffic is around its *perimeter*, in a counterclockwise rotational pattern. This rotational pattern dominates shoppers' movement in the store, and echoes many rotational patterns in nature, such as migration of elephant herds. For shoppers, we know that substantial majorities are right-handed, and a right-handed person, pushing a shopping cart, is going to tend to push with their right hand, giving the cart a natural tendency to turn left; that is, in a counterclockwise direction.

The next question is why is there the heavy traffic through the center of the store, several aisles after the shopper begins crossing the rear of the store? In examining store after store, this phenomenon is often repeated, with the first dominant path from the back of the store to the front being the first aisle where the checkout area can be clearly seen. This is a manifestation of the "checkout magnet," which draws the shoppers toward it, like a vortex.

Walgreens Finds Profits in Two Directions

One of the best-performing Walgreens stores was located on Michigan Avenue, north of The Loop in Chicago. It was on the southbound side of the street, convenient to traffic heading into the city. Walgreens then located a second store right across the street on the northbound side, convenient to traffic leaving the city. The result: two high-performing stores at essentially the same location but addressing traffic going in opposite directions. Similarly, in looking at in-store traffic, to maximize sales, we not only have to consider the volume of traffic going by a certain point but also traffic *direction*.

The second back-to-front dominant aisle is near the end of the checkout area, and through, in this store, the frozen food aisles. But we should also note that it is through the *wide* frozen food aisles. The wideness is significant because "open space attracts." Thus, there are at least three forces driving traffic down this aisle: It is the last visual opportunity to return to the checkout; it is wide and accepting; and it contains frozen food. This third factor—the actual products—probably accounts for the least number of shoppers down this aisle, although the perishability of frozen goods means that shoppers tend to like to buy them at the end of their trip (see the sidebar, "Shoppers Save Frozen Foods for Last, but Not Produce").

Shoppers Save Frozen Foods for Last, but Not Produce

It is interesting to compare shopper behavior in buying frozen food and fresh produce. Frozen food exerts a strong force on the order of the trip. That is, no matter where the retailer locates frozen food, it will often be visited near the end of the shopping trip. So, the aisle nearest the entrance of the store will ordinarily be shopped first, followed by the second, third, and so on, across the store. But if frozen food is not placed at the end of the trip in terms of layout, shoppers will often skip it and return near the end of the trip—if they remember—or just skip it altogether.

Compare this to fresh produce. We could theorize that shoppers might prefer to have produce at the end of the trip, to avoid having fragile, crushable fresh produce on the bottom of the cart. We do not, however, see large numbers of shoppers skipping fresh produce, which is often the first category offered to them, although this undoubtedly does occur to an extent.

Of course, progression is not the only factor to consider. In this case, *fresh* produce sets the tone for the store's image, not only from the standpoint of being visually attractive, but also by conveying the message of naturalness and freshness about the entire store. (Having cut-price items prominently at the entrance can similarly convey a *value* message for the entire store.)

We can cite a number of principles seen on this shopper second flow diagram, as follows:

- Trips always start at the entrance, and end at the checkout/exit.

- After pausing at the entrance, shoppers tend to move to the back of the store, especially if that pathway is broad and attractive.

- Once at the back of the store, shoppers will tend to turn to the left, counterclockwise, and immediately begin to exhibit exit behavior.

- The appearance of checkout stands on their left, at the front of the store, will attract many to move there.

- Several extra-wide aisles will hasten the growing rush to exit the store.

Clockwise or Counterclockwise: The Coriolis Effect in Shopping

The pattern of movement in the supermarket is counterclockwise in the United States, but PathTracker studies in the U.K., Australia, and Japan show a much greater tendency for shoppers to move in a clockwise pattern there. This could be due to many factors, including more crowded stores, but it could indicate that although there could be biological or instinctual forces that drive this behavior (such as the dominance of right-handedness), traffic patterns in the store may also be affected by *vehicle* traffic patterns outside. In these small studies, we noted that in countries with right-hand driving, where traffic circles move in a clockwise pattern, shoppers in stores may be more comfortable moving the same direction. Like the Coriolis Effect in physics, where winds and currents tend to veer to the right in the northern hemisphere and to the left in the southern hemisphere, the movement of shoppers in a store may depend, in part, on where in the world you are located.

The Checkout Magnet

It takes less and less time for shoppers to make a selection as their trip progresses. Why is this happening? Shoppers come through the front door with a goal in mind. That goal is the checkout and exit (and beyond), and they behave as if drawn by an irresistible force toward it. The speed of their shopping increases as they near the checkout. The shopping trip is not so much an event, such as a movie or sports contest, as it is a road or pathway (or even a detour) on their way to somewhere else. Within the store, we can refer to this shopping behavior as the "checkout magnet."

The checkout and exit is drawing the shopper away. This may seem obvious because all shopping paths lead to the exit. But it is manifested also in the quickening pace of shopping within sight of an open (and short) checkout line (and by steadily decreasing time spent per item purchased as the shopper moves around the perimeter racetrack). The shopper will hasten to complete any shopping to get into the short line before other shoppers can lengthen the line. Retailers should thus plan for more leisure time at the beginning of a shopping trip.

Products Hardly Ever Dictate Shopper Traffic—Open Space Does

There is a great deal more that could be pointed out for this store, but the single most important thing to learn here is that there is nearly nothing about *products* that is required to explain this shopper traffic. This is radically at variance with very close to 100% of all thinking about shopping, which assumes that it is all about the shoppers and their relationships with this or that product or category. After all, people come into stores looking for products. Why wouldn't products be the driver of movement through the store?

> *The location hypothesis:* 85% of shoppers' behavior is controlled by the geographic location of the shopper in the store, and only 15% of behavior is controlled by product interactions.

Observations of millions of shopper trips have led to what I call "the location hypothesis": 85% of shoppers' behavior is controlled by the geographic location of the shopper in the store, irrespective of what products may be around them, and only 15% of behavior is controlled by product interactions. This hypothesis has been confirmed by two groups of independent researchers working to create models that predict shopper patterns across a single store (Wharton) and across multiple stores (Pepsi).

A recent study with Wharton provided additional confirmation of this hypothesis. The study examined the impact of changing locations of products in the center aisles across six matched stores. The results indicated that the product itself had very little impact on sales, whereas location had a significant impact.[2]

So far, we have discussed how produce and other fresh goods influence the initial shopper landing zone, forming an attraction for shoppers. We also cited the frozen food aisles in relation to channeling traffic back to the front of the store. But there are plenty of examples of shoppers *not* moving through produce to the back of the store, and even largely ignoring the produce if it is not on their natural path. Also, notice that on the frozen food aisles, we cited the *extra-wide* nature of these aisles. Products have a role to play, but they are not the primary driver of traffic patterns.

Open Space Attracts: The Call of the Open Aisle

This is one of the most powerful motivators to shoppers—*open space attracts*. This means that adding a foot or two to the width of any aisle is likely to generate more traffic. Convenience stores generally do a *much* better job of creating open space than do other types of stores, primarily because their fixtures tend to be not as tall. Retailers in larger supermarkets want to entice shoppers down steel canyons, but shoppers like open space and visual freedom. For a convenience store, this extends right on outside the store. If a driver passing a convenience store, particularly at night, can't see into the store, and preferably the *entire* store, they are unlikely to stop and enter. Hence, these stores are typically heavily glassed and lighted, inside and outside.

Drug stores, potentially very effective competitors to convenience stores (they're convenient, given a multitude of locations), could significantly enhance their traffic by getting rid of those fortress exterior walls (reserve that for around the pharmacy in the back corner, if necessary). But it isn't just glass and lighting. I would *never* build a store with fixtures over five feet high in any area where I expected significant traffic. These six-foot and higher displays are overt throwbacks to the retailer as warehouseman. There is a place for warehouse displays, but not where you want to attract shoppers—you need open space.

Narrow, crowded aisles like packed highways can lead to social pathology, and even "aisle rage." In one incident, two shoppers met in an aisle less than two feet wide. They exchanged words, and as the hapless patron arrived from the aisle to pay for his purchases, the fellow shopper from the narrow-aisle encounter clubbed him. The angry assailant escaped for the moment, but the security camera recorded his criminality. Few shoppers carry matters to such extremes. Rather, they avoid cramped aisles, and probably the stores that have them, in the same way that motorists avoid congested freeways if they can.

Using a few wide aisles as thoroughfares to move the bulk of shoppers around stores is, of course, common everywhere. Beyond those nice "drive aisles," there is a more nuanced question of the "aisleness" of stores. We define this as the extent a store is divided into aisles. There are several ways to approach computation of this measure, but the simplest is probably the percentage of the store occupied by products, fixtures, and staff compared to the remaining total shopping area (where shoppers can actually walk). The higher the aisleness, the more crowded the store.

We first identified the importance of "aisleness" while trying to unravel a puzzle at a chain of gift and card stores. We found that two stores had much higher sales than two similar stores. All the stores stocked the same merchandise and were matched stores, but the key difference was that the two underperformers had much higher aisleness. They were cluttered and hard to navigate. We started looking more closely at this issue across a number of stores and found it was correlated with the success of the store. (It should always be compared across a set of congruent stores.)

The point here is that space in the store is allocated either to the shoppers or to the overall effort to sell to them—products, fixture, and staff. As the products and fixtures swell, about the only thing the retailer can do is work to highly organize and expand this product space. This results in aisles rather than free space. More open formats—what we typically refer to as a "bazaar" shopping domain, referring to souks and less-structured shopping—are more like typical produce areas in supermarkets.

There are aisles of sorts in these open arrangements, but they do not limit a shopper's walking path. Center-of-store aisles, for example, are highly constrained for the shopper—no turning this way or that way. It is all usually toward the front or toward the back. Of course, those long aisles are often intersected by a transverse aisle about halfway back in the store. This is a highly recommended feature that decreases aisleness to some small extent but adds an extra rank of end-aisle displays.

The bottom line is that stores with a lot of aisleness necessarily have less freedom for the shopper. This doesn't mean that all aisleness is all bad, but it is *mostly* bad, so in general the ideal store will have a minimum of aisleness. Aisleness costs the shopper time, so shoppers penalize the retailer by spending more sluggishly. Looking at shopping efficiency across a series of stores tends to confirm this, as shown in Figure 9.2. As aisles become more crowded (higher aisleness), the time it takes for shoppers to spend a dollar increases. As we have noted, the faster customers spend money, the higher the overall store sales. Aisleness is a significant factor to consider in thinking about store navigation.

If you are a retailer, perhaps you have never thought of actually measuring your store's capital commitment to shoppers' space, instead of to the merchandise space. In fact, it is widely thought that investing in a massive product offering for the shopper is done to cater to their needs. But it is simply not true. Shoppers do *not* prefer to shop in a warehouse. Hence, the slow death of the center-of-store "warehouse."

So, what kind of fixtures should the ideal store have?

- A maximum of 66 inches (2.6 meters) high.

- Not more than 30 feet (9 meters) long, preferably 15 to 20 feet.

- Always pyramidal—sloping back from the shopper.

This does not mean that if you have a store with tight aisles, you have to tear down the store. If you intelligently manage the store, you might blow away competitors. If you have a store with high aisleness and you recognize it, you can intelligently manage it through use of devices such as sloping displays, as we consider next.

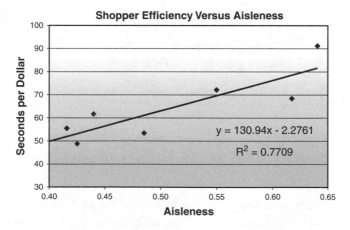

Figure 9.2 The greater the aisleness, the slower shoppers spend their money.

The Great Pyramids

The sloping back is well illustrated by a Pão de Açucar store in São Paulo, Brazil, as shown in Figure 9.3, but we have seen this feature occasionally in Europe, Asia, and North America as well. It creates a sense of greater openness and wider aisles without expanding the actual distance of the aisle at floor level.

We can see the shopper not only has the benefit of being able to see (more or less) over the top of the fixture, creating a great sense of openness, but the top of the fixture is recessed from the shopper by about 16", giving nearly three full feet of *apparent* extra aisle width, if this type of fixture is used on both sides of the aisle. This is of tremendous significance: With pyramid fixtures deployed in the typical seven-foot wide aisle, the shopper would react as if the aisle were nine or ten feet wide. Whether this would make possible a shrinking of total aisle width is uncertain, but it is most certain that shoppers are far less concerned about the crowding of their feet than they are about the crowding of their visual space.

Figure 9.3 Sloping shelves create a sense of greater openness without expanding the aisle width at floor level.

The old canard that "eye level is buy level" is quite simply untrue. The true shelf sweet spot is from the waist to the shoulder. The pyramidal fixture focuses on this sweet spot, sacrificing nothing in terms of facings, other than above "buy level." The shelf, however, serves as more than a vehicle to *display* merchandise (facings). It is also the primary vehicle for maintaining inventory (avoidance of out-of-stocks). So, the most serious loss is of "warehouse" space behind the facings, particularly at the top shelves. This seems a small price to pay for a greatly enhanced shopping experience.

A slightly less radical design is to use an offset. Rather than a smoothly sloping pyramid, the offset design uses a series of steps to move products away from the shopper. It maintains vertical shelf facing, but at about 40 inches, pushes the upper shelves back eight to 12 inches. This gains up to 2 feet of the precious visual space per aisle (assuming both sides are similarly treated). This design also allows for the addition of a sloped signboard of 8 to 12 inches width, the full length of the fixture.

Some early applications of in-store media, for all their hype, were close to worthless, but new approaches are now sometimes highly effective. The offset fixture may be the true future of in-store digital media, with several targeted messages or "kiosk" functions at perhaps five to eight foot intervals for the length of the fixture. Such deployments, automatically or shopper-activated, allow many of the functions to be found on mobile Internet devices, whether cell phones, PDAs, or custom devices such as Modiv Shopper and MediaCart.

New Angles

Before moving on from fixtures, we should consider something about their orientation and layout in stores. Another way to change the customer experience of the store is to shift the angles of the aisles. The angle of the aisles does not have to be from front to back. Rectilinear layout is a clear throwback to warehouse type thinking. The store shown in Figure 9.4 has aisles set at a 45-degree angle. This means that, among other things, shoppers will ordinarily be approaching these from a less acute angle, which may make them more inviting to enter.

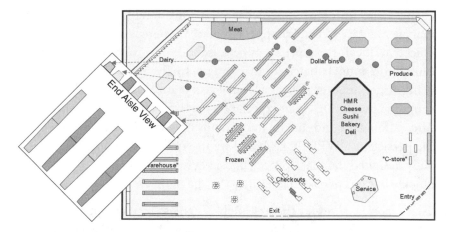

Figure 9.4 Angled displays change the customer experience.

These are shortened gondolas, laid out in a staggered pattern. So, if you are looking down any of those aisles, instead of being treated to a continuous view to the opposite side of the store, you see the endcap of a gondola in the next rank.

Notice also that every other gondola in each rank has been shortened, rather than shortening every gondola. In other words, as a shopper navigates down any of these "aisles," they will see on one side a gondola of standard height, about six feet, and on the other a lower gondola that they can see across, giving them a lateral visual expanse in the neighborhood of 20 feet—two "aisles" plus one gondola width. Also, because many fewer shoppers get to the center of any gondola/aisle, we suggest that giving the gondola a slight diamond shape, or otherwise providing some interruption of the surface of the gondola—vertical signage, for example, or convex shelving protruding into the aisle (referred to as "bump-outs")—is entirely acceptable, and likely to be a plus from the shopper's perspective.

You may notice also the nook nature of some of the perimeter shelving, as well as a designated "warehouse" area on the most remote perimeter. These are ideal locations for Long Tail displays, and will be discussed further as we look at the five basic ideal store designs.

Many of these ideas are conceived *not* to involve radical departures from existing operations. This is in recognition of the fact that radical changes may be foolish, since what *is* has considerable merit—including management inertia and shopper familiarity. There is no such thing as an objective "ideal" store, primarily because shoppers themselves have been thoroughly indoctrinated for many years, by the way things are already being done, and thus there is a level of acceptance and expectation by the shopping public. This is an expectation that is not based on strictly scientific, rational grounds but on the grounds of familiarity. (Remember that the persistent QWERTY keyboard we use on our computers was originally designed to separate mechanical keys that might stick if struck too quickly but has persisted long after the age of mechanical typewriters.)

These facts account for the well-nigh worthless results of many surveys asking shoppers how things should be done. For example, in surveys, most shoppers regularly report that they shop "most of the store" on each shopping trip, when in reality less than 2% shop as much as three-fourths of the store. There is nothing wrong with asking them, but the results will be a more accurate picture of their current perception than any reasonable plan for evolving the future.

Although we have stressed the wideness of aisles in drawing shoppers to them, products certainly play a role in attracting shoppers and causing them to spend time when they arrive. Frozen foods, as noted, benefit from a broader aisle, but also tend to take longer to purchase—two to three times as many *seconds* as the average item in the store. This is likely due to both the means of display (often behind closed glass doors) and the multiplicity of similar items that make choice difficult. This latter factor evidently also causes longer purchase times for canned soups, yogurt, and baby foods. (And although we generally advocate efficiency in making the best use of shopper time, there are cases such as canned soups where some strategic inefficiency works to the retailer's advantage, as discussed in the Alphabet Soup example in the sidebar, "Alphabet Soup: The Power of Inefficiency.")

Alphabet Soup: The Power of Inefficiency

Although we stress the importance of making the best use of shoppers' time, there is an exception to any rule. Years ago, Campbell's Soup recognized that its soup, with all those little red and white cans with identical labels in many varieties, represented some real challenges for shoppers attempting to find the specific items they wanted. The manufacturer realized that this variety might create significant angst for shoppers. Managers reasonably expected that they might reduce this angst if they could place the soups in a more rational order, so shoppers could quickly find cream of celery or chicken noodle without scanning through the whole selection.

It seemed like a reasonable assumption, so the company created a carefully controlled matched store test, with one test display of soup alphabetized (just like spices are). Sure enough, shoppers could find their targeted variety more readily—reducing angst. This would seem to be a good thing. As discussed in Chapter 8, money, time, and angst are the three currencies of the shopper, so one might expect that reducing angst would lead to higher sales. But Campbell's found that although customers were more efficient, they also bought less soup, presumably because they missed buying impulse varieties they just happened to come across while looking for their target varieties. In this case, making the experience a bit more inefficient proved to be a wise move. There is no substitute for this direct testing with actual shoppers. It is also clear that shoppers are complex creatures. To understand them better, we cannot use simple recipes. We need to use careful observation to study their true behavior.

Having wide frozen food aisles contributes to an accumulation of shopper seconds from the wideness of the aisles, as well from the nature of the product (and display). This illustrates the interplay of the *location hypothesis* with the *product hypothesis*. There is no point in pretending that the products play no role; simply that it is far less significant than generally thought.

Managing the Two Stores

There are two stores inside nearly every store—the main store (primary) and the promotional (secondary) store. These roughly correspond to the Big Head (promotional) and Long Tail (main store) we discussed in Chapter 1. Although retailers can't ignore the main store, the success or failure of the store is driven primarily by the promotional side of the store. This is not because the items there are *promotional*. As we have noted, promotions do not do much to drive traffic and sales. Instead, the importance of the promotional store is due to its location. Although the main store is located in the center aisles (with the exception of produce, dairy, and meats), the promotional store is on the perimeter, around the entry and the checkout stands or in special displays such as shippers and pallets.

How shoppers are reached in these two stores is illustrated in Figure 9.5. This is actual reach, by categories, measured on a million shopping trips in supermarkets scattered across the U.S. The actual reach in any single supermarket will vary from these averages, possibly significantly, depending on the store's design and layout.

One of the most striking observations here is the minor role of the main store, except for a few categories such as produce and dairy that predominantly appear at a single location, usually on the heavily traveled perimeter of the store. In other words, except for those few categories with large black bars, you could effectively shut down the main store and still reach nearly all the shoppers with the category! Even though the promotional store contains only a small fraction of the total number of items in the store, it delivers something like 40% of *all* store sales.

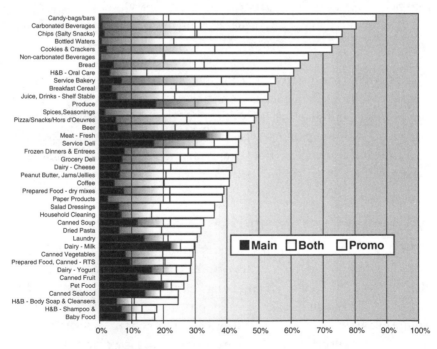

Figure 9.5 How shoppers shop the "two stores."

Take a category such as cookies. Across a wide selection of stores, retailers offer this category to 78% of all the shoppers in their stores. They "reach" 30% of their shoppers in the main aisle, on the gondola. Virtually all of those main aisle shoppers, however, have been reached by at least one promotional display. This means that the main display adds *nothing* to the reach of cookies. The promotional displays deliver more than twice the total sales of the main aisle—5% of store shoppers versus 2% for the main aisle.

Scattering displays around the store increases sales. In one store, for example, several of the cookie displays occur in alternate aisles, not in the usual promotional locations. But *any* alternate display, even on an aisle not frequently visited, has more potential to increase incremental sales than another, expanded main aisle gondola location. Of course, the reasonable expectation is that "cookie" shoppers will be found in the cookie aisle. But this is only true in a *very* limited way, since a high percentage of cookie purchases occur outside the main category aisle. Not only that, but we know that a large share of shoppers going down *any* aisle are not particularly interested in the merchandising in that aisle. Instead, they're simply using it to get from one place to another. In other words, they are navigating the store, which is what the shopper spends the majority of time doing. So placing cookies in an unrelated aisle is not necessarily a bad strategy.

Five Store Designs

Given these insights on shopper behavior and movement within stores, what are the implications for store design? There is clearly no one right answer for all occasions. Retailers need to design the best store for their customers and products. But it is useful to think about where the insights into shoppers would lead. A supermarket executive once challenged me to provide him with ten new ideas to increase sales—with the proviso that they needn't *all* be immediately workable. In that spirit, we discuss five models for store design that take advantage of our knowledge of shoppers.

As discussed in Chapter 7, there are three distinct groups of shoppers: quick trip, fill-in, and stock-up. For simplicity, the store designs discussed next take a layered merchandising approach to accommodating two types of trip: a combination of quick/fill-in trips, simply designated as *quick*, and the ever-desirable *stock-up*. Any loss in matching the needs of diverse groups is more than made up by the practicality of execution in the store. For the quick trip, there are a few hundred thousand U.S. stores that specialize *only* in the quick trip—the convenience stores—so I would look there for what is working best, in terms of store design, layout, and merchandising selection and display.

However, some things are crystal clear:

- The quick trip store *must* be near the entrance to permit a quick in and out.

- The merchandise is mostly a *selection* of big head items, not entire categories.

- No promotional pricing is needed—premium and high margin should dominate.

- Visual enticement to the rest of the store should saturate the experience without being intrusive.

The Enhanced Perimeter

The enhanced perimeter design is pretty much the direction that retailers have evolved the modern supermarket. That is, there is a broad perimeter aisle, which we sometimes refer to as the "racetrack," around the entire store. They have retained the classic center-of-store self-service "warehouse" but have gradually built a very attractive high-volume service belt around it (mixed with self-service, for sure).

There is nothing stunningly creative about this approach, but tens of thousands of sharp minds have created and refined this structure. It doesn't matter that the reasons for its existence have largely to do with the fact that shoppers need "stuff" and will solve almost any retail "problem" adequately for their own purposes. Another advantage of the enhanced perimeter store as ideal is that it can compete effectively with the other designs we will consider, with less draconian changes to traditional store format. These stores are going to be with us for some time to come and can function at a high level without *revolutionary* changes.

In this format, retailers focus mostly on the profitable (for them) perimeter and cede the center-of-store "warehouse" to the brand supplier—with category management and aisle management being a cooperative effort. The brand suppliers who have successfully escaped the center-of-store dungeon have been the direct-store-delivery (DSD) categories like carbonated soft drinks and, to a lesser extent, the salty snacks. Pulling magazines and candy into the checkout lanes blesses those businesses, too. Otherwise, access to the majority of the store's traffic, for brand suppliers, is limited to end-aisle displays and occasional lobby or other promotions, for which the all-important promotional dollars are required.

The Inverted Perimeter

This store is essentially the enhanced perimeter turned inside out. That is, all of that center-of-store merchandise is moved out of the way, and the perimeter departments migrate into the center of the store. Of course, then the former center-of-store merchandise is properly arrayed, probably still in its "warehouse" fashion, around the perimeter of the store.

Within five miles of my office is a store based on this design, which regularly does a million dollars of sales *in a single day*! Of course, it is not a supermarket, but a big-box Costco, the highest volume store in the chain, that pushes nearly $300 million per year in sales. There are obviously a lot of factors at play here other than store design. But the center-of-store is a very large open area, with low displays—a bazaar design—similar to other high-producing displays.

Surrounding this are true warehouse shelves, all visible from nearly anywhere in the center-of-store, where the majority of shoppers spend the majority of time. But all that warehouse merchandise is there, just a few steps away, without cramping the shopper's visual space. No wonder sales in a store like this, for an individual shopper, are often double what the shopper intended when they came in. But they like it! Think of all the money they are saving!

In fact, Marsh Supermarkets (the people who introduced electronic grocery scanning to the world) built a store like this a few years ago. This was a remodel from an earlier conventional perimeter store (see Figure 9.6).

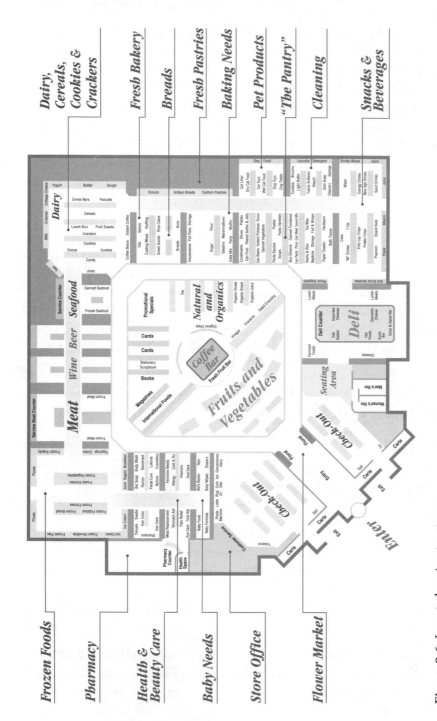

Figure 9.6 Inverted perimeter store.

Initially, shoppers did not care for this "radical" new design. Nothing in their shopping experience prepared them for such a concept. As time passed, however, shoppers adapted, comfort levels grew, and after several months, the desired sales lift was achieved. The nerve-wracking transitional period has, though, dampened the appetite of management for further digression from shopper expectations. None of this deterred HEB from undertaking a similar approach with its now highly successful Central Market concept. We see validation and a growing body of thinking and data favoring the inverted perimeter style of store.

The Serpentine Design

There is no question that part of the angst issue in most stores is, 'where is the ...?' This problem is greatly alleviated at Stew Leonards by eliminating navigation! How is this done? Simple, there is only one aisle in the store! That is, the store mostly consists of one wide aisle that snakes its way through the store, so that as shoppers traverse this one aisle they are exposed to all the merchandise in the store. Although most supermarkets do $10 to 30 million in annual sales, he is doing $100 million in sales. As discussed, he gains an additional $80 million in sales by significantly pruning shopper choice, reducing choice angst and wasted time, and then streamlines navigational angst by creating a single serpentine path through the store—not to mention his superior customer service. But the serpentine design takes advantage of natural shopping behavior and creates an experience for customers moving through the store that is directed by the retailer. As long as the selection of products and their display are right, then the shopper only has to follow this road and put products in the cart.

The Compound Store

The fourth "ideal" store is less a single store than an aggregation of stores. Of course, one can create a compound store by deliberately aggregating distinct stores. In this sense, the typical shopping mall is a compound store. But what we are referring to here is rather the fact that somewhere between 40,000 and 80,000 square feet (4,000 to 10,000 square meters), stores begin to fragment into substores, which then constitutes a compound store. Below this size, the store is shopped more or less as a unitary whole. That is, even though shoppers typically only shop a small portion of the store (less than 25%), they cruise and can see enough of the store to at least have all the square footage as a part of their consideration set. This fragmentation does not require distinct walls demarcating the various stores. Instead, we have found "virtual walls" that divide up the store, defined by shopper behavior.

This means that in a standard supermarket, you can think of the entire population of the store, at any given time, as a single population. However, as the store grows in size, eventually there will be distinct populations in the different virtual substores of the compound store. If there are two substores, few shoppers visit both the stores. One crowd visits one, and another crowd visits the other, with little crossover. When looking at detailed performance measures, the figures will be distorted because we need to separate out the performance of the two stores.

The Big Head Store

This final store focuses exclusively on the Big Head, an approach popularized by retailers such as Trader Joe's and Tesco stores in the U.S. southwest. Instead of a promotional store and then a main store, this store is just the promotional store. By introducing a 10,000 to 15,000 square foot store, and offering only 3,500 different items, Tesco aims to replace long stock-up trips with many more short- and medium-size trips. I think an even smaller store would be adequate to the purpose, and the aisleness is probably higher than it needs to be, depressing shopping efficiency. This, however, is offset by lower gondola fixtures, resulting in the very attractive, greater openness that is common in the convenience store channel.

We note with approval, also, the 45-degree angle of the aisles in Trader Joe's, rather than the less ideal rectilinear, as discussed earlier in the chapter. The much smaller size offsets the navigational issue to a significant extent. I don't know that I would recommend the serpentine path here, but certainly fewer fixtures with better full-store visibility—think Costco—would be helpful. There is no problem with having tall fixtures as small nooks around the perimeter, if there is a desire to include the first few percents of the Long Tail.

Where the Rubber Meets the Linoleum

Changing store designs requires understanding the Big Head and Long Tail, courage in challenging tradition, and specific insights into shoppers measured in the store. Notice that the first two designs I discussed included both the Big Head and the Long Tail in their strategy. I don't know how to put this more plainly: Whether brand or retailer, you *will* learn to manage the Big Head and the Long Tail distinctly, or enjoy your retirement in the not-distant future.

If your store design is not a result of direct measurement of the shoppers in your stores, it isn't real, unadulterated shopper insight. To my knowledge, there are only three people (and their organizations) in the world who got their insight from studying shoppers in the store, through observation and measurement of various aspects of the overall shopping experience. That would be Paco Underhill of Envirosell, Siemon Scammell-Katz of TNS Magasin, and, immodestly, myself. Like they used to say of EF Hutton, when Paco and Siemon talk, I listen. That doesn't mean we always agree, but at least we are pretty much the only ones drinking from the pool that should matter to you. This doesn't mean that no one else does good, valid research. But they don't live on the sales floor—Paco's rubber-soled shoes, if I might. Given the source of our data, we have collectively lived on the selling room floor for upward of 100 years. So I salute my colleagues Paco and Siemon, and the *millions* of our colleagues in the retail and supplier businesses to whom we have dedicated so much of our lives. It is the indomitable spirit of the retailer that delivers to the masses of the world the things they need and must have. It is our goal to help them do it better.

Review Questions

1. What are the traditional (passive) retailers' views about shopper traffic and navigation in-store?

2. What are the most crucial areas in a store? What principles should be followed in designing and managing shopper traffic in those areas?

3. Why is the position of the entrance of a store important? What does this tell us about shopper navigation and how retailers can utilize it in establishing a Dominant Path?

4. What are the main patterns in shopper navigation in a store?

5. What is the significance of open space and how does it facilitate shopper navigation? How do the height of shelves and other fixtures influence shoppers' perceptions of open versus closed spaces? What are the ideal height, length, and shape of a shelf? Explain what makes these dimensions ideal.

6. What is meant by *aisleness* of a store? How does this quality relate to shopper navigation? Describe what is meant by a "bazaar" environment within a store. How do shoppers navigate such a space?

7. Discuss the five store design ideas. How does each design reflect the diversity of shopping trips (quick-trip/stock-up) and types of merchandise (Big Head/Long Tail)? Think of examples of real stores in your geographical area for each type.

Endnotes

1. Whyte, William H., *City: Rediscovering the Center*, Doubleday, 1988, p. 100.

2. The study was conducted by Wharton student Jacob Suher.

PART III

Conclusions

10

Brands, Retailers, and Shoppers: *Why the Long Tail Is Wagging the Dog*

"Whenever an individual or business decides that success has been attained, progress stops."

—Thomas J. Watson, founder of IBM

AUTHOR'S NOTE

We have discussed how many bricks retailers have long viewed the Long Tail as a vital asset, allowing them to assure their shoppers that they could find any obscure product within their miles of aisles at any time. Retailers have been able to ignore the true cost of warehousing thousands of items in each store—despite the fact that shoppers rarely, if ever, purchase these items—due to the retailer's relationships with the brands and suppliers that stock their shelves. But with the emergence of online retailers like Amazon, who can now offer their shoppers both the Long Tail and the Big Head without the expense and logistical demands on the retailer or the frustration and impediment of the shopper, the urgency for bricks retailers to learn how to efficiently and effectively manage the Long Tail is at a critical point. Understanding the history of the Long Tail and the complex relationships between manufacturers and retailers is important for any bricks retailer ready to transition to active retailing.

There is a famous story about when Tesco started trials of its loyalty card, Clubcard, in the mid-90s. The retailer called on the services of dunnhumby, a company specializing in data analysis. The results of these first trials were delivered to the Tesco board in November 1994—which led to a prolonged and awkward silence.

The board chewed over a 30-minute presentation about customer response rates, the impact on like-for-like sales, and a dazzling array of data collected from 14 stores. It was Sir Ian McLaurin, then Tesco chairman, who broke the silence with a now apocryphal remark. "What scares me," he said, "is that you know more about my customers after just three months than I do after 30 years."[1]

It might seem odd that a very successful retailer would know so little about its customers or what they do while shopping. Tesco and other retailers obviously are increasing their understanding of shoppers (although loyalty cards just tell what happens at the checkout, not in the store). In many ways, the massive problems in this industry are caused by everyone assuming that supermarket managements are the repositories of deep insight into the shopping process. By and large, they are not. There are a few exceptions—but they prove the rule.

There is a reason why retailers have historically paid so little attention to their shoppers—they are not rewarded for doing so. The economics of retailing are completely biased against it. We cannot explore the mind of the shopper without expanding our view to look at the broader—and shifting—relationship between retailers and the manufacturers of brands on their shelves. This complex and uneasy relationship helps explain much of what may appear to be counterintuitive about how retailers work. Understanding this relationship also highlights opportunities, which we discuss in this chapter, for brand owners and retailers to collaborate more effectively in selling products. Brand owners can help retailers redesign their stores to maximize sales and can also take advantage of powerful merchandising promotional planning programs to pitch the emotional messaging of each category more precisely.

Where the Money Is in Retail

If shoppers are ignored, it is because they contribute the least to retailers' bottom lines. This may be surprising, because on the surface the entire business model of a retailer seems to be to sell products to shoppers. But a closer look shows that this is only a front for the true business. The main sources of supermarket profits are, in order of importance:

- **Trade and promotional allowances from the brand suppliers:** The number-one source of profits consists of rebates of one variety or another from those manufacturers who want to "warehouse" their merchandise in the retailer's self-service stores. The sometimes-maligned slotting fees are, in reality, a rational warehouse operator's recovery of storage costs from those who want to take the available space. It has been noted that supermarkets make their money by buying (from the supplier), not by selling (to the shopper).

- **Float on cash:** Stores necessarily manage very large amounts of cash. In fact, one executive pointed out to the author the large amount of "abuse" the store receives from shoppers, but then pointed out that this is compensated for by the fact that they leave "their cash on the counter." This cash is hurried to the bank to begin immediately accruing interest, or *float*. Float will multiply until the necessities of business require the dispersal of cash to suppliers, employees, and others, days, if not weeks later. In any event, the store wants to begin *instantly* accruing interest on its portion of that $15 trillion annual turnover of the retail industry. A few seconds of that interest would suffice to maintain most households for decades. This is the second major source of profits.

- **Real estate:** Every major chain maintains a large real estate department that finds real estate to develop for stores, often in developing communities. In a few years, that developed real estate will likely be worth multiples of the initial investment— not carried on the books as profit, because it will be unrealized until the sale of the property itself—often decades later after the underlying business has paid for it many times over.

- **Margin on sales:** This fourth source is not to be sneezed at, largely consisting of *service* departments, operated on the retailers' own prime in-store real estate—the wide perimeter zones or other high-traffic areas. This includes things like the meat department, in-store deli, pharmacies, and so on. Another growing area of profit is contract outsourcing, where outside suppliers manage certain aspects of the operation (such as cafes/restaurants or flowers) and the retailers get a share of the margin from the contractor.

When these sources of profit, and the inherent nature of self-service or passive retailing, are made clear, it is not surprising that retailers don't know a lot about the actual behavior of the shoppers in their stores. Why should they? The shoppers have been assigned responsibility for their own shopping-essentially, unpaid stock pickers, and they aren't really complaining. But this is a dangerous and complacent position for retailers to be in because this passive methodology is increasingly being strained by the diminishing effectiveness of outside-the-store communication.

The reason the Long Tail is wagging the dog in retail is that brand owners are investing in promoting their many products in the Long Tail. As long as manufacturers are putting up the money, it makes sense for retailers to keep their large warehouses well stocked. But if shoppers are buying largely from the Big Head store, could retailers and manufacturers work more effectively in meeting this need?

Massive Amounts of Data

In addition to this economic imperative, there is another major factor driving the lack of interest in what is going on *inside* the store. That is the massive amount of information about what is coming *out of* the store, or the veritable flood of data spewing out of the scanners around the world. This scan data has spawned two major industries in their own right: compilers and resellers of the categorized data—Nielsen and IRI being the preeminent examples—and the advanced analytics relating this data to specific shoppers through the use of loyalty card programs, demonstrated by dunnhumby and related businesses.

As positive as these derivative businesses are, neither speaks well of the retailers' own understanding of the shopping process. First, for decades, electronic barcode scanners contributed little more than an expedited method for ringing up the shoppers' purchases. Of course, sales data was more reliable for inventory control than the older warehouse velocity measures such as those provided by SAMI, which measured movements of goods based on warehouse withdrawals to the stores. But pricing and inventory control hardly bathe the retailer in glory for its use of shopper insights.

In fact, the salutary effect of dunnhumby on Tesco only serves to highlight the deficiency of the retail giant's previous approach to the business.

And now there is an ever-growing cadre of dunnhumby-type firms who are surely accelerating business and profits for any number of retailers through advanced analytics of the scan data linked to the loyalty cards of individual, specific shoppers. So just imagine the impact on profits of going even further and measuring what is going on in the actual *shopping process* in the store.

This is the stark reality that drives a good deal of retailing. It's not that retailers and suppliers don't seek to have a relationship with shoppers, but that their own mutual relationship tends to cause those to the shoppers to pale into insignificance, and, as a result, to remain somewhat distant by comparison. This is the reality of the self-service, warehouse-based view of the store. Sometimes my views may seem too critical, but there are certain absurdities in the industry that are driven by the economic structure. In the U.S. alone, fully one trillion dollars is paid by brand suppliers for the supermarkets to manage their supermarkets in a certain way.

To me, this is the emperor with no clothes. This is why supermarket managers measure inputs and outputs of the store but are largely blind to the process occurring in the store. And this blindness is shared by their brand suppliers. It is essentially the $1 trillion that the brands are paying retailers that justifies their leaving the $80 million per store on the table through not understanding and serving shoppers better. Of course, we have no illusions that there really is, in aggregate, an extra $80 million per store available to every store. But exceptions such as Stew Leonard's, with its $100 million stores, show that much more is possible, for any individual store.

Shifting Relationships

The relationship between manufacturers and retailers is already shifting with the rise of private-label brands and the increasing marketing sophistication of retailers. In an October 2008 article in *Advertising Age*, Jack Neff reported how retailers are hiring talent away from consumer goods companies, measuring shoppers, and building their own brands—"raising big questions about the balance of power in the industry."[2] Retailers are increasingly focused on building their own brands rather than turning over their stores to manufacturers. This is neither good nor news to the brands. However, the role of brands is often not well understood or represented at retail. It helps to consider that when shoppers purchase branded items, they are acquiring three distinct values:

- **Intrinsic value:** A carbonated beverage will quench your thirst and meet your physiologic need for water.

- **Added value:** Packaging the beverage and delivering it to you in a convenient, and possibly chilled, form adds value to the intrinsic value of the water.

- **Creative value:** This third value is in the mind of the shopper and is the essence of brand value.

Because this third, creative value sometimes seems to be a gossamer wisp, it tends to be misunderstood and abused. It obviously has considerable commercial value, because all profits derive from the difference between costs and prices. The cost of intrinsic value is properly regulated by competition for basic, commodity resources. The cost of added value depends on manufacturing and distribution efficiency, including such things as cleverness of design. So what is the cost of creative value? Unit cost is zero, because once created, there is no additional cost, the more of it is sold.

Once created, creative value is a bountiful source of profits. This is its strength and its vulnerability. The vulnerability is because those who do not own the brand are probably unwilling, at some level, to pay for it. This is the reason brands spend so much time and effort trying to convince the market that their value is really intrinsic or added. There is nothing wrong with a better mousetrap, and part of the value of the brand is the assurance that the brand will provide the "better" product.

But whether designer jeans or bananas, there is that something about the brand that makes a customer feel very good about spending a few pennies—or more than a few dollars—for it. In fact, that additional creative value is an important part of accelerating the upward growth of society. Think of that creative value as aspirational, something in the soul that longs for improvement and betterment.

In times of economic distress, there is always a call for a retreat to only intrinsic and added value. Retailers' first ventures in competing with their brand suppliers historically involved offering intrinsic plus added value private-label products only. The cutting edge today in retailing, however, is heavily dependent on building strong own-label brands, far removed from the old white label generics, as can be seen in retailers such as Trader Joe's. This is shifting the balance of power in retailing and placing more emphasis on understanding how shoppers interact with brands in the store.

Although retailers have learned how to create brands (creative value), they have long assaulted the concept of brands by insisting on cutting prices to promote them. This strategy suggests to customers that brands were overpriced at their regular retail prices. Although the relationship between the manufacturer and retailer is often seen as a great struggle over the value created from shopping, this does not have to be the case. In fact, as we consider next, both retailers and brand owners can often do better if they work together to serve the shopper better.

A Refreshing Change: Working Together to Sweeten Sales

Assuming that both retailers and manufacturers want to sell products to consumers, if they understand shoppers better, they can work together more effectively to use in-store marketing in more sophisticated ways. ID Magasin, for example, worked with chewing gum manufacturer Dandy, a business unit of confectionery giant Cadbury-Schweppes, to increase category sales by as much as 40% by introducing "refreshment cues" in the pre-checkout area of Swiss retailer Pilatus Markt.

In-store research in 2001 examined how shoppers interacted with chewing gum displays at the checkouts. The company filmed, interviewed, and counted thousands of shoppers at three checkouts, each of which was merchandised differently to enable comparison of different concepts. Representative customers were also fitted with a point-of-focus/eye mark recorder to identify the visual cues used in purchasing decisions. Researchers discovered that customers had stopped actively shopping by the time they reached the checkout. Because the customers were no longer shopping—just visiting—the products didn't have a chance of stopping, holding, and selling.

The researchers realized they needed a trigger to reignite the shopping mode at the checkout. And, because "freshening" is the overwhelming motive for purchasing chewing gum, researchers recommended that refreshment cues be introduced in the approach to the checkout area. The company then employed a group of experts to establish the visual elements that signal refreshment. The group recommended imagery that strongly communicated refreshment and which shoppers could instantly decode and associate with chewing gum. Dandy next commissioned in-store marketing material based on these signals for use in the key pre-checkout area. There were four graphic directions, each of which could be adapted for individual retail customers to promote the entire chewing gum category.

The next stage of the project was to confirm that refreshment and breath-freshening cues in the pre-checkout area do increase sales in the chewing gum category, and by how much. Dandy undertook research in two stores in Denmark, Kvickly supermarket and OBS hypermarket. Overall, nearly 20,000 customers were filmed at four checkouts in each outlet. Two checkouts per outlet had the trial setup and two provided experimental control. Dandy found that the new point-of-purchase material did indeed stimulate consumers to revert to shopping mode and attracted more of them to that checkout area. The new strategy increased the sales of all the categories represented in the display by an amazing 40% and Dandy's sales by up to 44%.

This is a major boost in sales just by retailers and manufacturers working together to understand shopper behavior. The retailer had to rethink its checkouts. The manufacturer had to rethink its in-store marketing. This is a different relationship than a passive retailer receiving stocking fees from a brand owner to gain shelf space. This is creating a more compelling sales opportunity for shoppers, reflecting an understanding of the three moments of truth for the shopper. If visitors are not converted to shoppers and shoppers are not converted into buyers, there is no sale. Working together, the retailer and manufacturer increased sales, which benefits both of them.

Beyond Category Management

As this example illustrates, collaboration between retailers and manufacturers can help both. This partnership between manufacturers and retailers moves beyond traditional category management to active cooperation in management of parts of the store, or even total store management.

To understand this evolution, we need to consider the evolution of the concept of category management over the last decade or so, as retailers and their brand partners began to realize they needed to take a more shopper-centric approach. Category management began in the early 1990s when Brian Harris of The Partnering Group set out a number of "best practices" for collaboration between suppliers and retailers. Basic category management, still in widespread use, involves retailers and suppliers using sales data to answer questions such as: How should the products on the shelf be segmented? What should the layout be? How can SKUs be optimized? How many items should be on the shelf? Which ones? More brands or fewer brands? What about different pack sizes?

The next level, category reinvention, has come to the forefront over the last few years. This is far more extensive, going beyond segmentation, assortment, and pricing decisions to include such elements as themes, fixtures, signage, size, layout, location, paths, adjacencies, flow, assortment, and planograms. This approach is becoming more prevalent because it is more engaging and encourages higher levels of conversion by offering a more emotional experience. A meat department, for example, might be creatively reinvented to look like a butcher shop. The coffee aisle might be redesigned to give a coffeehouse experience.

A New Era of Active Retailing: Total Store Management

Category management, aisle management, and even store management are blunt instruments. They lump products and categories together. Item management, on the other hand, is a scalpel, targeting the small number of items in the store that are major levers for sales. The typical approach to category management is for every category to have its place in the store. But if the individual products were instead totally randomized through the store, the shopper would be more exposed to more categories. Taking this approach to this extreme might lead to chaos, but secondary placements in the store do move retail in this direction by putting items in unexpected places, and managing individual items that drive store sales. The Long Tail of the store may be organized by categories, but the Big Head should be placed where shoppers can find it.

A third and higher level of category and aisle management is emerging, which is a natural progression from category management and the drive to create a real partnership between active brand owners and active retailers. Total store management takes a much broader perspective, with manufacturers working with retailers to design their total store layouts. This goes to the specifics for all the major categories, both in organization and arrangement in the main store, as well as in the promotional store. This progression from category management to aisle management and on to total store management can be seen as part of the accelerating movement from passive to active retailing that is now underway.

There are several reasons why this approach is attractive, particularly to larger brand owners. First, they often have products all over the store. Coca-Cola, for example, has products in the water section, in juices, in teas, and so on. Anything the brand owner can do to maximize the performance of the total store is going to improve its business. Second, when companies have a very large category—confectionery, say—overseeing the store in a holistic way means they can exploit their positions not just in the primary display areas, but also in the secondary, promotional display areas such as endcaps and the checkout, where an average 30% of purchases are made. Instead of fighting for space in the center aisles where shoppers are reluctant to come, manufacturers can take their brands out to the shoppers more effectively by looking at the total store.

A sophisticated large European confectionery manufacturer, for example, worked with a major retail partner to determine the ideal layout for stores, addressing the following questions:

- **Identifying leaders:** What are the steering categories in the retailer's stores, which genuinely move traffic? Remember, there are typically a small group of categories that do move traffic, the leaders—the rest are just along for the ride.

- **Arrangement:** In which order should different categories within a given arrangement ideally be placed?

- **Interaction:** In what way is the usage of different categories influenced by the location of other categories?

- **Order:** What is the optimal order of planned categories, impulse categories, and the categories "in between" (if they exist)?

All these questions are essentially *behavioral* questions. That is, if we can understand exactly how all the shoppers *behave* in the present store, this will serve as the foundation guide to how it might be altered to enhance that behavior to the mutual benefit of shoppers, the retailer, and their brand suppliers. To study shopper behavior, researchers began by analyzing how shoppers move through the store. In this case, data was collected by "shadowing" shoppers, recreating their trip with various behavioral annotations on a web tablet, as illustrated in Figure 10.1. The paths of individual shoppers were charted, as shown in the right side of the figure, and then paths of many shoppers were amalgamated. The methodology used here, *Personal PathTracker*, is one of many methods for creating this data, including radio-frequency idenification (RFID) tracking, video tracking, or shopper vision tracking.

Figure 10.2 shows the trip progression of these many shoppers in a stylized form. The numbers indicate how far along in the average shopping trip the shopper is, beginning at the lower left (0.7 = 7% of the trip) to 1.8 and 2.8 to the right, and so on, through the store to the 9.2 at the end of the store. The numbers are across many shoppers so the reason it doesn't go from 0 to 10 is that no matter how many people are heading one direction, there is always someone going the other direction. If nearly everyone ends their shopping trip at the checkout, there will be someone who begins there and moves in the opposite direction, both in terms of traffic flow, on the right, and time point (progression) in the trip. The arrows in the right side of Figure 10.2 represent the dominance of traffic, not the volume of shoppers. (A small arrow, for example, means that the number of people flowing both ways is about even. A larger arrow means that traffic is predominantly in that direction.) The researchers used the metrics summarized in Table 10.1 to understand shopping behavior in the store.

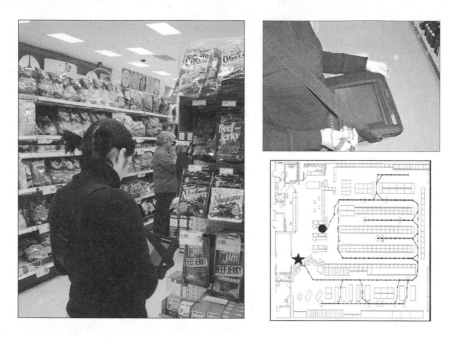

Figure 10.1 Shadowing shoppers, researchers follow shoppers and take notes on a web tablet.

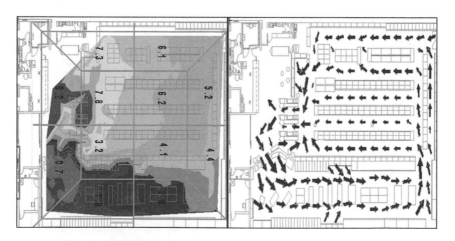

Figure 10.2 The progression of shoppers, showing patterns of movement.

Table 10.1 Metrics for Shopper Behavior

For Every Category in Store	For Every Shopper
Reach (visit %)	Duration of shopping trip (seconds)
Stopping (shop % divided by visit %)	Proportion of store visited (%)
Closing (purchase % divided byshop %)	Proportion of categories visited (%)
Holding: of buyers (buy time—seconds)	
Holding: of buyers and nonbuyers (dwell time—seconds)	
Trip progression (% of trip completed at the point in the trip)	
Walking speed (feet per second)	

The complete flow and adjacency analysis produced six key insights, as follows:

- **Understanding store and aisle traffic flow, hot spots and cold spots, and target shopper segments:** Researchers gained insight into the dynamics of movement of individual shoppers, as well as the overall flow of the crowd. This allowed identification of points of congestion and fixture location issues that might restrict traffic flow to all parts of the store. The goal was to open up and encourage traffic in an orderly way, to maximize the opportunity to offer the shopper the right merchandise at the most receptive point in their shopping trip.

- **Identifying "leader" categories—high performers for stopping and buying power:** These "leaders" may be identified in the Vital Quadrant™ analysis discussed in Chapter 2, "Transitioning Retailers from Passive to Active Mode," There we saw that there is not an iron-clad identity of these across all stores, but certain categories do appear again and again on the leader list. We also identified a series of categories through statistical clustering of shoppers by their trip behavior, which are common to the largest groups of shoppers, whether for quick, fill-in, or stock-up trips. Even though the metrics and analytical approach are not identical, there is significant overlap between the groups.

Other independent groups, working with RFID trip data, using intelligent agent modeling, found a similar group of categories whose impact on the shopping trip accounted for the total store traffic, in terms of density and flow. This type of convergence from multiple analytical approaches gives us added confidence, not only in the role of the leader categories, but also that the great majority of categories in the store *do not* drive shopping behavior and that purchases occur largely incidentally to those driven by the leaders.

- **Determining the ideal placement of "leader" categories to maximize performance and improve flow throughout the store:** Categories with high stopping power (visitor to shopper conversion) are given priority early in the shopper's trip (progression). This gets the shopper started off on the right foot, by beginning to fill the basket early. This also means that they're willing to spend more time on these purchases, making more of them, because they will tend to shop faster and faster, or spend less and less time, the longer they are in the store. It is also helpful to consider category buy time, trip type, and level of planned or impulse purchasing of the category.

- **Identifying leader category "affinities":** Affinity means that when one product is purchased, then another is often purchased as well. This analysis helps determine the placement of these affinity categories to maximize their performance and improve flow throughout the store. Because we have data on trip progression, we can then place these affinity categories in the right order in the path of the shopper.

- **Placing remaining categories using similar analysis procedures:** Once the leaders are positioned, the remaining categories can be placed based on margins and relevance to the other categories, as well as the guidelines offered for niche, high interest, average, and underdeveloped categories.

- **Identifying ideal placement, contents, and messaging for promotional (secondary) displays:** This is done through visual audits of stores—what's seen and what's not seen—as well as a detailed accounting of the exposure to shoppers of various endcaps in stores.

The results for this specific store were impressive, with post-redesign surveys showing that shoppers were very satisfied with the results and were likely to recommend the store to others. Specific sales lift improvements cannot be disclosed, due to proprietary concerns, but management consistently reports sales increases from a few percentage points to double digits after active retailing redesigns.

Pitching a Category's Emotional Tone More Precisely

One of the biggest questions retailers and brand owners have to answer is how to promote individual categories in the store. What should the emotional tone of each one be? Siemon Scammell-Katz introduced a set of powerful tools for merchandise promotional planning to address the type of promotions appropriate for various categories.

The foundation of the methodology was the evaluation of in-store shopping metrics from a large number of shoppers in a single U.K. supermarket linked to data from the same shoppers, as tracked over years in the TNS World Panel. Researchers found that two of the most significant variables in conversion rates are *buy time* (how long the purchase takes in minutes) and *purchase frequency* (on an annual basis). This analysis helped identify the emotional involvement of different categories. The categories are divided up based on these metrics and then restated in terms of the emotional mindset that shoppers are likely experiencing, given their investment of time in the purchase and its frequency, as illustrated in Figure 10.3.

Those emotional mindsets then provide guidance for appropriate communication strategies, to reach shoppers with the right type of messages, for the right emotional states associated with specified categories. For example, the categories that are high frequency but low involvement are most likely to be staples (in the lower-right quadrant). This in turn leads to a rational communication strategy appropriate to the category. For staples, for example, it should be about range reduction and ease of shopping. For "enjoyment" categories, it should be "theater," and for "involvement" products, the focus should be on providing information. Although this is a practical scheme for managing communication strategy in the

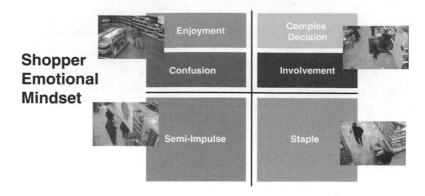

Figure 10.3 Connecting with the shopper's emotional mindset.

store, it does not, of course, dictate the creative strategy. As noted earlier, a hot pink package might capture attention but may not make the sale, so there is plenty of room for creativity in communication.

The examples we have used for illustration are largely drawn from supermarkets and consumer-packaged-goods (CPG) or fast-moving-consumer-goods (FMCG) retailing. Our largest experience has been in this arena. But the most valuable asset here is not the massive normative database providing insight to CPG/FMCG, but rather the organized, scientific approach to retailing. We have applied this schema across a broad spectrum of retail trade around the world, including sectors such as autoparts, home electronics, phone stores, gift/card stores, clothing, jewelry, and so on. Moving from country to country, and across classes of trade changes the values of the metrics, but it does not change the organizational paradigm. Wherever we have gone in the world, we have found that most people are right-handed (hence the inherent trend to navigate a store in the counterclockwise direction). In similar fashion, across wide swathes of human behavior, there is more that makes us alike than different.

Retailers Control Reach

One challenge in the traditional relationship between retailer and brand owner is that the retailer controls the first stage of the sale: reach.

Retailers control the design and layout of the store, so brands usually need to work within this framework. The passive retailer views reach as visiting: It's the shopper's responsibility to visit a product if they want it. Passive retailers also want to keep shoppers in the store as long as possible, so if products are difficult to find, or inconveniently placed, they reckon they are doing their job well. This attitude, which is locked into so many retailers' minds, is unhelpful. Supermarkets, for example, usually put the milk at the far corner of the store because they believe it will make people go there. Well, they very possibly won't. Instead, they may stop at the convenience store or a competitor if it's easier.

This creates great problems for brands because brand suppliers have to work through retailers to accomplish *anything* in terms of reach. First, people tend to shop with the subconscious expectation that they are going to buy just so much "stuff." When they have the right amount, they are going to leave the store as quickly as they can. They are not going to anguish over whether they have Brand A or Brand B. In fact, even if they usually buy a particular brand, and the retailer moves it elsewhere, the shopper might not realize it and no longer use that brand for some time, if at all. This is the real challenge for the brand owner: The retailer is relatively indifferent about what people buy as long as it is a reasonable amount and they do so with some frequency and efficiency. Brand owners try to address this careless attitude through promotional fees, but it is a crude instrument. Brands make the real difference in stopping power—after the shopper comes into the product's orbit. But the shopper first has to get close enough to see the brand. To address this challenge of reach, brand owners need to work with retailers to more effectively position the brand in the store.

After the shopper comes into reach of the product, its "visual equity" from branding and packaging makes a huge difference, particularly among the crowded Long Tail products. Packaging is the number-one communication vehicle at retail. It is the most viable method the brand has for communicating with shoppers. The shape and color of the package—visual equity—that consumers associate with the brand (such as Coca-Cola's color red) allow the consumer to quickly identify products among the clutter at the point of purchase, in the pantry, or on the tabletop.

The Urgent Need for Retailing Evolution

Retailers are harvesting massive cash from the brand manufacturers for representation in the promotional area. Meanwhile, brand manufacturers are spending further billions on researching how to manage the main store. The two parties are both distant from actual shopper behavior—to the financial detriment of both. These economics are the foundation of the supermarket's profits but are killing the brands, whereas the shoppers tolerate this modus operandi because so far there are few other options.

We reemphasize here that we are not advocating retail revolution but are excited about the continuing evolution and hope to contribute to it and perhaps accelerate it. What we want to eliminate is the thinking that says: "Shoppers are in the store, and it is just too difficult to conduct research there. And it is also much too difficult to master the promotional store. So we, as the brands, will continue to invest in aisle/shelf management. And we, as the retailers, will continue to develop our promotional store for ourselves." They should both be focusing more attention on the promotional store—the Big Head. That is where the money and the opportunities are.

We also suggest that the strategy of putting promotional pricing on the items on the endcaps is seriously misguided. Instead of trying to train shoppers to think: "If I want to get a deal, I should just grab something right here," they should think: "If I want a deal, I know I'm going to go down that aisle to get it." Retailers and brand owners should understand that their pricing and promotional strategy is highly irrational.

Brand suppliers, meanwhile, need to know how to maximize and optimize their secondary display performances: where the displays should be, what kinds of products should be on them, the type of message to attract the shopper and convert them to buy, and so on. It is not that brands do not work in this second store but that, because it is far more complicated and difficult, the focus tends to be on the section of flat wall in the main store over which they have some influence or control, and which is much easier to study and understand.

Promotional spending of big brands distorts the shopping experience in ways that are not good for the shopper, the retailer, and, often, even the brand owner. If I were a retailer, I would fiercely manage the Big Head strictly for the benefit of the shopper, and insist that the promotional "crack cocaine" not override the behaviorally expressed wishes of my shoppers. If you don't know how to manage the Big Head part of the store strictly in the shoppers' interest, learn or retire. I would continue to allow the Long Tail to be a battleground for the brands—and profitable for them, too. But the rational ones of them will want to know what they are getting from their share of that trillion dollars of retail spending. No problem. It is urgent that you know the value of every inch of real estate, every aisle location, every end-aisle display, every shipper, every lobby display, and all the in-store media. I'm talking about approximately monetizing every inch of the store.

Alphabet Soup: The Power of Inefficiency

Although we stress the importance of making the best use of shoppers' time, there is an exception to any rule. Years ago, Campbell's Soup recognized that its soup, with all those little red and white cans with identical labels in many varieties, represented some real challenges for shoppers attempting to find the specific items they wanted. The manufacturer realized that this variety might create significant angst for shoppers. Managers reasonably expected that they might reduce this angst if they could place the soups in a more rational order, so shoppers could quickly find cream of celery or chicken noodle without scanning through the whole selection.

Seeing Items in the context of their Brand, Category, and the Full Store

As we've pointed out before, much of the suboptimal performance at retail is a direct consequence of the gulf between shoppers, who buy individual items, and very few of them in comparison to what the other three retail management tiers must deal with. The issue is focus, the natural province of shoppers who only buy a few of what the brand, category, and full store have a large variety of. So here's a way to look at one slice of data most closely related to the shopper, with the context for the brand, category, and store:

| | | Store Total | $30 million | | Category Total | $894,976 | | Brand Total | $82,607 | |
| | | | | | Share of Store | 3.0% | | Share of Category | 9.2% | |
Item #	Brand Item Sales	Share of Store	Cum Shares	Item Rank in Store	Share of Category	Cum Shares	Item Rank in Cat	Share of Brand	Cum Shares	Item Rank in Brand
05	$21,098	0.10%	14.1%	100	2.4%	8.3%	3	25.5%	25.5%	1
03	$14,587	0.00%	18.8%	171	1.6%	15.5%	7	17.7%	43.2%	2
13	$10,229	0.00%	24.7%	294	1.1%	32.8%	20	12.4%	55.6%	3
01	$9,392	0.00%	26.3%	336	1.0%	34.9%	22	11.4%	67.0%	4
12	$6,717	0.00%	33.6%	535	0.8%	46.4%	35	8.1%	75.1%	5
09	$5,054	0.00%	39.9%	770	0.6%	54.0%	47	6.1%	81.2%	6
06	$3,721	0.00%	46.6%	1,117	0.4%	67.9%	75	4.5%	85.7%	7
08	$3,643	0.00%	47.2%	1,143	0.4%	68.3%	76	4.4%	90.1%	8
10	$3,208	0.00%	50.3%	1,349	0.4%	72.1%	86	3.9%	94.0%	9
04	$2,820	0.00%	53.7%	1,593	0.3%	75.8%	97	3.4%	97.4%	10
90	$2,138	0.00%	61.1%	2,205	0.2%	83.6%	126	2.6%	100.0%	11

This is essentially a brand table. It lists the 11 items in this brand within this store in the first column, and the items' total store sales in the second column (as a fraction of $30 million in total store sales). The critical factor is the ranking in the last column. Notice that four of the brand items deliver two-thirds of that brand's sales. For the brand, improving sales is a matter of focusing on those four, in the order of priority that they represent to shoppers.

The greatest opportunity for increasing sales for this brand is to increase sales of item #05—the top-ranking item for this brand. In fact, a 12% increase in sales for just that one item will increase the total for the brand by 3%. Not a bad lift for a quarter. Throw in just a little focus on items 03, 13, and 01—say 5% lift for those three—and you will have another 2% total brand sales increase. Add that to the 3% from the Top Seller impact the brand achieves, to give a 5% total sales lift.

But notice that we are ranking by dollar sales to focus on the top, and looking at the accumulating contribution of every item to the total brand sales. Help the winners win more and you will make the shoppers happy, because they are shouting at you, "this is the one that we love." Make the shoppers #1, and they will make you #1.

Now look at the rest of the table for your context. Notice the impact of the excellent performance of the top four items in this brand—and then look at that in the context of the category. The brand's top 1, 2,

3, and 4 are ranked 3, 7, 20, and 22 for the category. The category manager probably has #1 and several other top sellers in the top half dozen of category sales in his own brand. Unless the brand has #1, or #2 in the category, they are unlikely to be in the pole position of category captain.

This demonstrates why few brands have any real ability to drive merchandising and category management in the store. Any but these large-selling brands are likely to have only a small impact on the full store. The small brand has to do nearly all of their outreach to the shopper through their own package—their "voice in the store."

But small brands, take heart! Every small brand contributes something to total store sales—look at the first three share-accumulative-rank values of this particular brand in the context of the total store. The key to growing your brand is relentless focus on what the shopper wants—1, 2, and 3. Listen to what the shopper wants.

Review Questions

1. Discuss how the development of the retail industry caused retailers to ignore shoppers and shopper behavior focusing on other KPIs? Why should this change now?

2. Describe how the evolution of retailer own or private label brands could change the power balance between national brand manufacturers and retailers.

3. Thinking of category management—what actions could retailers and brand manufacturers consider together to improve shopper experience in the category and profit outcomes for all stakeholders?

4. Reflect on the key differences between a traditional tool of category management and a more progressive approach of aisle and whole store management. How do relationships between retailers and manufacturers need to change to make this new approach work?

5. Discuss the concept of "leader" categories. What is the role of the "leader" categories in shopper stopping and buying power and the whole store-management approach?

6. Describe the main sources of supermarket profits in decreasing order of importance and contribution.

7. What does the author mean by "reach" as a shopper metric? What is the difference between how passive and active retailers influence reach? What challenges passive approach to reach present to brand manufacturers? Discuss why putting milk at the very back of a store could be a problem.

8. Discuss the elements of retail evolution. Which parts and practices of a passive store could be improved and how?

Endnotes

1. www.thecrossbordergroup.com

2. Neff, Jack, "Brand Giants Weakened as Retailers Get Savvier," *Advertising Age,* October 6, 2008.

11

Conclusion Game-Changing Retail: A Manifesto

I n the seven years since we published the first edition of this book, retailers around the world have practiced and proven the scientific retailing principles summarized below. Here is a distillation of critical action points that will lead to double-digit sales and profit increases. Some retailers have achieved as much as *five times* more sales over the past many years by deploying these principles.

The single greatest update to the first edition of this book is our analysis of the relative strengths and weaknesses of both bricks-and-mortar retailers *and* online retailing. Both modes have inherent strengths, but 100 years of successful bricks retailing with little change in the rules of competition have imbedded weaknesses and unrealized strengths in that mode. The emergence of online and the entirely new set of rules it brings poses both opportunity and risk for the bricks retailer.

Amazon is not the only competition for bricks retailing that is winning by the new rules. Globally, all of the Big Head stores are knocking the ball out of the park. Costco has now climbed to the #2 global position, behind only Walmart. Lidl and Aldi are also thriving with Big Head stores, as has Stew Leonard's for many years.

In spite of this, Long Tail stores like Walmart continue to disastrously manage their Big Heads and are a long way from posing any serious long-term competition to Amazon. In Chapter 1, we outline the problem in more detail, including an outline plan for the way forward. Here we again outline a manifesto, with distinguishing programs for retailers and their brand suppliers.

The adage "The good is the enemy of the great," is possibly nowhere more applicable than in retailing. With a global population nearing seven billion, the world demand for goods and services is swelling. The movement from developing societies using traditional retailing to highly developed societies adopting modern retailing continues apace. *Demand* alone has been the driving force behind good retailing, globally.

A striking feature of good retailing has been an almost single-minded focus on matching the right selection of merchandise to the customer base, with little or no regard to the *time* it costs shoppers to acquire the merchandise. Good retailers, with their suppliers' complicity, regularly squander 80% of their shopper's time. Great retailers will make productive use of that lost time. This is the dominant advantage of Amazon's selling: Amazon can match specific products with specific shoppers with incredible *efficiency* that bricks retailers largely ignore (see Chapter 3).

A new movement in retailing will change the global game. The principles outlined next are listed roughly in terms of urgent priority for those who aspire to survive and thrive when their competition is not simply good, but *great*! In most cases, the advance is one of recognizing important distinctions, and responding appropriately and distinctly, rather than leaving it to shoppers to sort it out for themselves. Although all of these principles are relevant to both retailers and their brand suppliers, the first five deserve the greatest attention by retailers, whereas the last five are most relevant to suppliers:

- **Focus on the short trip.** For supermarkets around the world (the same principle applies to all classes of trade), half of all shopping trips result in the purchase of five or fewer items, with one item being the most common. These short trips typically account for one-third of store sales. The new strategy is to increase the size of each of those baskets by one or two items. Quick trippers spend money very fast, and getting them to buy one or two more items is far easier than motivating stock-up shoppers to buy ten or twenty more items. This focus on the quick trip could deliver an easy 30% sales lift and a lot more when the synergies with other types of trips become apparent.

- **Focus on the vital few items that drive success.** Fewer than 1,000 items, and perhaps as few as 100, make the difference between good retailing and great retailing. Which ones are they? Just as the store transaction log tells how many items are in each shopper's basket (Focus 1), it also identifies the exact items. Dump all the baskets together, sort them by item (SKU, UPC, EAN, PLU, and so on), count each item, and rank them from the highest-selling to the least-sold. Your shoppers vote every day for what they want to buy. Good retailers don't know or don't care about this, but great retailers do. Good retailers are obsessed about what they and their suppliers want to sell to shoppers. Great retailers are obsessed about what shoppers want to buy!

- **Display the vital few (or the Big Head) along the Dominant Path your shoppers take.** Good retailers expect shoppers to find the merchandise they want. Great retailers learn all they can about what the shoppers want and take it to them! This, of course, presupposes a modicum of understanding about the shopper's Dominant Path. Good retailers are unsure. Great retailers have this down pat. Points #2 and #3 are components of the new science of item management, a far sharper instrument than the category management used by all good retailers. Point #3 distinguishes high-value real estate within the store from the rest.

- **The most important promotion is place, not price.** In a typical store, retailers promote 2% of the total items in the store at any one time on end-of-aisle displays or other secondary promotional displays. This 2% of items may constitute a full 30% of all the sales in the store. However, half the shoppers who purchase an item from one of these promotional displays are unaware that it is at a reduced price. Of the half of the shoppers who are aware, half of them do not care about the price. Good retailers are locked in a mindset that price considerations dominate shopping. Great retailers realize that there are other currencies that matter to shoppers in addition to money: time and angst. Great retailers focus on value and convenience. Convenience means fast. Using less of the shopper's time will lead to more sales. Hence, Sorensen's primary principle of retail sales: The faster you sell, the more you will sell.

- **Open space attracts!** Shoppers compete with products for space in the store. Good retailers might be oblivious to this competition, and freely tip the balance in favor of the products over the shoppers. Jamming the store with products creates lots of narrow aisles and psychic discomfort for shoppers. Great retailers refuse to sacrifice shopper space, and use wide promenades to lead crowds of shoppers through a speedy, efficient, high-dollar trip. The allocation of open space is of paramount importance in store design, but there is no single recipe for success.

The following five principles are more closely aligned with the concerns of brand suppliers:

- **Balance the role of your store's vital few with the rest of your extensive line.** Keep offering the Long Tail, but make it easier for the shopper to reach the vital few items they want to buy: the Big Head. Although sales of the other 30,000 plus items, the Long Tail, do add up to significant sales and profits in aggregate, on an individual basis they are not consequential in total sales. They play a far different and distinct role. The Long Tail attracts shoppers to the store, but when they get there, they buy a habitual, predictable, select few items from the Big Head. Amazon's reputation as the "Everything Store" reassures me that I can always find the few books I want to purchase each month among the 50 million they have in stock. But Amazon would go out of business if every time I logged onto their site I was forced to spend hours searching through thousands of books that did not interest me in order to find the one or two I wanted to buy. Amazon has reached the pinnacle of retail (conceptually) by quickly and efficiently delivering to its shoppers exactly what they want, exactly when they want it. This is the challenge for all retail stores, online or offline: How do they maintain the huge product selection that assures shoppers the store has anything they might desire without suppressing sales by burying the vital few items they will buy from that massive selection? The key is distinction, so that the shopper can immediately reach and *recognize* the vital few.

- **Paying to get your own vital few into favorable placement within the store makes sense, depending on the "reach" of the location.** To make a sale, you must reach the shopper with the product, then the product must stop shoppers, and then you close the sale. As noted in point #4, place is more important than price.

In fact, charging cut prices at high-value promotional locations devalues both the real estate and the brand. *Selective* price promotion would be more appropriate for Long Tail items displayed in-aisle, and particularly for those items that are closest in sales rank to the vital few.

- **Focus on the vital few within your brand and that of your competition. Some of your own vital few will not make it into the retailers' vital few.** Just as retailers can more readily obtain double-digit sales increases for their vital few, so you can more easily turn your top few sellers into super performers than bring up the laggards. Again, Long Tail principles apply—the Long Tail attracts, and the vital few sell. Maintaining a reasonable Long Tail is essential both for purposes of attraction, as well as for the competitive imperative. Make clear distinctions in your planning and thinking on these issues.

- **Reach you can buy, but stopping power and closing power are inherent to the product, primarily through the package.** Both stopping power and closing power can be measured for individual products, as well as for categories. The significance is that some products are good at attracting attention but poor at closing the sale, whereas others are good at closing, but can't seem to stop the traffic. Besides remedial package design, appropriate shelf management and promotional strategies can increase the stopping and closing power of existing products.

- **Stores are excessively verbose. Products and packaging are a significant part of the clutter.** Using iconic images, colors, shapes, and appropriate emotional totems is a better way to connect to shoppers than more words. Using category reinvention, you can upgrade the emotional feel of an entire aisle or department. The coffee aisle, for example, can be redesigned to give it a café ambiance. Remember, the goal is to make your winners win bigger. This will be more easily done with large displays that you can dominate—appropriate to your vital few. And now on the near and far horizon, digital media, even interactive media, is a tool of greatest value to you as the brand owner. This means that you can win even in good retailers. Great retailers will expect and appreciate your cooperation with game-changed retailing!

The Package Is the Brand's Ambassador

In general, there are two types of research: *laboratory* and *real-world* (or *natural*). The laboratory variety typically consists of conducting experiments in a carefully controlled environment, where everything *except* the factors being studied are held constant. This type of research presumes that the researcher *knows* what needs to be studied, and can hold all factors not being studied constant.

Then one factor is varied systematically, to see its impact on another factor. The vast majority of my retail studies have been conducted in stores, where controlling things is nearly impossible. Not all of my research, but a large share of it, is real-world. Here's a small study with large implications—the evolution of four brand images over time, varying over anything from a few weeks to a century. You'll see why, and hopefully learn some valuable things about *brand* value and the use of packaging for communication. Consider the four examples in Figure 11.1.

Figure 11.1 After potentially billions of impressions to the subconscious of millions of your customers, make changes to your identity with fear and trembling!

In every case, the reality is that the package on the top was *much* more successful than the one on the bottom. In general, the images on the top seem simpler, cleaner, with the images on the bottom being more cluttered, and therefore actually poorer in communicating with shoppers.

Without going into confidential detail on any of these, the first example (the two gums on the left) illustrates an Olympic promotion that actually *suppressed* sales, just as the third example (the two orange juices) seriously suppressed sales when shoppers actually could no longer find their familiar orange juice.

The second example (the two soaps) had two things going for it in raising sales of soap. Obviously the top image (and text) is much simpler and cleaner. But it also makes use of the "crowd-social marketing" we highly applaud. That is, why wouldn't anyone, unless totally committed to something else buy something that is "America's favorite?" And sure enough, the simpler, cleaner package delivers more sales.

The fourth example (the two soup labels) illustrates the "evolution" of a label over a 100-year period! Actually, it is more like *non*-evolution, given how slight the changes. But this is brilliant marketing, fully leveraging the massive investment in the brand—by shoppers—over a very long period. This is habitual marketing at its best. The first three are not total disasters on this point—well, maybe #3 is. Remember Neale Martin's "Habit: The 95% of Behavior Marketers Ignore?" #2 Makes a change by replacing a complicated statement with a simple statement, whereas #3 virtually obliterates anything that might be associated with the brand at the habitual, subconscious level, built up over probably billions of exposures.

These are just a few of the principles that can be extracted from the research that informs this book. Although these general principles hold across many retail settings and types of products, precise solutions need to be tailored to the specific context. Above all, *great* retailers and brand owners continue to experiment. They test to find out what works, and what doesn't, so they can continue to improve their strategies. This rigorous investigation and testing is how we arrived at the principles discussed previously. Good retailers and brand suppliers, on the other hand, stick with the tried-and-true conventional wisdom. But as the world changes through new technologies, consumer shifts, and new competitors, the great retailers and brand suppliers create the new conventional wisdom and tailor it precisely to their own situations. In that context, the preceding ten points represent an initial hypothesis for this process of ongoing experimentation.

Review Questions

1. Why should an active retailer focus on short trips?

2. How do you identify the few critical items of the Big Head?

3. What is the role of the Big Head and Dominant Path in item management?

4. Discuss why price discount might not be as important to promoting a product in a store as the prime location in-store.

5. What is the role of open space in shopper navigation and directing shopper traffic to achieve better reach?

6. Consider the role of the Long Tail. How do you manage it more effectively?

7. What can brand managers negotiate with retailers to increase reach to their products/brands?

8. What can retailers and brand managers do to reduce in-store clutter and streamline shopper environment in a category? In an aisle? In the entire store?

9. What is the role of packaging in shopper navigation? What principles should be used in packaging design to make it work in-store in the long term?

Afterword

Endcaps and the "Promotional" Store

A fter completing the second edition, I am uneasy about "the elephant in the room," so-to-speak. But let me give you a few thoughts before I clarify that—and then some more interesting/validating data!

The "science of shopping" rightly has as its focus first on the shopper and *then* on the products. But there are actually at least five entities directly connected to that two-point nexus of shoppers and products. More or less in their order of priority *from the shopper's point of view,* they are:

- The shoppers themselves.

- The products those shopper seek, plus the host of "also ran" products that are relatively rarely purchased.

- The store itself—the building, displays, fixtures, and various supplements (restrooms and so on).

- The retailer, in the sense of the staff, management, and the whole corporate image.

- The suppliers of goods (manufacturers, particularly branded), and sometimes services.

Interestingly, the suppliers have invested billions in studying the shoppers—#5 studying #1—but a large share of that research was basically trying to understand *people* and, secondarily, their reaction to the products—#2—with an increasing focus on that interaction inside real stores—#3. (That real interaction in real stores was a large part of the impetus for the growth of Sorensen Associates in the 90s, a lot of preparation for which occurred in the 80s.)

The retailers'—#4—major role has been the management of the physical store—#3—including staff and inventory—#2—and the all-important business relationship with suppliers—#5.

The "elephant in the room," so to speak, about these five prime components of retail is that they *all* are subject to changes that can range from hourly/daily/weekly to more glacial changes that occur over quarters/years/decades. The most active changes occur amongst the shoppers and the store merchandising. Just as an example, the Ehrenberg-Bass Institute has been prominent in discovering the inconstancy of shoppers—loyalty is a myth—and the necessity of steady recruitment of new shoppers for a store, just to stand still with respect to growth.

But the inconstancy we want to draw attention to here is about the perimeter of the store where most of the endcaps are, as well as a lot of "drop shippers," temporary displays prestocked with merchandise and shipped to the store, ready to be "dropped" anywhere on the floor there is space and availability to shoppers.

Now, endcaps are one of the most constant displays of promotional merchandise, usually—but not always—with prices reduced. A few of these, like the "battery endcap," are relatively constant even from year to year, but most of them change on a regular schedule of weekly, biweekly, and so on. And, appropriately, as valuable instore "media," that is, with exposure to shoppers, they are competitively priced for the suppliers—#5—to fund the retailer—#4.

From a research point of view, this regular churn of endcaps and a good deal of the store perimeter, is a serious impediment to the type of detailed xyz-t (location and time), both of products—#2—and people—#1—that has driven our scientific research of shopping. At present, it is very difficult to be as detailed and scientific about endcaps and promotional displays as we are about aisles. In aisles, both shoppers and products are regimented into orderly rows (aisles) and columns (shelves) which move—both in terms of sales and physical organization—at a glacial pace compared to the "promotional store." That is, a very large share of total store sales come from the dynamic "promotional store," not from the relatively static center-of-store aisles.

At a time when industry-standard thinking was that maybe 10% of total sales come from endcaps, by eye-tracking shoppers through one super-market we found that 50% of all Coca-Cola product sales came from promotional locations, mostly endcaps, and not from the aisles. In the much larger RFID-PathTracker study across nine nationally distributed, diverse supermarkets, we learned that across all the products in the store, 43% of the products are purchased from the perimeter/promotional part of the store, which probably has something like 20% of the individual item SKUs on display. What this means is that any given item displayed in the highly fluid area of the store is about twice as likely to be purchased as one displayed in the center-of-store aisles.

Predictive, Mathematical Modeling of Shoppers' In-Store Behavior

See: Guide to Shopping Norms—Dashboard; and Shopping Category Norms for Observe-Measure-Think. You may also want to visit Atlas, where all the normative data cited in these references were modeled into a center-of-store layout, with associated endcaps—but not the rest of the perimeter. You will need the user name (demo) and password (12345) to access an interactive online model that allows you to shuffle categories around, including endcaps, both by location and size of aisle displays, and to see the calculated performance of that design based on its actual performance across a national sampling of stores with millions of shopping trips.

But here's the problem: Our measurements are likely far more accurate for the center of the store than for the highly fluid endcap/promotional area. Thus, we understand more accurately the least important part of the store. This means our carefully measured category management and planogram design approaches some measure of scientific validity, but the management of the far more important promotional side of the store is still mostly a matter of art and horse-trading.

We often cite what we refer to as *the hierarchy of truth* in shopping research, in which exactly what shoppers buy in the store—as evidenced by the transaction logs—is at the pinnacle of the truth pyramid. This is not because the Tlog is a perfect report of sales in the store. And again, center-of-store aisles are the most reliable. But for those items, when they are sold in secondary locations, like endcaps, there is *no* simple way to determine which of multiple locations they might have come from. Our RFID PathTracker methods were very good for this, based on linking measured paths, foot by foot, to the scan-audit of the exact xyz location of every item in the store, and linking these to the shoppers' purchases at the checkout. However, these very costly methods are not practical for widespread, everyday use.

But there are many items in the store, particularly in the promotional part of the store, that don't even have a UPC look-up code for scanning, but may have a PLU, "price-look-up" code, particularly if it is an item sold by weight. This is just the tip of the iceberg, *at the pinnacle of truth* in the store. That is, the highest selling items often are least well identified in the transaction logs, because they are *not* standard, branded/coded merchandise. And they are also *most* fluid in moving around the store, whether on endcaps or other "promotional" locations. Another way to look at this is that the most important information about shopper behavior in the store (products and shoppers) is most difficult to obtain, reliably.

It's very easy to have a simplistic view of shopping. Some researchers either don't recognize the environment they are working in or simply sweep the complications under the rug. Okay, at times even I have been guilty on both counts. But I applaud the serious efforts my colleagues at Ehrenberg-Bass are making to identify exactly how much of each item is being sold off of each endcap, daily. At Accelerated Merchandising, we are making a special focus on the accurate measurement of the amount of time shoppers spend, in aggregate, before each and every display in stores. We're working through the details of that problem in some small stores, where the problems are as small as the stores. Figure A.1 shows a graphic from an endcap display study at a full-size supermarket.

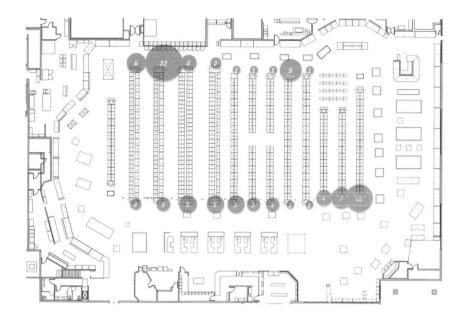

Afterword Figure A.1 Indexed shopper exposure to the end-caps in a supermarket.

Our goal has been to produce an accurate measure of exposures at end-caps. You can see that two or three endcaps get the lion's share of shopper exposures in this store. This should parallel the measurement of purchases at endcaps—see the sidebar "Endcaps Audit: Do Retailers Reduce Visual and Choice Complexity?"

Endcaps Audit: Do Retailers Reduce Visual and Choice Complexity?

Prior academic research has suggested that the effectiveness of an endcap could be due to the display featuring only one (or a few) brands, which means that the endcap's reduced visual complexity, competitive clutter, and choice overload makes it easier for shoppers to identify the product.

A new study by Australian researchers (Caruso et al., 2015[1]) conducted store audits of 550 endcaps across multiple retailers. It confirmed that retailers indeed practice what shoppers are likely to appreciate as a clutter-reduction approach. On average, 78% of endcaps had only one category present, 18% had two and 2% had three categories on display. These categories were most often high-penetration categories such as soft drinks, chips, and snacks. At a brand level, 47% of endcaps had one brand present, 20% had two brands, and 13% had three brands. Researchers also discovered that 93% of endcaps on price promotion have catalogue/advertising support, which suggests retailers are trying to highlight these products to shoppers before they even come to the store.

Endnotes

1. Source: Caruso, W., Bogomolova, S., Corsi, A., Cohen, J., Sharp, A. and Lockshin, L. 2015 Exploring the effectiveness of endcap locations in a supermarket: early evidence from in-store video observations, ANZMAC, Sydney.

Index

angled displays, 216–219

angst

Angst purchase state, 37

long-cycle purchasing, 194–195

anxiety, 142–143

assisting shopper navigation. *See* navigation

Autopilot purchase state, 37, 206

B

"bazaar" shopping designs, 213

behavior of shoppers. *See* shopper behavior

Berra, Yogi, 77

bidirectional search, 2–3

Big Head

Big Head stores, 226

creating easy access to, 256

displaying on dominant shopping path, 255

explained, 38–39

focus on, 257

managing, 59–63

most frequently purchased items, 169–170

product placement, 256–257

big-store strategy, 59

birth of self-service retail, 26–32

B. J.'s, 59–60

Bluetooth, measuring time in-store with, 54–55

Bohr, Niels, 15

BOPIS (buy-online-pick-up-in-store), 129

brand strategies

brand suppliers, 256–257

brand table, 249–251

brand value, 235–237, 258–260

context, 249–251

emotional tone, 245–246

need for retailing evolution, 248–249

packaging, 258–260

private-label brands, 231–237

reach, controlling, 246–247

retailer/manufacturer relationship, 237–239

stopping and closing power, 257

vital items, 256–257

brand suppliers, 256–257

bricks-and-mortar retailers

Amazonian techniques

affinity sales, 104–106

case study: Seattle store, 107–112

crowd-social marketing, 104–106

curated information, 107

immediate close, 101–104

Long Tail, 106

navigation, 96–101

selection, 101

BOPIS (buy-online-pick-up-in-store), 129

as convenience stores, 136

weaknesses of, 253

buy-online-pick-up-in-store (BOPIS), 129

C

Cadbury-Schweppes, 237–239

Campbell's Soup, 218–219, 249

capital, parked, 39

categories

categories purchased most often on quick trips, 167–168

category management, 238–239

category reinvention, 257

context, 249–251

destination category, 61–62

F

Fader, Peter
interview with

G

H

hedonic-time dimensions, 33

higher-cost purchases, 142–143

highest-selling items
    creating easy access to, 256
    displaying on dominant shopping
        path, 70–71
    focus on, 254–255, 257
    product placement, 256–257

history of retail, 25–32

holding power, 188–189

I

IBM, 231

iconic images, 257

ID Magasin, 237–239

ideal self-service retail experience,
    41–43

IKEA store design, 6

immediate close
    Amazon online sales, 90–91
    Amazonian techniques for bricks
        stores, 101–104

immersive experience, 147–149

impressions, 182–188

impulse category, 61–62

indecision, 142–143

inefficiency, power of, 218–219, 249

information, providing to customers
    Amazon online sales, 94–95
    Amazonian techniques for
        bricks stores, 107
    information acceleration, 118

information seeking, 147–149

insight needs, 156

in-store media, 182–188

in-store migration patterns
    checkout magnet, 210–211
    clockwise versus counterclockwise,
        210

importance of, 201–204

location hypothesis, 211

main store versus promotional
    store, 219–221

metrics, 205–206

open space
    "aisleness" of stores, 212–214
    offset shelves, 216
    orientation and layout, 216–219
    overview, 211–212
    sloping shelves, 215–216

overview, 199–201

PathTracker, 201–203

product hypothesis, 219

shopper direction, 207–210

shopper movement through stores,
    204–205

store design
    Big Head store, 226
    compound store, 225–226
    enhanced perimeter, 222–223
    inverted perimeter, 223–225
    overview, 221–222
    research into, 227
    serpentine design, 225

store entrances, 206–207

in-store visibility, improving,
    176–177

The Intel Experience, 149–150

Internet, effect on behavior studies,
    116–117

intrinsic value, 235–237

inverted perimeter, 223–225

J-K-L

journey of shoppers, 151–153

Kantar Retail, 15–16

labels, evolution of, 259

laboratory research, 258

layout of shelves, 216–219

leader categories, 243–244

leveraging purchase states, 26–28

Lewis, Robin, 93

licensing, 120–121

Lidl, 163–164, 253

life changes, 150

Linden, Greg, 88

location hypothesis, 211

Long Tail
    Amazon
        case study: Seattle store,
        110–111
        online sales, 93
        techniques for bricks stores, 106
    explained, 38–39
    managing, 76–81
    product categories, 80–81
    webby stores, 135–137

long-cycle purchasing
    consumer anxiety and indecision,
        142–143
    desire, building, 144–147, 149–150
    overview, 141–142
    romancing the sale, 144
    shopper engagement spectrum,
        147–149
    shopper's journey, 151–153
    shopping process, 143
    time, role of, 143

loyalty card programs, 234–235

M

Machado, Antonio, 199

main (primary) store, 219–221

management

Big Head, 59–63

category management, 238–239

Long Tail, 76–81

shopper navigation of store
    checklist, 71
    dominant shopping path, 67–71,
    255
    importance of, 63–71
    open spaces and sightlines, 5–10,
    66–67, 255–256
    shopper behavior, 63–66

shopper's time in-store, 53–59

total store management, 239–245

manufacturer/retailer relationship
    collaboration between retailers and
        manufacturers, 237–239
    private-label brands, 235–237

margin on sales, 233

marketing, crowd-social
    Amazon, 91–93
    bricks-and-mortar retailers,
        104–106
    definition of, 18–21

Marsh Supermarkets, 223–225

Martin, Neale, 37, 76

mathematical modeling of webby
    stores, 129–135

maximizers, 190

McDonald's, 207

McKinley, William, 173

McLaurin, Ian, 232

media, in-store, 182–188

MediaCart, 216

mediated sales, 85–86

meeting of the minds, 85–86

merchandising
    Accelerated Merchandising, 10
    Guiness case study, 176–177
    merchandise promotional
        planning, 245–246

P

pace of shopping trips, 121

packaging

importance of, 247, 258–260

stopping and closing power, 257

verbosity, 257

Paley Park, 200–201

pantries, stores as, 35–36

Pão de Açucar, 215

The Paradox of Choice (Schwartz), 93, 122, 189

parked capital, 39

passive retailing, 49–51, 246–247

path-to-purchase, 151–153

PathTracker, 201–203, 241

patterns of movement, 242

Penn, Allen, 5–6

perimeter

definition of, 207–208

enhanced perimeter, 222–223

inverted perimeter, 223–225

per-item time, 56

personal selling, 85–86

Pilatus Markt, 237–239

placement of vital items, 256–257

Polinchock, David, 188

pop-up promotions, 123–124

prediction, challenges of, 15

pricing, promotional, 21, 255

primary store, 219–221

Principle of Social Proof, 93

private-label brands, 231–237

produce, location of, 209

product benefits, 150

product hypothesis, 219

product placement of vital items, 256–257

product/shopper allocation, 3–5

profits in retail, sources of, 232–234

promotional (secondary) store, 219–221

promotions

buy time, 245

promotional (secondary) store, 219–221

promotional allowances, 233

promotional displays, 255

promotional pricing, 21, 255

purchase frequency, 245

purchase states

Frustration/Angst, 37

leveraging, 26–28

Now!, 35–36

overview, 33–35

Routine/Autopilot, 37

Surprise/Delight, 36

purchasing, long-cycle

consumer anxiety and indecision, 142–143

desire, building, 144–147, 149–150

overview, 141–142

romancing the sale, 144

shopper engagement spectrum, 147–149

shopper's journey, 151–153

shopping process, 143

time, role of, 143

pyramid shelving, 215–216

Q

quick trips

appeal of, 158–160

categories purchased most often on, 167–168

characteristics of, 157–158

consumer considerations influencing where and how to shop, 161